Bill Mack's Memories
from the Trenches of

BROADCASTING

An Autobiography by Bill Mack

For information, contact: UNIT II, P.O. Box 8161, Fort Worth, Texas 76124.

Library of Congress #2004556088

ISBN   0-9752630-0-5

FIRST EDITION

Branch-Smith: Printing

Credit to: Sandra Beddow and Christy Blackwell for guidance.

Dedicated to Mom,
who took the time,
and to Cindy,
who continues.

Introduction

I met Bill Mack around the time I recorded 'Delta Dawn", when I was 13 years old. He was one of the very first D.J.s to play my record.

Right away, I knew I had a friend and supporter in Bill. What I didn't know then was that he would become like "family", to me.

In this business, it's sometimes hard to tell who is a true friend. Bill Mack is the <u>real deal</u>! Whether I had one hit or twenty, I knew he'd be right there with me.

I feel my career accomplishments pale in comparison to Bill's. He did "all-night radio" for over 30 years, cranking out quality programming with the 'Bill Mack Show". His loyal listeners knew him back then as 'The Midnight Cowboy". Now, of course, he's even <u>better known</u> as "The Satellite Cowboy", *since joining* XM Satellite Radio, *where he can be heard all over the world, clear as a bell!*

Bill is truly a trucker's best companion during those long hauls on the road.

And that voice! It's warm, sincere, and makes you feel comfortable and safe, as if you were with a friend ... and which you are!

Bill doesn't stop with his radio shows. He reaches out to his fans and friends with a monthly column, writing books, and, of course, winning Grammys *and other trophies by composing some of the best songs ever heard!*

Bill's longevity and enthusiasm for this business are a constant inspiration to me.

In my book, Bill Mack is the <u>top D.J.</u> More important, I'm proud to call him my friend.

—Tanya Tucker

Table of Contents

Special thanks to:

Elite Document Management
Marty Rendleman-Rendleman Management Group
Acuff-Rose Music
Road-Ahead Music
Bill Mack Country, Inc. - www.billmackcountry.com
Larry Shannon
Radio Daily News-www.radiodailynews.com
The *Grand Ole Opry*
NARAS
The Country Music Disk Jockey Hall-of-Fame in Nashville
The Country Music Hall-of-Fame & Museum in Nashville
The Country Music Association
The Texas Country Music Hall-of-Fame in Carthage, Texas
The Tex Ritter Museum in Carthage, Texas
The Academy of Country Music (ACM) in Los Angeles
Beau Tucker
Mel Foree
Imperial Records
H. W. Daily
Kenyon Brown
"Snuff" Garrett
Wesley Rose
A. J. Lockett
David McCormick
Merle Kilgore
Budd Wendall
Junior Brown
Howard Crockett
Wynn Stewart
Audrey Williams
Frank Mull
Ray Chaney
Glad Music
The Mills Brothers
"Major" Bill Smith
Every Country Music Disk Jockey on the Planet Earth!

FORWARD

I had the pleasure of being in the company of one of my best pals, Willie Nelson, on his birthday a few months ago. I mentioned I was in the process of writing my book. "Have you ever given thought to writing another book?" I asked.

Without hesitation, Willie laughed, "No. Matter of fact, I never gave much thought to it when I was writing my book!"

Willie's book, *"THE FACTS OF LIFE and Other Dirty Jokes"* (Random House-New York), is entertainment through-and-through, although it isn't a compilation in print you would normally send to your mother as a gift. Some of the jokes are a bit hairy ... but funny!

Come to think of it, your mother may have already heard the jokes if she knows Willie!

Of great importance to me was the fact that Willie sent me pages of the manuscript for his book as he wrote them on his bus. I have those raw pages in my "precious-memories" collection. He autographed them, making them even more special to me.

I love Willie. So, what else is new? Everybody who knows the man automatically attaches to him. And it's a "lifetime attachment". Nobody ever walks away from Willie unless he (or she) has committed an act of brutal disassociation.

"Even the members of your band never leave you," I said, as we sat on his bus. "You still have the same pickers in your band that were with you thirty five years ago ... or longer (Paul English, drummer)."

Willie's reaction: "There are no ex-musicians, just as there are no ex-wives. You just add *more* wives."

Willie's laughter, which I recorded during the interview, ran for 10 seconds following that voluntary remark.

Willie Nelson is an acute study in realism. Could be, he's the most real person I've met, in or out of show business. Study his eyes. He doesn't have to say a word. The "Full Nelson" is revealed in his eyes. Soul! Love. Sometimes, anger. Most times, I'm told, any anger is very subdued.

Old friend Ray Price called me the other day, on his 78th birthday, and laughed: "Subdued, my butt! Willie can go into a rage like th' rest of us, when he's pissed!"

Ray, who loves Willie like a brother, is aware of the fact that anybody leading a band and attempting to formulate entertainment has to blow his stack from time-to-time.

Ray said, "It's a necessity! Show business folks have to 'let-go' every once in a while! Otherwise, they'll haul you out of th' hall on a stretcher!"

Price, like Willie, is very special. Strange ... but special!

While Willie's biography, set to perfect print, was a fun assignment for him, I had gone through a very cruddy, uncalled-for experience, and promised myself I would never again attempt to write my book.

One of Nashville's better known writers had been after me for a couple of years to "team up and write a book." He made these suggestions every time he visited my radio show, plugging his latest typewritten creation. Most times, he was accompanied by the "subject" in the book.

The writer, and a book publisher out of Nashville, flew into Fort Worth, came to my house, and approached me with what sounded like a winning proposal pertaining to my bio. I agreed, and began sending chapters to both, the publisher and the writer. The publisher kept assuring me it was exactly what he wanted, that the book was going to be a "best-seller", etc. After over 100,000 words had been put to the pages, the publisher suddenly decided the book wouldn't work because I was no longer associated with WBAP, the radio station I had spent over 30 years with, shelling out country music and running with the trucks. Obviously, the publisher expected a bunch of free "plugs" on that

show, although it was never a stipulation in our contractual agreement. Besides, my gig with WBAP had become an over commer-
cialized piece of crap. The sales department had managed to take
over programming. The fun and enjoyment that at one time had
made my all-night radio show something I looked forward to on
a daily basis, had become a dread; a study in embarrassment.
There was no room for entertainment left for me at the 820 spot
on the AM dial, which also fed my programs to a restricted network of other radio outlets around the country. The telephone
and mail reaction to the five hours of nightly re-heated hash had
begun to fizzle. When making appearances at trucking conven-
tions, country music shows or wherever, the people would side
up to me and ask, "What 'n hell has gone wrong with your radio
program? Nothing there but commercials anymore!" Or words to
that effect.

When program directors give-in to sales, as is what happened
to my show, it's bye, bye baby. Listeners are more selective now.
They can switch to FM, which most have done, or scan the dial
until they find a talk show of some sort, if they are determined to
hang in on the AM band.

The brightest broadcast star in the skies is satellite radio: *XM
Satellite Radio*! It makes limitation in coverage, as is the case with
both AM and FM, something akin to the dinosaur. Soon, anything
with static and coverage restrictions will be placed on the shelves
with 78-rpm records.

Back to my bad memories with the book publisher and co-
writer:

Like me, the writer who was signed to help me with my book
received a nice bit of up-front loot from the publisher. Trouble
was, he couldn't cut it! The bits of my typing that were sent to
him for editing and re-writing came back to me a total mess! I
honestly couldn't decipher what the dude was chipping out on
paper for my approval. Later, I was to find out that several of the
other people the *"Hemingway of the Hillbillies"* had attempted to
"capture" in previous books, had gone through similar unhappy
experiences. After hearing that the woozy scribbler had been set
as the co-author for my manuscript, a couple of those "subjects"
called me, advising me to "drop him immediately, even if it means
paying an editor out of your own pocket!"

Even the publisher admitted the writer's "contributions" were
lousy. "Do you think he's on drugs or booze?" He asked, after

going through a tough telephone conversation with the writer. "He sounded very off-centered to me!"

I agreed to refund my up-front money to the publisher, in order to reclaim my 100,000 words of typing.

I was told the rotten writer had been involved in a recent lawsuit with a well-known singer. With me, he found a safety zone from any more lawsuits by declaring bankruptcy! He kept thousands of dollars for an assignment he never attempted to fulfill. When I approached him about the idiotic scenario, he couldn't remember many details. Instead, he bobbled on the telephone about his various malfunctions in life, sounding like a sick animal stuck in the swamps of humanity. He informed me he was not interested in writing any more books about entertainers. He screamed, "All entertainers are pains in th' ass!" Instead of focussing on singers, disk jockeys and the likes, he told me he was in the process, at that time, of writing a book about "fishing".

From the few advance pages he submitted to me while working my manuscript, he could have been writing about "fishing", then!

Since splitting with the writing fisherman, I've heard rumors he is ill. The nature of his illnesses vary, depending on which of his former, angry subjects you are talking with. It's a sad state to be in, and I honestly don't wish him bad health, but the "master of the printed word" is most obviously "out of focus" in the attic.

When the writer visited our house in Fort Worth, under the pretense of planning the book, he would tell Cindy and me horror stories about the other subjects that he had helped put in book form. These "off-the-cuff" bits ranged from extreme cocaine habits to group sex. One tale he whispered, although there were only the three of us in the house, was how one of his past book subjects had a teenage son who wasn't potty-trained! "He still wears diapers!" he laughed, maniacally.

After the woozy writer had excused himself and walked to our bathroom, Cindy was in a state of complete shock as she whispered, "I wonder what he'll have to say about us after your book is completed!" She also noticed something else that grabbed my attention. She asked, "Have you noticed that every time he returns from the bathroom that his nose is running? Does he have a cold?"

I will always believe the dude was being restricted from his writing assignment with me due to a hidden "problem". This is one of the rumors making the rounds when his name is brought up, which is seldom. He has become a very unimportant fixture in the ranks.

Cindy and a few others claim that my decisions to cut all ties from the publisher and the weird writer were blessings in disguise. Looking back on the wad of discomfort they put me through, I totally agree.

The publisher, obviously hoping I would back out on the book after I had refused to extend my contract with WBAP Radio, put pressure on me. He ordered me to rush my writing, demanding the completed biography be submitted to him a couple of months earlier than the original contract stated.

I did as he suggested, but wasn't satisfied with the rapidly written manuscript. Now, I can type out the pages (yes, I do my own typing) in my own personal style of presenting words. It may not be the best form of writing, but it'll be me, not a garb of manufactured paragraphs.

Possibly, I shouldn't take on the self-assigned venture of telling my story in life, but I'm a Gemini. I just can't seem to leave well-enough alone. Besides that, I am now celebrating 50 years among the greats and the not-so-greats in broadcasting … and I have a few stories to tell.

Here goes:

CHAPTER ONE

Down through 50 years in the business of country music, I've been asked several times: Which do you consider most important in your career? Is it your years as a disk jockey, or is it your songwriting that rings the loudest bell?

Both avenues have been very beneficial to me and I'm grateful. Honestly, it's a complete separation. When I'm "on-mike", doing my radio show, I seldom think of my songwriting. When I'm writing a song, most everything is blocked out of my mind except the lyrics and melody being set in my brain.

I certainly wasn't thinking of what I was going to say next on radio when I composed *"DRINKING CHAMPAGNE"*.

I was just going through my scrapbook, which my wife, Cindy, has done such a wonderful job of creating and stocking, and ran across Paul Bain's column in *"The Round Up"* publication, dated September 24, 1995.

Under the heading, *PAUL BAIN'S TOP TEN SONGS OF ALL TIME*, the writer lists his Top Ten favorite songs of all time, mentioning they are not his "top ten favorite records", but is a list of what he considers to be "the best written songs ... words and music", that *he has ever heard.*

In the list are *"Stardust"*, written by Hoagy Carmichael and Mitchell Parish; *"Always"* by Irving Berlin; *"Old Dogs, Children and Watermelon Wine"* by Tom T. Hall; *"City Of New Orleans"* by Steve Goodman and others.

13

In the midst is *"DRINKING CHAMPAGNE"*, written by Bill Mack!

Talk about an honor!

I've been asked many times, down through the years, how the song came to mind.

The words and music came easy. Come to think of it, all of my more successful compositions have come fast, requiring very little backtracking or deep study. That's why I've always said *songs are gifts*! Every songwriter I have known has said, basically, the same thing: "If you have to tug and toil at the song to make it work, walk away from it. Try later."

Well, anyway, *"DRINKING CHAMPAGNE"* came to me very fast.

The year was 1966 and I was traveling from the golf course on my way to my home in Fort Worth. It was close to the *Thanksgiving* and *Christmas* seasons and I saw the billboard on the side of the road reading, *"This Holiday Season, Serve Champagne!"*

I hadn't intended to write a song. I just started singing the lyrics and the melody as they came to me, and decided I would whiz over to a recording studio that was owned by a good friend.

By the time I had arrived at Johnny Patterson's recording studios in Fort Worth, the song was completed in my mind. I had fought the late afternoon traffic, but still managed to retain the lyrics and melody in my head.

I walked into the studio and asked Johnny to loan me a guitar and set a tape. I wanted to capture the song while it was still whirling in my brain.

I don't recall ever writing the lyrics down on paper. Patterson, who is still very active in music, doesn't remember me asking for a pencil and paper. He said that he does remember me asking for something to drink. I suppose the word, *champagne*, had been flopping around in my thoughts so long that it had made me thirsty.

I don't remember drinking champagne, though. It's not among my favorite drinks.

I do remember Johnny walking into his control room and setting up a reel-to-reel tape recorder. After messing around with his control board, he yelled through the studio speaker, "Are you ready?"

Holding a guitar, and seated in a chair with a microphone directly in front of my mouth, I informed him I was set to go.

Johnny shouted, "Tape's rollin'!"

Picking the old acoustical Martin guitar, I warbled:

"I'm drinkin' champagne, feelin' no pain, 'til early morning,
"Dining and dancing with every pretty girl I can find,
"Havin' a fling, with a pretty young thing, 'til early morning,
"Knowing tomorrow I'll wake up with you on my mind.
"Guilty conscience, I guess,
"Though, I must confess,
"I never loved you much when you were mine.
"So I'll keep drinking champagne, feelin' no pain, 'til early
*   morning*
"Knowing tomorrow I'll wake up with you on my mind."
(Published by Acuff-Rose Music-BMI)

Next day, Johnny Patterson called my house and asked me to drive by his office because he "had something to listen to". He had a surprise for me.

After I had laid the words and music on tape, accompanied by the guitar, Johnny took the time to *over-dub* several guitars and a bass-fiddle to my vocal. Except for my simple strumming of the guitar, every single instrument heard on my original recording of *"DRINKING CHAMPAGNE"* was performed by one man: Johnny Patterson.

Kapp Records, a subsidiary of *Decca*, took my "audition" recording, made by Johnny, and released it as a single record.

Now, over thirty-five years later, close to one hundred artists in the country and pop fields have recorded an old song that was inspired by a billboard and mastered on tape by a very talented old friend who had a lot of confidence in my song.

"DRINKING CHAMPAGNE" may not be a masterpiece, but it was to eventually win me the very honored distinction of becoming a member of the *BMI MILLION-AIR CLUB*, indicating my song has been played *over one million times* on radio and television!

Receiving that *Special Citation of Achievement*, certified and signed by my friend, Frances Preston *(BMI)*, is one of the greatest compliments ever handed to me.

I'm also most grateful to George Strait for recording the song, allowing me to receive both, a *gold* record and a *platinum* record, indicating his releases of *"DRINKING CHAMPAGNE"*, as a "single" and in several of his albums, have totaled millions of copies in sales.

Cal Smith, a tremendous talent, was the first to peg the charts with *"DRINKING CHAMPAGNE"*. Cal's version of the song is still a winner in my mind. He lit the fuse for many to follow, and I often wonder if *"Champagne"* would have ever become a hit if Cal hadn't believed in it many years ago.

I've got to be honest, here. I don't believe any artist will ever top Ray Price's version of *"DRINKING CHAMPAGNE"*. Like everything this old pal tackles and decides to sing, his rendition of the song makes the hair stand up on my arms.

Trouble is, the Ray Price version of *"CHAMPAGNE"*, on *Columbia Records*, recorded in 1970, has not been transferred to either, CD or cassette.

As I write this, Ray Price has hit the 78 mark, yet sings better than ever. He is in the same class as Tony Bennett. Like fine wine, these super pros improve with the years.

God! Can you imagine the music scene without Ray Price and Tony Bennett?

We are blessed.

Incidentally, I always thought *"DRINKING CHAMPAGNE"* was a "natural" for Dean Martin. I had him in mind when I first wrote and recorded it. Dean finally recorded the song … fifteen years after I had composed it!

Dino liked my little composition, telling my music publisher, "I should have done that song years ago! What happened?"

My music publisher, *Acuff-Rose Music*, replied: "You didn't open your mail, Dean! We've mailed you at least 25 demo recordings of the song, since 1966!"

Cindy and I were watching a video titled, *"DEAN MARTIN IN LONDON"* the other night. Dean sang *"DRINKING CHAMPAGNE"* for members of the British Royalty and a sold-out audience. It brought a combination of thrills and chills. A few subtle tears came to my eyes. Dean has been gone for years, but watching him on the videotape, singing my song, made me very grateful.

I'm certain that "DRINKING CHAMPAGNE" would have never come into existence if Johnny Patterson had not been in his Fort Worth studio that late afternoon in 1966.

Thank you, Johnny.

16

"*BLUE*", written eight years before "*DRINKING CHAMPAGNE*", also came easy. I wish I could say I was "inspired by romanticism", since the song sold millions of recordings, but I had nothing in mind when I composed it. Really, I was practicing on my guitar in my home in Wichita Falls, Texas. I was just learning to "pick" the guitar and found the chord change from "C" to "E" a bit interesting. I began humming the song and then, without any needed inspiration, started singing: "Blue ... ooo ... ooo ... ah ... ooo, oh so lonesome for you ... why can't you be blue over me ..." It all came to me within a matter of minutes. The completed rendition was set and ready in my mind. I didn't utilize a recorder. You have to remember that this was 1958. Audio recorders weren't something you found laying around the house, as is the case today. Back then, the recorders were reel-to-reel. Cassette tapes had not made the scene.

Just a thought: Today, cassette tapes have been updated by CDs. Tape is being replaced by digital audio discs.

I telephoned Sally and Lewis Nesman at Nesman Recording Studios, one of two recording studios in Wichita Falls at that time, and told them I would be over with some musicians later to record a new song I'd just written.

That night, I recorded *"BLUE"*. As I remember, it was done in one "take", after rehearsing it with the band. It may have required two takes, but I believe it was all wrapped in a single run-through. It was no big deal ... at the time.

I signed with *Starday Records* to release my recording of *"BLUE"*. I also signed the song over to *Starday Music* as publisher. Don Pierce was the owner of *Starday Records* and *Starday Music*. Pierce was from the same school as Bill McCall. Pierce and McCall had worked together at *4-Star Records*, referred to as the "outlaw label", out of California. Bill McCall had a reputation for shortchanging his artists (Rose Maddox, Webb Pierce, Slim Willet, T Texas Tyler, etc.). Slim Willet, composer of the hit, *"DON'T LET THE STARS GET IN YOUR EYES"*, flew from Texas to California and placed a gun to McCall's head, growling, "Pay me what you owe me! Do it now ... while you can still open the safe!"

McCall humbly opened his safe and forked over thousands of dollars to Slim. It was money rightfully owed to Willet after McCall had made a ton of loot as the music publisher of Slim's song.

Don Pierce might not have been quite as shady as McCall, but there was a strong resemblance in the way they juggled the books with the artists recording and writing songs for their record labels and music publishing companies.

I was like the majority of others when I entered the songwriting and singing arena. I was willing to pay to have recordings made. Pierce set a plan for suckers like me. I would pay all musicians and recording studio costs out of my own pocket and then pay Pierce several hundred dollars to have 500 45-rpm records printed on the *Starday* label. Catch here was, Don Pierce also placed my compositions in his publishing outfit, *Starday Music*. During the time I recorded stuff for *Starday*, I never received a royalty check from Pierce. My only happiness here was when Pierce sold his publishing company, which included my song, *"BLUE"*, to a more honest outfit. I'm sure he made a ton of loot by selling out. Had he had the professional business sense to keep *"BLUE"*, that song, alone, would have made him a millionaire.

I feel fortunate Pierce wasn't King of the Hill when LeAnn Rimes recorded *"BLUE"*. I'm sure I would have been highly short-changed if my checks were due from *Starday*.

I didn't write *'BLUE'* for Patsy Cline, as was stated after Rimes hit with the song. LeAnn copied Patsy's styling and it made good print. I read a couple of newspaper articles stating LeAnn was Patsy, reincarnated. One dude even went so far as to say LeAnn believed she was, in a former life, Patsy Cline. This was a piece of junk, which might have been set up by Rimes' promotion people in order to grab attention and sell more recordings.

As would be expected, the subject has arisen many times: What do you think of LeAnn Rimes?

Answer: I hardly know LeAnn Rimes.

Except for seeing her perform several times as a youngster, most of those times while singing my song, "BLUE", there haven't been many occasions for me to visit with this talented chirper of songs. I had seen her as she belted tunes on the *Johnny High Review* in Arlington, Texas, located just a few miles from my home. As best I can remember, it was there that I first met her. It was also the first time I heard the kid perform. After hearing her sing *"I Want To Be A Cowboy's Sweetheart"* and a couple of Patsy Cline songs, I was a bit overwhelmed. I believe she was ten-years-old at the time. She may have been younger.

Shortly after meeting LeAnn, she and her parents, Belinda and Wilbur, visited our home one evening. She was the typical, pretty little girl who was quite taken by our dogs and our swimming pool. I'll always remember her looking at the pool and saying, "I'm going to have one of those, some day." At the time, the Rimes family lived in an apartment in Garland, Texas, near Dallas, where Wilbur worked at a couple of jobs to make ends meet.

Got to hand it to the daddy, he moved to Dallas with full determination to make his daughter a singin' star.

My first chance to spend any important time with the youngster was when her manager, Marty Rendleman, brought her to my house in Fort Worth for a visit and interview after she had recorded *"BLUE"* in the *"ALL THAT"* album, released on her own independent label.

Let me mention something of importance here: Marty Rendleman, a very genuine, talented music agent, was responsible for the *"BLUE"* happening. She telephoned me one day and asked if I had a song for her protégé, who was yet to hit her teens. Normally, I wouldn't have responded very seriously, since pre-teeners without a record contract weren't the subject of many conversations at the time. Had it not been for Marty's friendship and my great respect for her as a music representative, I might have suggested the child sing, *"A TISKET, A TASKET (My Brown and Yellow Basket)"* or *"JESUS LOVES ME"*. However, I realized LeAnn was talented and, remembering the way she presented Patsy Cline songs on the *Johnny High Show,* I thought of my old song, *"BLUE",* which a good singer in San Antonio, named Joanie Hall, had recorded as a demo for my use in 1962. Joanie sounded very much like Patsy Cline. I told Marty I would make a cassette copy of the song and meet her in a couple of days at the *Denny's* restaurant, located between Fort Worth and Dallas on I-30.

When the day for my meeting with Marty arrived, it was chilly, and there was a heavy rain falling. I told Cindy to call Marty and move up our scheduled get-together. I growled, "Who wants to ride in the rain all the way to Grand Prairie to deliver a tape to a kid without a record contract?"

Cindy replied: "Marty's our friend! We're not going to let her down! Now, get the cassette and get in the car. We're going to Denny's."

She then put the grand slammer on the conversation by adding, "I'll drive!"

Of this, I am certain: Had it not been for Marty Rendleman and Cindy, *"BLUE"* would never have happened.

Often, I thank God for Marty, Cindy and Denny's.

"BLUE" was more than a song, it was the Overture to Drama.

I had been asleep for possibly an hour when I was awakened by Cindy, informing me the news department at WBAP, where I was doing my all-night radio show, had something important to tell me. It was around seven o'clock in the morning and I was holding on to a cup of coffee Cindy had handed to me as she placed the telephone into my other hand.

I growled a confused and sleepy, "Hello."

To this day, I can't remember which newsman placed the call to me, saying: "Good news, Bill! Your song, 'BLUE', has put you in nomination for two *Grammys*!"

Over thirty years had passed and the song I had written in a matter of minutes was now complimenting me with the possibility of receiving the greatest achievement award in music, the *Grammy*. This was equal to an actor receiving the news he or she was in nomination for the *Oscar*!

The *Grammy Awards* were held that year at *Madison Square Garden* in New York. "BLUE" was in nomination for the *Song of the Year 1996* and for the *Country Song of the Year 1996*. Honestly, I didn't believe I would win either of the nominations but, thank God, I received the comforting shock of my professional life when I heard: " … and the Country Song of the Year is 'BLUE'! The writer, Bill Mack!"

LeAnn Rimes received a *Grammy* for *Female Country Singer*. I was thrilled for her and really didn't give too much thought to the fact she mentioned everyone except me in her acceptance speech. I was still in shock from winning my Grammy!

Cindy whispered, "She should have mentioned you."

No big deal. The kid was nervous.

A few days after receiving the *Grammy*, I received a package from Washington DC. Opening it, I noticed the American Flag and a certificate that reads:

This Is To Certify That This Flag Was Flown Over The United States Capitol On February 27, 1997 At The Request Of The Honorable Kay Granger, Member of Congress.

The Flag Was Flown For Mr. Bill Mack In Recognition Of Being Selected As The Songwriter For The Grammy Award Winning Song, "BLUE".

Signed: Alan M Hantman AIA
Architect of the Capitol

The flag is now in a beautiful frame located near our sofa. I look at it daily.

Proud? Yes.

"BLUE" also won the trophy for being the *Country Song of-the-Year 1996*, at the *Academy of Country Music Awards* in Los Angeles. LeAnn received the *ACM* award for Female Country Vocalist. Again, she failed to mention me when making her acceptance speech on nationwide TV. Cindy was a bit ticked, but I still wasn't too concerned. However, the press caught it and when I returned to my hotel room, there were many *calls-to-return*, most of them to various members of the press and to a gob of radio and television stations. More than half of those I chatted with brought up the subject of LeAnn ignoring the writer of "the song that made her!" Several close pals in the media utilized special wording when referring to Miss Rimes, many calling her "an ungrateful little brat!" Some used stronger words of reference.

An act that really caught my attention took place in Los Angeles while Cindy and I were having breakfast with LeAnn's attorney and personal-manager, Lyle Walker, in the hotel coffee shop. This was the morning after the little girl had received her second giant award for recording my song. Her daddy, Wilbur, approached our table, and without uttering a "good-morning", tossed a music cassette onto the table and growled, "This girl don't need to be sangin' country music!"

It was then that I realized LeAnn might have considered herself much more important than *"BLUE"*, *Country Music* and me. I could now understand her ignoring my name in her little acceptance speeches.

I received a press release, dated February 6, 2004, announcing LeAnn is set to headline the *NEXTEL TRIBUTE TO AMERICA*, the pre-race extravaganza leading up to *Nascar's* most prestigious race ... the *Daytona 500 ... on* February 15.

Rapidly catching my attention, the press release shouts: *Double Grammy award-winning superstar, LeAnn Rimes, whose hits include "HOW DO I LIVE", "CAN'T FIGHT THE MOONLIGHT, and "WE CAN" will headline the big blowout!"*

My song, *"BLUE"*, that made those grand awards possible for the little lady, wasn't mentioned.

As I look back, I realize LeAnn may have been jealous of the song that made her a star. It's been hinted that she now considers *"BLUE"* a bit *too-country* for her new approach to music, and that there is almost resentment toward me for writing it!

We would never be close.

The *"BLUE"* album sold over 9-million copies. The style that made LeAnn a star had an obvious Patsy Cline touch to it. I recently read a current bio on LeAnn's website where she refers to her recording of *"BLUE"* as having a Patsy Cline *"twang"*.

Kiss my grits!

It was so visual in every direction: The Rimes group was not able to handle "overnight success". The big figure checks began rolling in, and LeAnn was in demand. She was the biggest name in country music. Daddy took charge of things, with the aid of Lyle Walker. Marty Rendleman, the lady who ignited the fuse and was responsible for LeAnn's initial success, was fired. I will always believe this was the first of several serious mistakes made by the new Rimes regime. Just as his daughter had become an overnight success as a singer, Wilbur considered himself to be the *producer-of-producers*. He needed someone to handle the bookings, keep up with the taxes, "and all of that stuff", so he chose Lyle Walker, a qualified attorney.

Things were buzzing so busy on the road that Wilbur personally designed LeAnn's tour bus. He came up with the idea of half-bus, half *Peterbilt* truck. He christened the uncomfortable piece of junk, which LeAnn claimed looked and felt like a cattle truck, *"The Peter-Bus!"*

By this time, the Rimes marriage was beginning to peter out.

LeAnn's mother, Belinda, was a good mother and a good lady. When the loot was piling in, and LeAnn was spending most of her time in the *Peter-Bus*, Belinda's main concern was her daughter. She was beginning to feel the discomforts of show-business. Several times, she mentioned to Cindy and me: "I wish things were like they used to be. I'm worried about my daughter!"

Not only was LeAnn tired, she was suffering with the dreaded skin condition, Eczema. She was also tossing temper tantrums. It wasn't a pretty scene.

Wilbur, however, wasn't showing any signs of wear. He informed me, "You've gotta make it while it's hot!" He was also beginning to enjoy the attention he was receiving as the father of the hottest little act in show business. He set aside his brogans, purchased some nice zip-up clothes, and, dammit all to hell, fell in love with another woman!

"That there's just part of show business!"

Wilbur had also decided Dallas was "too small a' town". He bought property in Nashville, a city with a population approximately one-quarter the size of Dallas, and moved east. Trouble was, Nashville didn't take a strong liking to LeAnn. Granted, there was a lot of jealousy in *Music City USA*. If your CDs were selling better than Carlene Carter's, th' town wasn't big enough for two! Unfortunately, LeAnn had made the unforgivable mistake of having the hottest record in the grand ol' town, and most of the oh-so-proper ladies in Music City were snubbing their noses.

LeAnn and Belinda moved back to Dallas. Wilbur bought a ranch near Nashville. He was determined to "stay where the action is!" He was now a recognized hit record producer. "Dallas ain't no place to be when you're a damned hit record producer!"

It wasn't long before LeAnn felt Dallas was a bit too small for a *super-star*. She and Mama moved to Los Angeles. *Hollywood!* By this time, Wilbur and Belinda had decided to divorce. Wilbur had chosen another woman and LeAnn and her mom had decided to exit the *Peter-Bus* for good. First, though, there was some serious accounting to do. Belinda and her daughter hired themselves a front-seat attorney and sued ol' Wilbur and his saddle pal, Lyle Walker, for seven million big ones! The daughter and ex-wife claimed Wilbur and Lyle had been hidin' some big loot on the *Peter-Bus*!

I've never seen worse timing in show business. Cheating around, boozing it up, and fighting in public ... all seem to run with the natural flow of *Hollywood*. These are normal happenings in *Tinsel-Town*. It's the same in Dallas!

You can do just about anything you damn well please ... but don't sue your daddy!

Going completely against the grain, LeAnn was determined to take her papa to court. Lyle Walker, her attorney, was also set to stand beside ol' Wilbur in the courthouse.

All hell broke loose via the media. Members of the press, radio and television began calling me! Most of the concerned news people had already formed opinions toward LeAnn. The stock question was, "Why couldn't they have settled this thing out of court?"

Answer: An issue too hot to handle. Perfect *meat for the media!*

To add fuel to the explosion, LeAnn decided she would sue

Curb Records, claiming she was "too young to comprehend" when the contracts were signed with the big Nashville recording house. I never could figure this one out! The way LeAnn's claims were placed on the legal tables, she should not have signed any big bucks agreement until she was *of age*. That would have been six or seven years <u>after</u> selling millions of recordings and receiving the *Grammy!*

Give me a break! Show me one sensible person who will honestly state: "No! I don't want that *Grammy* or that *Academy of Country Music Award* until I turn eighteen! And you can keep your measly millions, too!"

Everything was settled in court. Now, LeAnn had decided Hollywood wasn't big enough for her <u>and</u> her mother. Belinda headed back to Dallas, leaving her precious and demanding daughter in her own little mansion in the *Hollywood Hills!* Shortly after moving back to Big-D, Belinda married LeAnn's official photographer after the *Kodak Kid* divorced his wife.

Now, things were going a bit goofy. To stiffen the stinkin' atmosphere, LeAnn wore a T-shirt on a nationally televised awards show, making fun of her daddy! There were very few laughs in the audience. Mostly, you heard, "Oooh!"

Here, I blame television producer Dick Clark for allowing such foolishness to happen.

Next thing we knew, the child had come-of-age. She was engaged!

Cindy and I weren't invited to the wedding.

As I look back, there is sadness. I will always be grateful to LeAnn for talking her daddy into allowing her to record *"BLUE"*, the song ol' Wilbur didn't see fit for recording. LeAnn also recorded my song, *"CLINGING TO A* SAVING HAND", doing a wonderful job. The album, consisting of this song, would also sell millions.

In 2003, *"BLUE"* was chosen as one of the *Top One Hundred Country Songs of All Time* (CMT). Cindy and I were invited to Nashville for the television airing of the *"Top 100"*.

Naturally, we were proud as LeAnn sang *"BLUE"* on the show. After the program was completed, we saw her rushing to her dressing room. Wanting to thank her for doing such a good job with my song on the television show, we went backstage and gave my card to the backstage guard, asking him to deliver it to

LeAnn's dressing room, and inform her that Cindy and I wanted to say a fast *hello* before going back to our Nashville hotel.

The guard walked to LeAnn's dressing room, and knocked on the door. The door opened, and I saw LeAnn take a fast glimpse in our direction. Then, I saw Belinda and her husband look in our direction before darting into the dressing room!

The guard, obviously embarrassed, returned to his desk and informed us, sheepishly, "Miss Rimes has left the hall."

("Elvis has left the building!")

I'll never understand the Rimes scenario, but can honestly say I don't feel any hurt. Really, there is no anger ... as there shouldn't be. After all, *"BLUE"* not only opened doors for LeAnn, it also brought a lot of extra meals to my family table, as well as presenting opportunities for me to meet a lot of important people outside of the country music scene.

Gotta mention this: One of the most enjoyable days of my professional life took place in Chicago in 1997 when I was invited to be the guest of Oprah. To be honest, I seldom viewed her show, although Cindy was a big fan of the lady. Now, I am also a true believer in Oprah. Once you meet her, you're automatically attached! She is a sincerely warm, thoughtful and beautiful host.

Oprah makes you "feel at home".

I've been asked several times: Of all the songs you have written, which is your personal favorite?

The answer to this one is easy. It's a song I wrote on a cold, dreary morning in 1970 titled, *"CLINGING TO A SAVING HAND"*. I had been doing my all night radio show on WBAP out of Fort Worth for over a year. Although I was recognized as the *Number One Overnight Country Music Disk Jockey in the Nation* that year, I was finding it difficult to track true happiness.

I had everything to be thankful for: Good money, good company, good food ... everything! And still ... there was a sadness. There was emptiness in my life.

I will never forget that special morning. I had finished my radio show and decided to work on a song that I had in mind. I took my guitar and set up shop in the WBAP Production Studio.

The song in my thoughts was titled, *"TAKE ME FROM THE SHADOWS OF THE TREES"*. It was about an atheist who was dying.

A portion of the lyrics in my head:

"Don't send me any red or yellow roses,
I don't ask for your prayers on bended knees,
Don't bury any bible with my body, I beg you,
Just take me from the shadows of the trees."
(Road-Ahead Music, BMI)

It was about 5:30 a.m., and the day was beginning with cold rain. I was feeling depressed as I set the reel-to-reel tape on the recorder, and the lyrics to that song in my mind sent a chill through my body. I could feel the presence of evil.

Suddenly … new lyrics entered my heart and mind. Utilizing the same tune I had set for *"TAKE ME FROM THE SHADOWS OF THE TREES"*, the new song was born and completed in a matter of minutes. It was easily titled: *"CLINGING TO A SAVING HAND"*.

Of all the songs I have written, *"CLINGING"* will always be my personal favorite. I had been a Christian for many years when *"CLINGING TO A SAVING HAND"* entered my life, and the song gave me new strength because I was certain it was a gift from God.

My beautiful little friend, Connie Smith, was the first to record the song. She gave it a perfectly constructed "soul" treatment! Soon, many others would record *"CLINGING"*, including Conway Twitty, Bill Monroe ("The King of Bluegrass Music"), the darling Linda Plowman and dozens of others.

As mentioned, LeAnn Rimes also recorded *"CLINGING TO A SAVING HAND"*, although I've never heard her sing it "live". I honestly doubt I will ever have such a privilege.

Oh, well.

"CLINGING TO A SAVING HAND" has been performed in countless churches and at many funerals. Thankfully, today it is considered a standard gospel song with new recorded versions released every year.

"CLINGING TO A SAVING HAND" is my personal prayer.

Every time I hear the song, I feel *His* warmth.

CHAPTER TWO

I was born and named Billy Mac Smith, in Shamrock, Texas. I was blessed with two wonderful parents, Ernest and Irene, and a younger brother, Clois, whom I will always refer to as *The Greatest!* I have no sisters, although I consider my cousin, Doris, to be closer than a sister to me. Doris Coleman Goodson, in reality, is my *Super-Sister.*

Geographically, the Texas Panhandle town of Shamrock rests 93 miles east of Amarillo and 14 miles west of the Oklahoma line on Interstate 40, better known as Route 66 to the old timers who still live in the good town.

Do you, by chance, remember the old '40s hit by Nat "King" Cole titled, *"Route 66"* (*"Get your kicks on Route Sixty-Six"*)? Well, we citizens of Shamrock were a bit put-out when we noticed they had left our town out of the lyrics, which boasted: *"Oklahoma City is mighty pretty ... See Amarillo ... Gallop, New Mexico!"* I was always of the opinion the composer could have squeezed Shamrock in between Oklahoma City and Amarillo, since that is where the proud town is located.

Although it is referred to as "The Irish City", Shamrock had very few authentic Irishmen within its' territory that I can remember.

If you saw the motion pictures, *"To Kill A Mockingbird"* or *"The Summer of '42"*, you might have an inkling of what life was like during my beginning years: Small town, population about 3,000, a most dedicated Volunteer Fire Department, a couple of five–and–dime stores, three drug stores, all of them capable of making the best toasted tuna sandwiches and the thickest malted milks to be served anywhere.

We had two movie theaters: the *Texas* and the *Liberty* ... both of which I patronized regularly.

There was the municipal swimming pool on the southwest edge of town, with outdoor speakers wired to a jukebox inside blasting Tommy Dorsey's *"Boogie Woogie"* while we burned our bodies and studied the pretty girls in their one-piece bathing suits during the sweltering summer months.

Shamrock had several cafes. The *K. C. Steakhouse* was my personal choice, featuring the best hamburger steaks in town. I believe, though, that the *U-Drop-Inn* was the most popular eating spot. Most town meetings were held at the *"U-Drop"*.

My favorite hangout was the pool hall, which was located in the rear of a barber shop, where a black friend nicknamed "Tight Eye" could put the best shine possible on your shoes. He was a master at his calling.

In the narrow hallway leading to the pool hall was *"Jay's Hamburgers"*, a spot where a simple gas hotplate, controlled by a fine man named Jay Burkhalter, turned out the tastiest greasy hamburgers on the face of the earth. If you don't believe me, ask anyone who ever tasted a hamburger made by Jay.

Let me insert here:

Many years after leaving Shamrock, Roger Miller and I were seated next to each other at one of Nashville's awards banquets, attempting to cut into our tough steaks. Roger nudged me and said, "Bill, what would you give for a good old Jay's hamburger right now?"

Roger, one of our real super-stars in entertainment, was born in Fort Worth and raised in Erick, Oklahoma, located about a half-hour's drive from my hometown. He married a Shamrock girl.

Shamrock was in the center of Bob Wills country. What *Arthur Fiedler* and the *Boston Pops Orchestra* were to Boston, *Bob Wills and his Texas Playboys* were to Shamrock!

There was no *class distinction* in our town, as I remember. Oh, perhaps a limited few attempted to "put on the dog", but they didn't fool anybody. Big houses and big cars were simply an indication that the owners were a little more in debt than their more humble neighbors.

There was no *race discrimination* in Shamrock. No one ever heard of those words. Back then, blacks were black and whites were white. There were no problems between the colors during my growing years.

The blacks lived in a section of our town known as *"The Flats"*.

Rumor had it that more bootlegged booze was available in *"The Flats"* than could be found in Amarillo, where liquor was legal — - if you had the loot to spring for a bottle.

I well remember an extremely hot summer night during my high school years when Bill Setzler, Bill Green, Jack Worley and I piled into Setzler's old Plymouth, drove to *"The Flats"* and attempted to purchase some beer. Not only was a door slammed in our faces as we stood on the dilapidated wooden porch, three or four vicious red dogs roared from under the house and, almost on cue, attacked the four of us. No effort was made by the black witnesses to call off the dogs. Instead, they laughed convulsively until the dogs finally halted their biting and ran back under the house.

All of my outlaw pals and I left bits of our butts in *"The Flats"* that humid evening.

Madden Street in Shamrock, the street on which we lived, was referred to as *"Snuff Street"*, because you would go a block <u>and take a dip!</u> Really, it had more dips than any street or road I've ever set wheels on. It was a common sight watching the town constable, John Cox, chasing villainous vehicles down Madden Street, his loose muffler on his old Dodge creating an array of sparks as it dropped to the pavement at every miserable dip.

I could never understand why the city never placed a better means of travel in the hands of the constable, although I was grateful they didn't. There were several times when the dedicated lawman was giving chase to my gang, only to have his old car peter out on him.

By the way, I had a special uncle who laid claim to having spent part of a Saturday night in the Shamrock jail as a guest of John Cox. He said he would have spent the entire night, had he not noticed the cell was unlocked! It seems the lock wasn't functioning right and the importance of repairing it was far down on the list of things that needed 'tending to' by the city. My old uncle informed me with a certain amount of pride that he simply opened the door, strolled out of the jail and walked out on to the busy, crowded sidewalk. He added that as he was jogging to his car, anxious to hit the road home, Constable John unexpectedly walked out of the *J. C. Penney* store and came face-to-face with Uncle Jack! It was obvious that the lawman's memory was bad when he smiled at my old uncle, whom he had supposedly locked up less than an hour before, and shouted, "Howdy, Jack! How are your folks?"

Another incident that comes to mind pertaining to the constable occurred during my senior year in high school when my regular set of weird pals and I struck out on a trip to Texola, Oklahoma, 14 miles to the east, to buy some beer. Shamrock was, still is, and always will be <u>dry</u>, by law, when it comes to sales of alcoholic beverages. We were in Bill Setzler's old Plymouth, making good time, when we noticed a somewhat confused figure standing beside an old Dodge which was setting idle on the side of Highway 66. Then, we noticed it was Constable Cox. He was waving frantically for us to stop, which we did. He walked toward Setzler's open window and informed us that the battery on his undependable machine had failed him. "Give me a push, boy!" He ordered in tones resembling the cartoon character, Yosemite Sam. As a matter of fact, there was actually a physical resemblance in John Cox and Yosemite Sam, complete to the big hat, fat belly and outrageous mustache.

Setzler acted like he was happy to oblige the lawman, believing it would put him in good standing with the local police department.

After a short bumper-to-bumper shove, old John's Dodge sputtered off on its' own into the darkness of the night, making a U-turn, back toward Shamrock.

Bill Setzler shoved the gear into high speed as we all laughed about the constable's old broken down crate. We were cruising nicely when, suddenly, we noticed a red light blinking madly behind us to the accompaniment of a loud siren. "Damn! It's th' law!" Shouted Bill, bringing his car to a halt.

It was the law, indeed. It was non-other than Constable John Cox in the sluggish Dodge we had just helped jump-start! He approached Setzler's window and growled, "You was speedin', boy! I'm givin' you a ticket!"

John scribbled some weird wording on a yellow sheet of paper, handed it to Bill and said, "Now, git your butts back to Shamrock 'fore I throw all of you in jail!"

Come summer, it was expected of my gang to steal watermelons. One of my first serious associations with a trucker was related to the theft of watermelons.

It was a late summer night when we noticed the old truck exiting the Shamrock city limits, headed toward Wellington, Texas, 28 miles to the south. He was chugging at low speed and his truck bed was loaded with huge watermelons. We decided to follow the old rig in Setzler's Plymouth, with a well-planned idea on how to lift the melons from the rig to the car. While the old vehicle was grunting up the steep hill near the Red River Bridge at approximately 10 miles per hour, Setzler steered the Plymouth close to the rear of the truck. All went as planned. I made it to the bed and began picking up the watermelons, handing them one-by-one to Jack Worley, who was squatted on the hood of Setzler's car. He carefully shoved the stolen goods through the passenger's window to Robert Lee. The poor trucker was doing all he could to get his ancient vehicle to the top of the hill, which he finally managed to do. Then, after getting on a more flat surface of Highway 83, he stepped on the gas. In no time, I noticed the truck was leaving the Plymouth behind. I also noticed the Plymouth stopped, Worley jumped from the hood, got inside, and the car turned around, high tailing it back to Shamrock!

My thug friends had deserted me!

The rig pulled into Wellington and stopped at a service station. As I hunkered down in the bed of the heap, amidst the watermelons, the driver gave me a couple of minutes to become more frightened by taking his good easy time in approaching me. Finally, I heard him say, "Get your ass out of there."

I crawled to the back of the truck bed and eased out on to the ground.

"What were you doing back there?" Asked the driver.

I lied: "I was looking for a watermelon to buy from you."

Strangely, the trucker snickered a bit and then said, "Let's get a cup of coffee."

We walked into a small café adjacent to the service station and sat down at a table. I thought it best to remain silent as the driver ordered a couple of cups of coffee.

"Want a doughnut?" He asked.

"No. I'll just have some coffee."

Finally, after sipping from the coffee cup, he said: "I saw what you and your pals were doing. I also saw them back out on you, leaving you to take the rap." I could only manage, "Yeah."

The trucker said, "Well, I know you guys took me for about a half dozen melons and that won't be any problem. I figure you can help me empty my load here in Wellington and that'll make us about even." He slurped some more coffee and added, "Does that sound fair to you?"

"Fair enough", I said, although my heart wasn't in it.

For an hour or so, we stopped at various spots in Wellington and unloaded melons. Then, we headed back toward Shamrock in the old truck. The driver informed me he lived near Wheeler, 17 miles north of my home, and knew several of my relatives who lived close to his farm. He also let it be known that I shouldn't have put myself in the situation I had placed myself in with him. "It might just be watermelons," he said, "and I know you were just doin' it to have some fun, but it was still <u>stealin'</u>."

It was approaching five o'clock in the morning as we pulled up to the curb in front of my house and I was completely exhausted. The truck driver gave me a silent stare and then, with a smile, shook my hand before I got out of the cab.

As I walked slowly across my lawn toward the door of my house, he yelled, "I'm leaving a few watermelons on your lawn here for you, since you seem to like them so well!"

Then, I heard him laugh as he got back into his rig, started the engine and pulled the wheezing old vehicle away from the curb.

Outside of my dad, this was the first trucker to take the time to instill importance into my life. There would be many, many more.

Bill Mack
The Early Years

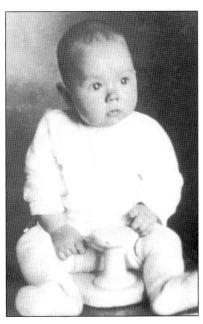

Enter...Billy Mack Smith

Ernest and Irene Smith with their son Billy Mack Smith

Ernest and Irene, Clois & Billy

Billy Mack Smith and his brother Clois Ralph Smith

Photos A

Bill in his high school play "Night Must Fall."

KEVA – Shamrock, Texas. My First job in broadcasting.

KEVA – Shamrock, Texas. As it looks today.

Grannie and Grandpa Sechrist

U-Drop Inn – Shamrock, Texas. My favorite hang-out.

Photos B

The late Leon Rusk (right). Had Mama not begged me to come home for Mother's Day, I might have died with him.

KLYN – Amarillo, Texas. Bill with his "all girl crew."

KLYN – Amarillo, Texas

Introducing Big Band Leader, Harry James in Amarillo, Texas.

Photos C

Publicity photo,
Wichita Falls, Texas

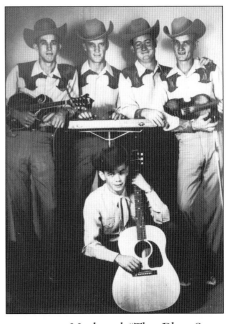

My band "The Blue Sage
Boys" (Buck White of The
Whites — far left).

KLYN – Amarillo,
Texas. World's
biggest pie

Bill, Jackie and
daughter Debbie
with dog Elmer

Photos D

Jackie and Me with Ernest Tubb (left)
and Cecil Boykin in Wichita Falls, Texas.

Publicity photo,
KWFT, Wichita
Falls, Texas

Eddy Arnold — Wichita Falls, Texas. Mid-50's

TV Show – Big 6
Jamboree every
Saturday night in
Wichita Falls,
Texas.

Photos E

Announcer for Bob Wills and the Texas Playboys. (Bill waving hand in the air) Mid-60's

KPCN – Grand Prairie, Texas

The Family

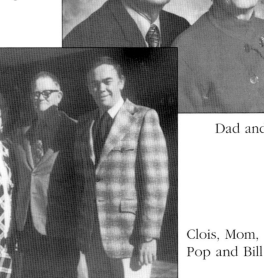

Dad and Mom

Clois, Mom, Pop and Bill

Photos F

Today with my Grandson Nicholas, Debbie and Mom.

Mom and Pop with "Hole-in-One" golf trophy.

Playing a round of golf with Clois and Pop.

Debbie, her husband Ronnie and their son Nick.

Photos G

Today with my
brother Clois.

Bill, Clois
and Mom

Clois' Family left to right; Andy, Mom,
Pam, Clois, Chris and Lisa, Scott and Laurie.
Clois and Pam have been blessed with
eight grandchildren.

Clois and Pam

Cindy – my wife of 31 years

Bill, Nana and Pop and Misty – 1975

Cindy, Bill, Clois and sister-in-law Pam

Misty, Sunnie, my Nephew Jeff and son Billy

Photos I

Easter 1992

Misty 7; Billy 3;
Sunnie 2

Christmas card 1995. Our 1973 MGB which we still own today. It was
Cindy's wedding gift.

Photos J

Sunnie 5; Billy 6;
Misty 10

My son Billy

Mama Jo,
Papa Bill
with great-
grandchildren
(Cindy's
Mother and
Dad)

My daughters
Sunnie and
Misty

Photos K

Billy, his wife April and son Julio

Papa with grandchildren Cody and Brittany

Cindy's sister Linda and her husband Dennis. Their son Jeff and his wife Janna with their children Melanie, Rebecca, Kevin and Dylan

Left to right; Billy, Brittany, Cindy, Cody (facing backwards), Misty, Bill, Sunnie, April and Julio

Photos L

CHAPTER THREE

I was approximately 5-years-old when my dad hauled cotton-seed in the Texas Panhandle area. I can still remember when he purchased me a toy shovel, allowing me to get in the bed of the truck with him and follow his mannerisms as he shoveled the stuff into some kind of huge container. Also most vivid in my memory is the taste of *Milky Way* candy bars. Pop would always stop at the Dozier store for our *Milky Ways* and *R. C. Colas*.

Later, my daddy would haul fuel. First, he transported kerosene throughout the Shamrock, Texas area, and then he switched to hauling gasoline to various service stations. Oft times, I would travel with him on those rugged jags. There was no air-conditioning in cars or trucks in those days and we were forced to keep the windows down on the old rig in order to have any cool breeze, if any was to be had. This led to another problem, dust. Not near all of the roads were paved when my dad was delivering fuel, most of his customers being in the rural areas. The misery of grit, dirt and dust was overwhelming. However, I was too young to allow the excess dust to bother me too much. One reason was, my mother always had Pop carry several clean, wet towels in the truck to dab away the dirt from my hands and face and to cool me if the weather was extra hot, as it was during most summers. My memory is so clear of my dad having one hand on the big steering wheel and the other holding a wet towel to my face in order to supply comfort to his "man".

Pop never referred to me as "Son" or "Boy". It was always, "Man." And that was the supreme compliment. I well recall: "Want a *Milky Way*, Man?" "Are you sure you don't want to put your head in my lap and take a little nap, Man?"

I don't remember my dad ever having a new rig. His were to be an assortment of oldies with different brands inscribed on the hood. One thing was certain; they all sounded the same. It seems every one of Pop's trucks had that grinding, growling echo and when he switched gears, it sounded like the transmission was literally screaming for relief.

One gear, in particular, caught my attention. Pop referred to it as "Grandma Low", and it was utilized to climb steep grades.

When I see the big, shiny rigs whizzing down today's interstates, my memory jumps back in time to those dear old pieces of rolling, grunting contraptions that my daddy used to handle so well, never complaining.

Once, while traveling with Pop to get a load of gasoline in Wichita Falls, Texas, I <u>know</u> he had <u>five</u> blow-outs during the 320 miles we geared the truck that day, and I never heard him complain. He would remove the inner tube and, with the aid of mixed patches, he would repair the defective tires on the side of the road, using a hand pump to inflate them, while I caught a nap under a tree. He told me "road heat" was the villain, causing the blowouts. This was during World War II, however, and it could be new tires and inner tubes were hard to locate or, more likely, were priced a bit above Pop's means.

Although he never griped about his bad luck on the road, I could see the hurt and weariness in his eyes.

Many times, I've wished I had been blessed with Pop's patience and with his attitude toward life. He attempted to instill those valuable traits in me, but this was his only failure, I'm sorry to say. Or, should I say it was <u>my</u> failure? I failed to follow his teachings, his examples, and I was to pay for it down through life

For many years, on my radio shows and in my printed columns, I have attempted to boost the image of the trucker, a false image created by people unfamiliar with the tremendous assignments that are placed on the driver. And one reason I have been so determined to boost that image is my dad. He understood and appreciated truckers, and passed his positive attitude toward trucking on to me.

Pop finally quit trucking, the competition being too tough and his rigs a little too hesitant to roll. Instead, he opened a Conoco service station on Route 66 and this was a fine venture for him. Business was good and it was an opportunity to do what he enjoyed most, meeting people. My job was to sweep up the place and hose the grime, dirt and oil leakage off the driveways. I was paid in nickels; most of them used to buy tickets to the Texas and Liberty theaters in Shamrock.

After getting the opportunity to purchase a bigger fuel stop on the west edge of Shamrock, still on *Route 66*, Pop secured a loan from the Farmer's and Merchant's Bank and took control of a place called, "*Bumper-To-Bumper*". It was to be Shamrock's only truck stop and, although it didn't measure up to most of today's big stops, it got the job done and was very busy most of the day and night, remaining open around the clock. There was also the adjoining restaurant, which was always filled with truckers and travelers.

When I entered my mid-teens, Pop decided to hire Bill Setzler and me to work the all-night shift, from midnight until 6:00 a.m., thinking it would be a good training ground for me to follow in his chosen field, the truck stop-service station business.

For a week before Setzler and I were scheduled to take over the midnight shift, Pop instructed us on the cash register, oil changes and the toughest job to be handled, the fixing of flat tires. In those days, you had to "break" the flat tire from the rim of the wheel, using a huge short handled sledgehammer and various other poking tools, remove the tube, patch it, put it back in the tire and put the tire back on the wheel! It was a time consuming pain in the butt.

In the 40s, we didn't have to deal with credit cards. Every purchase, all services, were handled on a cash basis, unless it was someone you knew very well, personally. From them, you could take checks. There were some that Pop had placed in his "special-book". This allowed them to "buy now, pay when you can". He told me one time, "Every trucker I put in that 'special-book', paid what they owed me. It might have taken awhile, but they were honest. They paid their bills."

The first few nights, while doing the midnight 'til dawn shift, went without hitches. Setzler and I would run to the windshields, cleaning them thoroughly, and then follow Pop's instructed words, "Can I help you?"

Back then, the standard order from most customers was: "Fill her up!" Then came the expected question, "Where's your rest room?"

Since it was summer, with many people enjoying their vacation time, there was a steady stream of cars and trucks on *Route 66* and there were several all-night service stations in Shamrock to handle the traffic, most of it heading toward California or, in the opposite direction, Chicago. Pop's "*Bumper-To-Bumper*" was on the north side of the highway, grabbing mostly westward California, New Mexico and Arizona bound tourists and truckers. As an aside means of income, Setzler and I sold horned toads, found mostly in the southwest. They're almost extinct now, but back in the 40s, you would find dozens of them jumping around in the many red ant beds and strutting within the vacant lots. We named them "Mini-Monsters" and sold them to tourists, mostly those from California, for twenty-five cents each. Our sales were limited, not because of the lack of horned toads, but because we couldn't find enough small boxes to hold them.

The lady tourists would look at the vicious appearing little creatures and scream, "Get that away from me!" The men would buy several to take home with them, but they had to be "boxed". Not even the men wanted to place them in their hands. Boxed, we would add a few dead red ants as food for the little creatures.

Working all night in the adjoining restaurant was a good looking girl named, Minnie Mae. She was probably 19 years old but, to me, was an "older" woman. Minnie Mae had just gone through a divorce from her husband, who was in the service, and had casually informed me that she was "lonely". She had light brown hair, beautiful brown eyes, ruby red lips and a "build" similar to Betty Grable, the *Twentieth Century Fox* movie queen.

When there was a slow-down in highway trade, Minnie would invite me to join her at the counter for coffee during those wee hours of the morning. Several times, she would say, "I wish I had something 'stronger' for us to drink!"

It finally got to the point to where Minnie Mae would lay kisses on me, saying such things as, "I like the young dudes!" or "Have you ever gone out with an 'older' gal, one who knows how to have fun?"

Naturally, I became extremely interested in Minnie Mae, looking forward to her arrival at the café around midnight. She would always pull into the driveway before parking, allowing me to clean her windshield and, sometimes, asking me to pump two or three gallons of gasoline into her white Chevy. Gas was cheap then, and sometimes I refused her attempts to pay. Being the big shot, I would say, "That's *on-the-house*, Minnie."

Pop was unaware of my gifts of "free fuel" to Minnie Mae.

Many times, Mom would look at Minnie Mae's perfect "build" and growl to me, "You stay away from her!"

The only dreaded times Setzler and I had during those hot summer nights at the *"Bumper-To-Bumper"* were when cars or trucks pulled into the driveway with flat tires. The timing was always bad and I remember one night when I had Minnie Mae in the storage room, located in the rear of the main buildings. She was laying some heavy kisses on me when I heard Setzler yell, "Hey, Bill! We've got a flat that needs fixin'!"

Minnie Mae did a sexy walk back into the café, giving me a suggestive "you-don't know-what-you-missed" smile while I flopped into the garage and patched the tire from the California car. Adding to my anger was when the California customer growled, "Fix it quick, boy. I'm in a hurry!" Then, he walked into the café and had several cups of coffee with Minnie Mae. As he pulled away in his Chrysler, after tossing me a quarter as a tip, Minnie said: "That guy is from Hollywood! He wants to put me in one of his movies!"

"I didn't know you could act, Minnie", I said.

"Lots of things I can do that you don't know about, boy!" She laughed, giving me a *Jane Russell* wink.

Setzler and I finally struck upon an idea that would save us a lot of misery and, at the same time, allow me more precious, uninterrupted moments with Minnie Mae. We decided to take the *"WE FIX FLATS"* sign away from its' obnoxious spot every night after Pop left the premises, headed for home. We would place it behind the building until shortly before 6:00 a.m., when Pop or one of the other hands was scheduled to come on duty, then we would shove it back in place, near the highway.

When cars or trucks would limp in with a flat tire, we would inform the drivers, "We don't fix flats, anymore." We would then send them back up the highway to P. B. Wooldridge's Sinclair station.

This bit of dishonesty worked for several weeks and Pop never mentioned the slow-down in tire repairs that I can remember. All things came to a turn, though, when P. B. Wooldridge dropped by one afternoon for coffee in the café. He asked Pop and me to join him. After talking about baseball for awhile, P. B. said, "Ernest, I want to thank you for the tire-repair business you've been sending me these past few weeks." Slurping some coffee, he added, "I didn't know you had quit fixin' flats after midnight."

Pop gave me a short glance, looked back at P. B. Wooldridge and said, "We're gonna start fixin' them again, tonight."

Setzler was fired from the job and I was placed on the 6:00 p.m. 'til midnight shift, causing a drastic intrusion in my nighttime fun. Adding to the discomfort, Pop was constantly working by my side, overseeing my actions.

Within a few weeks, Minnie Mae left town with the *Holsum Bread* deliveryman.

I sincerely believe that those days spent at the Bumper-To-Bumper Truck Stop in Shamrock were my roots with the industry on wheels. It was in that little service establishment that I caught the truckers in-the-raw. I was to pick up on their language, their mannerisms and their attitudes, all so very interesting to me.

While running the service stations and truck stops, my dad was a "stickler" for courtesy. His Number One rule was to say "Thank you. Come back," when taking loot at the cash register. Anyone caught not extending such courtesies was given one warning. If it happened the second time, the ungrateful employee would be fired.

This was a permanent pattern. No excuses.

"It doesn't cost a thing to be courteous," He lectured. "I've stopped at too many places where they acted like they were too busy to be friendly and to show appreciation. And there's nobody who deserves a 'thank you' more than those truckers out there on th' road."

That attitude toward rudeness I <u>did</u> pick up from Pop. To this day, if the cashier fails to utter words of appreciation for my money that she (or he) just piled into the cash register, I mark my mind to never trade there again. Of course, I've had to ease up a bit on being that finicky, since I've run out of places to shop in my neighborhood! Let's face it: Courtesy is no longer required at most business spots.

Pop used to say, "The two most important words in business are 'Thank you'."

Let me insert a little something here that I will never forget:

Even though there was a café adjoining my dad's truck stop, he would often take truckers to our house for lunch or supper, wanting to treat them to some of my mother's home-cooked food.

His reason for doing this? "They get tired of cafes. They need some home cookin', and there's no better place to get it than in our home."

Years later, Pop sold his Bumper-To-Bumper in Shamrock and he and Mom moved to Amarillo and took over a bigger truck stop on I-40. While visiting him one day, he informed me that a movie outfit was staying across the street at the Ramada Inn and some of the crew had been spending some time at his service spot, including the guy who was supposedly the leading actor, a "very nice young fellow who liked to talk and play the pinball machine."

"Can't be much of a movin' picture," he said, "since it's being made in Claude." Claude, Texas is a small town located about 40 miles southeast of Amarillo.

He also informed me that a nice little "Chinaman", who worked for the movie outfit, spent a lot of his casual time at the truck stop, drinking soft drinks, eating peanut patties and passing friendly, idle chatter. Pop said, "He's a very nice little 'Chinaman' and likes to hang out with me when they allow him some time off.

"He hasn't told me what his job is, but I'd guess he just does general help for them. He probably cleans up after they've finished for the day."

Out of curiosity, I went to the truck stop with Pop and, sure enough, there were several big rigs with "Paramount Pictures" printed in huge lettering on them, setting in the parking lot out back.

I was to find out that the "leading actor" was none other than Paul Newman, while the nice little "Chinaman" was James Wong Howe, who was to win an Oscar for his cinematography in the movie they were filming in Claude. It was titled, "Hud".

CHAPTER FOUR

I was blessed with wonderful, loving parents.

My dad was the greatest human being I have ever known. He was totally unselfish to everyone; a genuinely <u>good</u> man. To this day, almost 20 years after his descent to Heaven, I have people remind me of that fact.

My mother is that creation you read about in books. As I write this, she has her little apartment in Houston, still drives to the store, prefers to do her own cooking ... and she loves to cook for everybody! She's proud of her culinary skill, just as she <u>should</u> be.

Mom has always been a creative person. I'll never forget those bedtime stories she used to tell my brother and me, most of them she concocted as she told them. Great imagination! I've always thought that a good portion of whatever talent I may have had as a writer, songwriter and microphone hired-hand must have been instilled in me by my mother.

She is also a bit nervous at times, and reminds me, always in a loving, joking way, that I have made her a "nervous wreck" down through the years.

Mom has always been scared of thunderstorms. It's a fear which, I was told, stems back to her childhood when a torna-do came close to pulling her up into its' funnel. Anyway, I vividly recall the many wee hours of the mornings when my brother, Clois, and I were awakened from our innocent slumber with those oh-so-familiar words: "You kids wake up! It's comin' up a storm!"

We were then whisked to a storm cellar my dad had dug and covered without any professional help. The "*dug-out*", as it was called, was to play a consistent and important part of my life during those beginning years. During the more threatening thunderstorms, it was usually occupied by several yawning neighbors whom Mom had taken the time to telephone, notifying them of the impending disaster which never, ever occurred, I'm happy and thankful to say.

The setting in the cellar consisted of a dim kerosene lantern hanging from a hook on a rotten beam. And, to add to the excitement of those early morning hours, there were those special creatures found in the dark corners: Several scorpions, centipedes, spiders of different sizes and colors, rats and, on one occasion, a snake of unknown species!

My dad would open the door to the "*dug-out*" from time to time during the storm, and proudly announce that our house was still standing. He would also, inevitably, proclaim the "All's clear!" which was either an invitation for the sheltered neighbors to run into our house for a late cup of coffee or rush to their respective beds amidst the remaining innocent pelts of falling rain.

One thing I will always remember is the fact that my mother would never allow us to bring our cat, Troubles, into the storm cellar because "cats draw lightening". Had Troubles been permitted to be with us in the "dug-out", I'm certain there would have been less vermin in the corners. However, all of us might have been destroyed by lightening!

Who will ever know?

Mom used to place a card in the front window of our house, informing the ice man of how many pounds of ice he was to leave on our back porch. The ice, usually in a big 25-pound block, would be delivered by hook.

My mother kept the block of ice in a big tub. It was covered by a heavy insulated tarp in order to protect it from the heat of those sultry summers. Even though we had a *Kelvinator* refrigerator in good working condition, Mom always ordered the additional ice from time to time, when the weather was extra hot.

One hot June afternoon, my parents and an old neighbor, Mr. Nunn, were watching pea-size hail and sprinkles of rain falling from the threatening sky. My mother was delivering her usual commentary pertaining to what she was certain would be a dreadful weather situation, complete with her predictions that we were all certain to be blown away at any given moment, should the dark green clouds invade our territory.

It was during the early rumblings of the storm that my brother, Clois, and I struck upon an idea that was sure to break the dullness of an otherwise boring afternoon. While Mom was delivering her predictions of fear, we slipped back into the house, went to the back porch and, with the aid of an old broken ice pick, chipped a big slab of ice from the block in the tub. Then, like thieves in the night, we slowly walked from the porch to the side of the house and crawled toward the front yard.

After peeking around the corner, my brother informed me that our parents and Mr. Nunn were still studying the tiny hailstones falling around them. Then, I tossed the big chunk of ice over the house and it fell into the front yard in a perfect position to cause panic. We heard Mom yell, "My God, Ernest! Look at that!"

While my brother and I were bent over in silent laughter, our dad ran to the yard, grabbed up the ice and was running back to the porch as my mother continued screaming: "My God, Ernest, run! You'll be stoned to death!"

Our old neighbor was having trouble controlling his kidneys after witnessing all of the excitement and asked for permission to use our bathroom.

Within minutes, the storm had passed over our town and the frogs were making their usual sounds of tranquility. Mother wasted no time in getting on the telephone, informing all of our neighbors and kin of the "unbelievable hail stone" which my dad had placed in the freezer section of our *Kelvinator*.

In practically no time, our house was swarming with neighbors and relatives while my dad opened the refrigerator door every few minutes to proudly expose our treasured, frozen alien. "I don't want to open it too often," he informed our visitors, "because it might melt some of it!"

After awhile, someone from our hometown newspaper, *The Shamrock Texan*, arrived on the scene holding a camera with a huge flash unit attached to it. Dad opened the door of the refrigerator after being assured by the newspaperman that he was "certain the flash wouldn't melt any of 'it'".

By noon the next day, news of the fallen monster from space

had spread to the surrounding towns of Wellington, Wheeler and McLean, and there were many strange people entering our house as Mr. Nunn took my mother aside and suggested we charge admission to see "it".

I believe some serious thought might have been given to the idea before it was finally rejected. "It would make our house resemble a carnival 'freak show'," my mother said to Mr. Nunn.

"Be that as it may, Irene, them 'freak shows' make th' owners rich!" Mr. Nunn argued.

Around one o'clock that afternoon my mother came into the kitchen and asked who had chipped such a hunk of ice from the block in the tub. The guilty were rapidly found out as Mom removed "it" from the *Kelvinator*, carried the chunk to the big tub on our back porch and, as my brother and I sweated in anticipation of things to come, she placed it almost perfectly into the spot in the block of ice it had originally occupied.

Neither, Charlie Chan nor Sherlock Holmes, could have performed a more accurate study in solving a mystery.

My dad utilized "it" in his iced tea while mother made several humiliating telephone calls explaining her embarrassment to several neighbors and relatives. Most calls ended with Mom saying, 'Yes, it was Billy, and more of his foolishness!"

I've got to tell another one of Mom's favorite stories, one she had a hand in:

Bob Slemmer was a good ol' oversized Shamrock boy whose dad ran a print shop. Although he had never dated, Bob was always fantasizing about the women he was "slippin' around with" when he wasn't busy in the shop.

One day, Bill Setzler just happened to mention to Slemmer that he, Bill, had a cousin visiting from Amarillo who was a stunning beauty. Thinking quickly, Setzler said, "Her name is Mary Margaret and her folks are sending her here to stay with us for awhile because she is so 'wild'!"

When Slemmer was heated, his voice became slushy, resembling the sound of a flushing toilet. Hearing Setzler make the statement, Bob slushed, "Really?"

Then, Bill really laid the interesting news on him. "Yeah, she's crazy about men and her folks just can't control her. They think a smaller town, like Shamrock, might tame her." Pausing for just a moment, he added, "Would you like to meet her?"

Slemmer replied: "I most certainly would! When will she hit town?"

Setzler said 'Mary Margaret' would be in town the next night and, since Bob didn't have a car, he would even furnish the transportation for him and his 'blind date'.

The date was set and it was then that Bill told me how much fun it was going to be. I was to dress up like a female and date Bob Slemmer!

My reaction: "Not on your life, Setz!"

"Come on, Man, it'll be funnier 'n hell!"

I gave a few minutes of thought to the idiotic idea and agreed that it would be one great joke ... if it worked.

My high school principal was Mr. Edward Burkhalter. He was also a master at make-up, having done a lot of theater when he was in college. For some strange reason, Mr. "B", as we called him, agreed to dab the make-up on me and make a phony nose, since mine was extremely "pug", and would be most noticeable, should Slemmer give any serious study to my profile.

My mother, always there when needed, thought the idea was hilarious and volunteered to supply the skirt and sweater I would wear. Mom was a very little lady and, at the time, I was also skinny. The outfit fit me almost perfectly. Although I felt like a fool while she "straightened here and there", I must admit that when the make-up had been applied by Mr. "B", I was one good-looking chick! In my mind, I resembled Natalie Wood.

Mom said "falsies" would also be needed, even telling me how to place them, and Mr. "B" had located a cute, dark brown wig. I had also doused myself heavily with my mother's favorite *Avon* cologne.

There were a couple of *Band-Aids* on my legs, caused by a dull razor when I shaved them, but all-in-all, everything looked pretty good on my body. My feet were fairly small and I wore brown loafers and white sox, which were the trend at the time for both, boys and girls.

Plan was, I would drive to Setzler's house in my car and wait in his living room while he, Wayne Carver and Glenn Reeves went to pick up Bob Slemmer. Then, they would bring Slemmer back to the house where he "would call on me".

Might mention here: Glenn Reeves, a good Shamrock chum, would eventually move to Florida, get into country music and was *to sing the "demo" recording of a song written by our dear friend, Mae Axton, titled "Heartbreak Hotel". Mae informed me Elvis sang the song <u>exactly</u> as Glenn had performed it on the demo. She also said she had offered Glenn a percentage of the writers' credit/ownership, but he chose to accept a token of money for his efforts, instead. It was a decision Glenn would regret for the rest of his life.*

While sitting nervously in Bill's living room, I noticed his dad giving me a strange look as he glanced up from the newspaper. We hadn't informed Mr. Setzler of the joke and I honestly believe he winked at me as I sat there across the room from him. Obviously, he had no idea I was the little cutie, which gave me a bit of assurance Slemmer wouldn't be able to detect the bit of absurdity.

Soon, the doorbell rang. I walked slowly to the door, making certain the light near the door was turned off. As I opened it, I could see Slemmer's fat body, silhouetted by the big moon glowing behind him, and I heard the slurpy voice: "Mary Margaret, I presume!"

He then handed me a box of *Whitman's Candy*, took my arm, and led me to the Plymouth.

I couldn't utilize my normal voice, of course, and it was pre-decided I would speak in a whisper when the occasion arose for me to react to Slemmer. As an excuse for my whispering, Setzler had informed Bob that "Mary Margaret had almost lost her voice from screaming at her parents." It was also understood that the car would stay away from all bright-lighted areas, and when we neared a street light, I would turn my head from Slemmer.

While Setzler, Wayne Carver and Glenn Reeves were crowded in the front seat with the radio at full blast to drown out any upcoming laughter, it didn't take long for me to discover what countless females are subjected to. We were hardly in the backseat of the car before Slemmer placed his heavy arm around my shoulders and growled, "Come to me, baby."

I shoved him back, removing his arms from my shoulders.

Bob and I remained speechless for a moment, and then he asked, "Ever go *upstairs*, baby?"

I thought: "My God! This is getting out of hand!" I did manage to reply, in a very nervous whisper: "What do you mean?"

"I mean ... do you ever go up in the sky in airplanes?"

"No!"

Slemmer then went into one of his most vivid bits of bravado nothingness. He spit out, "Well, if you ever want to *go upstairs*, give me a ring. I'm a pilot. I have my own plane. It's nothing fancy, but it flys!"

I could hardly hold my laugh on this one. Here was a dude who couldn't drive a car, but was claiming he could whiz over Shamrock in his own, personal plane! And just as this absurd junk was crossing my mind, here came the arms again! Before I could defend myself, Slemmer was attempting to lay me down in the backseat while Perry Como was crooning *"PRISONER OF LOVE"* on Setzler's radio. I managed to escape, pulling myself back up in the seat. Adding to my misery and fear, as I was adjusting the "falsies", which had managed to move toward my side, I received a swamp-like kiss on the cheek from Bob, who was, without a doubt, in serious heat! I gave him a hard, loud slap and could hear the muffled laughter from the front seat!

There was no reaction from Slemmer after I slapped him. He seemed to be in a more calm frame of mind for a couple of minutes, and then he slobbered, "Let's get close!" Again, he tried to muscle me down in the seat and, again, I managed to get back in a sitting position.

I was scared out of my mind when Setzler brought the car to a halt near the Twitty, Texas cotton gin, located 7 miles north of Shamrock, a favorite parking spot for lovers in our area.

Twitty was the town Mississippi's Harold Lloyd Jenkins would find on the map and, combining it with Conway, Arkansas, would change to the professional name, Conway Twitty.

Setzler said, "We'll go over to the café and get some coffee while you lovebirds get better acquainted."

Shaking, I said, "I want to go home!" I was still whispering, not wanting Slemmer to catch on to the shenanigan that was getting out-of-hand. Honestly, I was afraid he would attempt to rape me before the night was over!

Slemmer grabbed my hand and growled, "Your hand's cold, baby! What's wrong?"

"I'm sick," I replied,

"Oh, is it 'that time'?" He asked, his voice allowing a bit of concern to be heard.

"Yes."

Slemmer nudged Setzler on the back and said, "Mary Margaret feels bad. I think we'd better take her home."

During the eight-mile trip back to the Setzler house, Slemmer kept mauling at me, attempting to kiss me, and I continued slapping back. Finally, after reaching our destination, he opened the door of the Plymouth, pulled me out and walked me to the door. He tried to kiss me goodnight, but I simply turned my head and pushed him away.

As he opened the door of the house for me, he slurped the words: "Tomorrow night, same time?"

Making every attempt to get away from him, I whispered, "Yes", before slamming the door in his face.

Setzler, Carver, Reeves and Slemmer headed for the *K. C. Steakhouse* while I removed my makeup, my sweater, skirt, wig, "falsies" and all other attachments. Then, I tugged on my regular clothes, jumped into my Ford and headed for the K. C. to join the clowns. Bob Slemmer thought I had been on a date with my girl-friend, Jackie, and was the reason why I hadn't been in their company earlier.

As I walked into the restaurant, I saw the smiling faces in a big booth near the rear. Seating myself next to Slemmer, I heard his first heavy announcement: "You should have seen what I <u>had</u> tonight."

"Really?" I asked in a tone of both, innocence and concern.

"Yeah," slushed Slemmer, a big smile on his face. "I <u>had</u> Setzler's cousin, Mary Margaret! Gorgeous!"

Setzler inserted, "Bob says she's crazy about him!"

I could only manage another, "Really?"

Then, Slemmer let the handle down. Spitting every word perfectly in my direction, he grumbled, "I'm <u>having</u> her again tomorrow night. Then ... after I'm finished with her ... she's <u>all</u> <u>yours</u>!"

Looking me square in the eye, Bob Slemmer released his trademark laugh, "Huak! Huak! Huak!"

Bill Setzler, Wayne Carver and Glenn Reeves also broke out in loud laughter while I ordered my hamburger, french-fries and *Coke*.

CHAPTER FIVE

My high school days were fun. Sorry to say, they weren't as educational as they should have been, but they were enjoyable. I didn't go out for sports, although I did try my hand at boxing for a short amount of time and I did this for the sole purpose of impressing my high school sweetheart, Jackie Briggs. Edward Burkhalter, my high school principal, had also dabbled in boxing as a youth and thought I should give it a try, since I would be fighting in the lightweight division and was blessed with a "pug" nose, almost unbreakable. I was told most great fighters had pug noses.

The annual Shamrock High School boxing tournament was coming up and I was set to go! I would put on my white shorts, have someone strap on the huge boxing gloves, and give the punching bags fits. My coach informed me I had a "built-in swing, the kind that lays lesser swingers 'on the mat'."

To make certain I would be ready for the big night, "working out" was a priority. I would spar with different boxers in the ring, none of us putting our hearts into it, not wanting to cause any "hurt" until it counted. My sparring partners built my confidence by informing me I was a true fighter with a powerful punch.

My first match was to be with a skinny little fellow named Red Peevey. He was referred to as "Little Red". Red was from the rural area around Samnorwood, Texas and it was to be his first official match in the ring, also.

I had seen Little Red walking around the gym area for a few days and I always felt a bit sorry for him because his red hair needed cutting and. since we were shirtless, I noticed his ribs were literally sticking through the skin, leaving the impression he might be hungry; undernourished.

I wanted to be friendly, although I certainly didn't want to over-do it. I growled, "How are you, Red?"

Little Red was shy. He looked down at his torn tennis shoes and replied, "Fine". His voice was barely audible, revealing the fact he was probably scared out of his lovin' mind, dreading the upcoming fight.

On the day of the boxing tournament, I was in the gym, practicing my punches, anxious for the ring of the bell. Excitement was in the air! I told Mr. Burkhalter I would like to be matched with someone other than Little Red Peevey because it would be a mismatch. I simply didn't want to hurt the little fellow. Also, Jackie and several others wouldn't consider me much of a hero by watching me beat the hell out of someone resembling a tubercular case! "I'm even willing to punch it out with someone a little heavier than me," I said, furiously slapping the punching bag.

"It's all set with Little Red," said Mr. Burkhalter. "We can't change the line-up, now. Besides, it's a big night for Red, too. It's his first official time in the ring and his relatives will all be here from out in the country."

Grabbing a sweat towel, I said, "Well, I'll go easy on him for the first few rounds ... before I end it!"

That night, the Shamrock gymnasium was packed to the rafters with screaming fight fans. There were a couple of minor matches before I was to enter the ring with Little Red and I was sitting in the workout room in the rear of the gym, dressed in my bright green shorts, matching green sox and white shoes, talking to some of the other guys who were scheduled for the ring that night.

I remember looking at Roy Don Brower, a heavyweight, and saying, "I wish I was matched with you tonight, instead of Little Red. Man, this is going to be embarrassing!"

Roy Don grunted, "Well, just get it over with! You don't have to kill him, you know!"

In a few minutes, the trainer came in and tied on my big boxing gloves. He said, "You're set to go in next."

As I entered the ring, I received a tremendous ovation. I

spotted Jackie and a bunch of my thug pals close to ringside. They were all giving me the "thumbs up" and shouting words of encouragement as I proudly galloped around the ropes. When Little Red entered, there was an embarrassing lull in the sound, except for a few people from the farming community where he lived, who were applauding him. My followers even had the audacity to "boo" the poor little man as he walked slowly to his corner wearing faded brown shorts, white sox and dirty gray shoes.

The referee brought both of us to the center of the ring, gave us the regular rules and instructions, adding: "Now, go to your corners and when the bell sounds, come out fighting."

I strutted to my corner, smiling, while Little Red walked to his corner and sat down on his stool.

I winked at Jackie, just as the bell sounded, and then galloped to the center of the ring, my arms already punching at the air, as Little Red approached me with both arms down, not even in a fighting position. I lowered my hands and yelled to him, "Let's fight!"

As I was being carried to my dressing room by the trainer and a couple of other people whose names I can't recall, I managed to ask, "Wha ... what happened?"

They laid me down easy on the workout lounge and applied cold cloths to my head while the trainer collected enough nerve to say, "You got hit pretty hard, Bill. That skinny little devil knocked you out!"

"How long did our fight last?"

There was a long pause before the trainer admitted: "About 18 seconds, I was told."

Since my attempts at becoming Shamrock's Kidd Smith in the ring had failed, Mr. Burkhalter approached me with the idea of me "announcing" the Friday night boxing matches. I was to sit at ringside and, utilizing the school's public address system, make all pertinent announcements during the fights such as, "Please step outside the gym to smoke." or "The concession stand is open if you would like to have hotdogs or cold drinks!" I would also announce the names of the fighters entering the ring and, of course, the winners.

It was while serving as the public address announcer for a couple of years that Mrs. Barkley, the wife of my dentist, approached me at the concessions stand and said, "Bill, you have a very good voice on the microphone. You should give some thought to getting into radio!"

At the time, I considered that a nice compliment and, as I look back, actually believe it might have been the statement that lit the fuse that instigated my interest in the field of broadcasting.

As far back as I can remember, radio has played a very important part in my life.

During my childhood, television was a thing of the future. A few isolated stations were in limited operation, most of them in the eastern part of the nation, but few people in the south were aware of them and could care less. It wasn't a big deal at the time and when World War II broke out in 1941, what television was being transmitted took a recess until the big war came to a close.

Radio was the big thing. It encouraged <u>imagination</u>. In my mind, I could actually picture the action of *"Jack Armstrong! The All-American Boy!* Brought to you by <u>*Wheaties*</u>, the <u>*Breakfast of Champions!*</u>" "Jack Armstrong", via the power of radio, literally forced me to make *Wheaties* the breakfast cereal that bumped my young body into action every morning.

I would rush home from grade school in order to catch the late afternoon episodes of those other gigantic heroes of the airwaves, *"Dick Tracy"* and *"The Lone Ranger"*. The combination of sound and imagination had me hooked to our *Philco.*

As a teenager, my taste in the airwaves changed to such biggies as *"The Jack Benny Program"*, *"The Bob Hope Show"* and *"Your Hit Parade"*.

Also, there were those powerful radio stations that became a part of our household. WBAP and WFAA out of Fort Worth and Dallas were favorites. KGNC, broadcasting from Amarillo, was another very important station at our house. This was because Amarillo was less than a hundred miles from Shamrock and KGNC would program features that were a little closer to home. KWFT, Wichita Falls, Texas, was also a very special spot on the AM dial. This was where I could pick up Blaine Cornwell's dynamic voice as he spotlighted the *"Top Ten Records of the Week"*.

My favorite programs were heard late at night. I loved to dial in the Old Mexico border stations such as XELO, Clint, Texas … XEG, Fort Worth, Texas and, my super favorite, XERF, Del Rio,

Texas. It may sound a little confusing when I say these were stations in Mexico while tagging Texas cities. Reason for this was Mexico set up post office addresses in the towns in Texas in order to make it easier for listeners to send money when ordering such well advertised goodies as baby chickens by mail *(" ... and any dead chickens delivered will be replaced by mail!")* ... razor blades *("These razor blades have been separately super-sharpened in order to give you the best shave of your life! And you can get one-hundred blades for only a dollar! Send one dollar to ... The Blade Man, Del Rio, Texas!")* ... and, believe it-or-not, a tablecloth from Heaven! It was a tablecloth featuring "a real picture of Jesus", guaranteed to bring you happiness and <u>wealth</u>! *("Yes, this is a <u>beautiful</u> table cloth that, when placed on your table at mealtime, will bring health, wealth and happiness to your family! And the cost? Only one dollar! That's right, only one dollar for this <u>specially</u> <u>blessed</u> tablecloth! Mail one dollar to ... Jesus, Del Rio, Texas!)* They would even spell it for you. *("That's one dollar to Jesus ... spelled J-E-S-U-S ... Jesus, Del Rio, Texas!")*.

Incidentally, this was before zip codes came into being.

I especially loved listening to Wayne Raney and Lonnie Glosson with their 15-minute radio shows peddling their harmonicas and songbooks. *("You can play the harmonica right there in the privacy of your own home or, like so many other fortunate folks, play the harmonica for your friends! We found out th' ladies <u>love</u> th' sound of th' harmonica! Make that little lady in your life happy! Play her favorite songs on the harmonica ... just like me and Lonnie do every night on this fine radio station! And we'll also send you our new song book which will let you <u>sing</u> <u>along</u> with us on the radio, right there in your own home! And there's also a picture of Lonnie an' me in th' songbook which we will be happy to <u>personally</u> <u>autograph</u> for you! Now listen! You'll git th' harmonica <u>and</u> th' songbook with personally autographed pictures of Lonnie an' me for only ... now, git this, friends an' neighbors ... only one dollar! Mail one dollar to Harmonica, Del Rio, Texas!*

That's Harmonica ... H-A-R-M-O-N-I-C-A ... Harmonica, Del Rio, Texas!")

I ordered a harmonica from Wayne and Lonnie and never received it!

53

Years later, I had Wayne Raney as a guest on my radio show and told him I had never received the harmonica he and Lonnie had advertised over twenty years earlier on XERF, even though I had mailed my hard-earned dollar to him. Laughing, he handed me a dollar bill and said, "For some strange reason, a lot of folks never received their harmonicas."

The reason Mexican border radio stations were so popular was because the Mexican government hadn't set any limits on the wattage power of the outlets located south of the border. *The Federal Communications Commission* in the United States set a limit of 50,000 watts for AM stations while the Mexican radio outlets were blasting out at 100,000 watts and more. Also, the cost of advertising in Old Mexico was cheap. Preachers and country music entertainers made a wad of loot off such memorable radio stations as XEG, XELO, XERF and a few others blasting the airwaves with 150,000 or 250,000 watts of radio power. At one time, the power went to 500,000 watts on XERF, but the Mexican government was forced to cut it back because of some problems outside of radio. I heard from several sources that the half-million watts caused the barbed wire surrounding fields and ranches to glow in the dark! The tin roofs on barns and outhouses would light up in an eerie red glow after sundown. Hard to believe, but many testified that they were picking up the border radios stations via the fillings in their teeth! Yes, I laughed at this bit of idiocy until an engineer at KWFT in Wichita Falls seriously explained to me how this could, indeed, take place.

Do you happen to remember the preaching of "*Brother Divine*" on those powerful boomers from South of the Border? *("I can _heal_ that arthritis. I can _heal_ that crippled foot! I can _heal_ that near blindness! All you need is my blessed _prayer cloth_! And I will be happy to mail you this beautiful, blessed prayer cloth for only one dollar! I would send it to you free ... but we need your _offerings_ in order to keep this program from God on the air! All you need to send is one dollar! And when your prayer cloth arrives, dial in this program, place the prayer cloth on the spot giving you trouble and I will say a special prayer on the radio and _heal_ that hurt! Just mail one dollar to Brother Divine ... that's BROTHER D-I-V-I-N-E ... Brother Divine, Del Rio, Texas! Don't put it off, brothers and sisters, get your dollar in the mail tonight! Don't wait another day to get rid of that pain! Mail one dollar to Brother*

Divine … that's BROTHER D-I-V-I-N-E … Brother Divine, Del Rio, Texas! Let me heal the hurt!")

Then, there was the *King of Medicine, Doctor Brinkley.* The old doc had been kicked out of the United States because of malpractice and assorted other questionable acts. He finally moved to Del Rio, Texas, bought time across the border at XERA (which would eventually become XERF) and began peddling his goat glands. That's a fact! The not-so-good doctor advertised on the air the good news that all men lacking in their sexual duties could "come to Del Rio to my clinic and I will replace those worn out glands that are embarrassing you, sexually, and causing so much hurt and neglect to that precious little wife … with the miracle of 'goat glands'! You will feel young again! Your little wife will feel young again … thanks to the miracle of goat glands! The surgery is almost painless and can be performed at a low cost to you! After all … what is money when it comes to 'home happiness'?"

Men with troubled sex and prostate problems traveled to Del Rio from all over the world in order to have their inactive glands replaced by those extracted from the hapless goats.

It's been said that the fastest animal in the world was a goat passing Doctor Brinkley's office.

Horrible joke performed by the comedy act, Homer and Jethro: Referring to Dr. Brinkley's "goat surgery", Homer said, "I wonder how that goat surgery worked."

Jethro, sounding like a goat: "Not b-a-a-a-a-d!"

The great old act, The Carter Family, also moved to Del Rio and presented their nightly radio shows on XERF for awhile. They would sell their phonograph recordings, songbooks, autographed photos, announce their personal appearances and live nicely, thanks to the Mexican powerhouse.

I might mention here that the reason all of the sponsors, preachers and singers bought the night time, early morning hours on the so-called border stations, is because AM radio reaches out farther during the night; when temperatures are cooler. That's still the case today and is the reason I would eventually spend over 30 years doing my radio show out of Fort Worth between midnight and dawn. The later the hours, the cooler the temperatures, the better the coverage when it comes to AM radio.

My dear friend Paul Kallinger, who had a country music show on XERF for many years, told me it wasn't unusual for him to receive mail from Australia, England and Japan on a regular basis.

"I received phone calls from Canada and other countries asking me to play Webb Pierce, Ernest Tubb and the likes," said Paul.

I wasn't into country and western music during my teen years. It was called "hillbilly" back then. My pals and I used to drive around town listening to the radio and poking fun at the works of the hillbilly stars. My favorites were such singers as Sinatra, Ella Fitzgerald, Perry Como and The Mills Brothers.

My granddad Sechrist was the one who brought any serious focus of country music into my younger years. He kept telling me, "Bill, you need to listen to this fellow, Eddy Arnold. Now, there's a real singer. He's the best there is!" Although I didn't agree that he was the "best there is", I did believe Arnold was better than most of the so-called rural stars on radio and records. His recording of *"Bouquet Of Roses"* played constantly on the old Wurlitzer jukebox at the *Green Frog Café*, located across the street from dear old Shamrock High. My pals and I used to sneak over to the *Green Frog* to smoke our *Lucky Strikes* and listen to the jukebox.

Country music really became an important sound in my life when my high school sweetheart, Jackie Briggs, and I had a serious falling out. Jackie and I were together constantly, patronizing the *Texas* and *Liberty* movie houses and dancing at the *U-Drop-Inn*. In between the movies and dancing, we would spend time at my house listening to records and eating homemade fudge. We were a very close couple, making big plans for the future.

One night, for some reason I can't recall, Jackie ordered me to "get lost!". Although the reason for our temporary split has long been forgotten, I do remember leaving her house in a very sad state of mind and picking up my old pal, Bill Setzler. Setz and I wheeled around the empty streets of Shamrock during those late hours. He drove while I smoked my cigarettes and released my words of sorrow. Searching for music, I stopped the dial at Radio Station WLW in Cincinnati where the great country music disk jockey, Nelson King, was doing his late night thing. Although I wasn't a real fan of country music, I enjoyed listening to Nelson because of his authoritative approach to radio. It was obvious that he was in complete command. Even his commercials had that distinctive one-on-one appeal. He didn't sound like he was <u>reading</u> a commercial. Instead, it was more like he was simply <u>telling</u> you what you should do if you ever came down with a case of hemorrhoids. I well remember Nelson King allowed me to forget my hurt over Jackie momentarily and break into a much needed laugh with Bill Setzler as he informed us of the benefits of using 'Preparation H'.

"Are you suffering from itching, burning, tormenting hemorrhoids, my friend? Well, don't you dare suffer another minute! Relieve yourself of the agony of hemorrhoids ... sometimes referred to as 'piles'. Take it from your old friend, Nelson King. Pick up a pack of Preparation H' at your drugstore. Maybe there's a store open tonight! Get a pack! Yes, try a few applications of Preparation H and say goodbye to those hemorrhoids. With no more 'piles', there will be many more smiles —- thanks to Preparation H'! "

Even though I had no problems with hemorrhoids, I felt like Nelson was speaking confidentially to me ... like a caring friend.

Soon the laughter subsided and Jackie jumped back into my thoughts. Then, adding to my hurt, I heard Nelson King announce: "Here's a great new singer from the state of Alabama. I love the way the man sings his songs. Here, my friends, is Hank Williams and a song he composed titled, '*MANSION ON THE HILL*.''

I truly believe it was at that very moment: Close to midnight ... on a dark street in my hometown ...listening to Hank Williams sing "*MANSION ON THE HILL*" ... that my avenue in life made a complete change.

CHAPTER SIX

I'm not going to dwell on my teenage romances, although I must mention Jo Nell Gamble. Without realizing it, Jo Nell was partly responsible for my entering the field of broadcasting.

Since my Shamrock High School sweetheart, Jackie, and I were in a split situation, I took a temporary shine on Jo Nell Gamble. Jo Nell and I both joined the Thespian Club, an acting class under the tutelage of Professor Fred Short at Shamrock High. Coincidentally, we were both aspiring actors and were cast for leading rolls in Prof Short's production of a play titled, "*Night Must Fall*". There was a special spot in the play where I was to give Jo Nell's character a simple, innocent kiss on the cheek, the way we had rehearsed it for a couple of weeks before the play was to be presented. However, on the night of the production at Clark Auditorium in Shamrock, I improvised a bit. Came time for the special scene and instead of giving Jo Nell a simple kiss on the cheek, I pulled her into my arms and, in front of the filled auditorium, including Jackie, I gave her a hungry kiss in the mouth that lasted for close to a minute, according to my cheering, applauding hoodlum pals. After the kiss was completed and the curtain was pulled, the audience headed for the exits, including Jackie.

I received a serious butt chewing from Professor Short, while Jackie decided she "had had enough!"

Eventually, Fred Short accepted me back into the acting group. since thespians were hard to come by in Shamrock, but Jackie was to take her leisure time in reopening her arms to me.

That would have been a crushing blow to my heart had it not been for good ol' Jo Nell, who was <u>waiting</u> <u>in</u> <u>the</u> <u>wings,</u> so to speak. She informed me that she loved the way I kissed … and she was also nuts about my *Avon* cologne, which I splashed on heavily every day. The cologne came easily for me, since my mother was an *Avon* sales lady and I knew where she kept the "samples".

It got to the hot point to where Jo Nell and I would synchronize our watches, ask to be excused from our respective classes at exactly the same time, meet at the water fountain on the second floor of Shamrock High and exchange sizzling kisses.

The hit show from Broadway, Rodgers' and Hammerstein's *"Oklahoma!",* featuring the original New York cast, was scheduled for a special appearance in Oklahoma City, located 180 miles from Shamrock. Fred Short thought it would be most beneficial to our Thespian Club if we took an overnight trip to the big town. He was most determined that his class of amateurs would witness the heavyweight performers in action.

The trip to Oklahoma City via Greyhound Bus was most memorable. Before reaching the Texas/Oklahoma border town of Texola, 14 miles east of Shamrock, I was holding Jo Nell's clammy hand in the back row seat of the bus. She had brought a green and white blanket, Shamrock's official colors, to keep us warm. "I hear it gets cold on these old busses," she said. I rapidly agreed.

Jo Nell and I puffed on our Camel cigarettes behind Fred Short's back. There were also a couple of chaperons seated up front, but they could have cared less about the activities behind them. As I recall, one of the chaperons was sneaking around with a coach from McLean, Texas while the other had a big crush on a wrestler in Amarillo. They were big sports fans.

By the time the bus reached Sayre, Oklahoma, 28 miles east of Shamrock, Jo Nell and I were making big plans. We had agreed to meet in the lobby of the Oklahoma City hotel shortly after the clock struck midnight, while Prof Short and the two needless chaperons were asleep. "We'll have fun!" She giggled, squeezing my hand.

"You can count on that, Baby," I inserted.

As I lit another Camel, she looked me square in the eyes and whispered, "My God! You are a wild man! Has anyone ever told you that you resemble Burt Lancaster?"

"No."

"Well, it's not so much that you <u>look</u> like Burt Lancaster, but you have his <u>wicked</u> laugh! Wild!"

Her words and actions had given me an overdose of encouragement and when the bus finally reached the hotel in Oklahoma City, my mind was at work on how to handle the heated Jo Nell. Jo Nell, however, had been snoring on my arm for over an hour. I had to awaken her as the rest of our crew was exiting the bus.

After checking into our rooms and freshening up with showers, we were set to meet in the hotel coffee shop for snacks before bedding down for the night. It was already past 8:00 o'clock before the group gathered for food. "You will want to get plenty of sleep tonight," said Prof Short. "Tomorrow will be a long and exciting day. We will meet for breakfast at nine o'clock in the morning."

Jo Nell was sitting beside me in the booth, munching on a hamburger. I squeezed her hand and whispered, "Meet you in the lobby at midnight."

I will always remember her expression as she looked at me and asked: "What?"

"I said … I'll meet you in the lobby of this hotel at midnight. Sneak out of your room prepared for one big night of it!"

She bit back into her hamburger and replied: "O.K."

It was an almost heartless statement.

Naturally, I was in the lobby of the hotel long before the scheduled midnight meeting time that had been set with Jo Nell. The only person in the huge room was a black porter wearing a red cap. He was snoozing in a section of the lobby marked: "Negroes". This was back in time when blacks and whites utilized separate sections. There were separate rest rooms, separate water fountains, almost everything was separate, depending on the color of skin.

The clock struck midnight and the only sound was that of a lonesome train whistle. I checked for elevator movement toward the lobby and there was none. Since all of our rooms were near the top of the big hotel, I was certain Jo Nell wouldn't take the stairs. The clock moved to 12:30 a.m. and, still, Jo Nell had not arrived. Finally, the porter awoke, coughed and said, "Can I help you with somethin'?"

"Waitin' on a woman," I growled.

"No problem, man," said the porter, smiling. "Got twenty dollars on you?"

"No!" I grumbled. "I've got a woman. She ought to be here any time now."

"All right, man," replied the porter, snoozing off again.

At 1:00 a.m., I accepted the fact that Jo Nell wasn't going to make the scheduled scene and went back to the room I was sharing with Jerry Berten. Berten was still awake as I entered. He asked, "How was she, Bill?"

"Unbelievable."

"Jo Nell Gamble!" He shouted. "You are one lucky dude!"

After I had finally crawled into bed, I heard him repeat: "Jo Nell Gamble! You are one lucky dude!"

Not wanting to reveal my failed plans with the lady, I replied, "Yeah. That Jo Nell is somethin' else!"

Next morning, I had made my mind up. There would be no more Jo Nell Gamble. Besides, I was missing Jackie.

As Jo Nell entered the coffee shop, she jumped into the booth next to me and whispered, "I'm sorry. I suppose I was suffering from bus-lag. I went to sleep as soon as I hit the bed. I was exhausted." Then, sipping some water, she asked, "Will you forgive me?"

I attempted to ignore her question. However, she kissed me softly on the ear and repeated: "Will you please forgive me? I promise to make it up to you tonight!"

"We'll see." I growled, feeling like Burt Lancaster.

After finishing our ham, eggs and coffee, Professor Short made the announcement: "We will catch the matinee of 'Oklahoma!', come back to the hotel for an early dinner and then, we are going to visit the studios of Radio Station WKY, located here in this hotel. I spoke with the manager this morning and he assured me that it would be the honor of the great radio station to have us as special guests."

Since Fred Short was also the speech professor at Shamrock High, he felt our witnessing broadcasting in action would add to our visit to Oklahoma City.

Everything went per schedule. We arrived via bus at the Oklahoma City Municipal Auditorium at least an hour before "Oklahoma!" was scheduled to begin. Jo Nell and I sneaked Camel cigarettes to and from our sweaty hands while walking far behind the rest of our motley crew. Even though I was traveling with limited funds, I did manage to purchase a couple of hot dogs and cokes for Jo Nell and me and forked over another dollar and fifty cents for a porcelain ash tray proclaiming, *WELCOME TO OKLAHOMA CITY!* in bold, black lettering. She later dropped the ash tray, breaking it into many pieces, while rushing to the ladies' rest room as the orchestra played the overture to "*Oklahoma!*" just before curtain time. She asked me to buy a replacement for her but I steadfastly refused, informing her I might make another purchase before leaving Oklahoma City, depending on how our late night plans came to pass.

After the "*Oklahoma!*" matinee, which I still consider to be the greatest of all Broadway shows, our bunch returned to the hotel in the dependable old bus for an early dinner. As we gulped and burped our tuna sandwiches and cokes, Prof Short reminded us we could, with proper training and real devotion, become Broadway performers comparable to those we had witnessed in action that afternoon. As I recall, we all responded with "Bravo!", having heard the mysterious word shouted by the audience following the conclusion of "*Oklahoma!*"

After we had our dinner, we were to go to our hotel rooms, shower and dress properly for the visit to the WKY radio studios. Professor Short suggested the boys wear coats and ties and the girls put on their dainty best. "Also," he added, "you might want to think of some questions to ask our hosts pertaining to radio."

Dressed as ordered, we again congregated in the lobby of the hotel and then took elevators to the floor where the studios of WKY were located. In the elevator, I snuck my clammy palm into Jo Nell's cold hand. "Love me?" I asked.

Her reply: "Where's th' damned ashtray you promised me?"

The elevator door opened, revealing the blazing letters, *WKY!*

As we waited for the rest of our group to arrive, I noticed the business of broadcasting in action for the first time. Soft music played from hidden speakers in the background as a kindly receptionist invited us into a huge waiting room and offered us soft drinks. Soon, our entire group was assembled in the waiting room, belching the complimentary drinks. Suddenly, from out of nowhere, a tall, thin dude with a huge Adam's-apple announced: "Welcome to WKY! Follow me, please, and keep your voices as low as possible. If you must speak, please utilize a whisper." Then, with a semi-smile, he added, "I … am your host." It was then that I noticed his Adam's-apple bobbing up and down just above his buttoned shirt collar.

Jo Nell immediately whispered, "God! He's gorgeous! And did you ever hear a voice as deep and beautiful? He's absolutely it!"

I was speechless. I was also allowing my jealousy to show as I tossed my empty coke bottle into a wastebasket. Naturally, the host heard the coke hitting the bottom of the basket, put his long finger to his mouth and whispered, "Shh! Don't forget ... this is a radio station."

As we followed the mysterious guide down the well-lighted corridors, we gazed at huge pictures of various stars of broadcasting who were popular at the time, hanging on the pastel painted walls. Under each picture was the name of the star and, under the names, were the proud letters: *NBC* with explanatory captions in smaller print proclaiming: "*The National Broadcasting Company*".

Our guide opened a heavy door to a large studio. Over the door was a brightly lighted sign which read: "Silence Please". Under that sign was an even more impressive bit of print, although it wasn't lighted, exclaiming: "ON-THE-AIR!"

The deep voice of the guide broke the temporary silence. "This is the main studio here at WKY. This is where most of our *live* programs are produced."

Jo Nell and I had hidden ourselves near a big ashtray in the corner of the dimly lighted room. "Sneak me a Camel!" She whispered.

"You can't smoke in here!" I replied, still ticked over her remarks pertaining to the tall host.

"What do you mean we can't smoke? Why is there an ash tray here if we can't smoke?"

In my know-it-all tone of voice, I said, "Well, the ash trays are for the radio bosses and sponsors. Announcers and performers don't smoke. Smoke ruins their vocal chords."

I had no sooner finished that stupid statement when the guide struck a match, lit a cigarette and informed Prof Short and the two chaperons: "You may smoke if you like."

Jo Nell gave me a look of total disgust as we walked toward the front of the studio and rejoined the rest of our throng in time to hear the tall one announce that we would now proceed to the News Room. "Sorry there is nothing of importance going on in our main studio tonight," he said. "Practically all of our live programs are aired during the early morning hours." He paused and added, "Perhaps you can arrange to join us some morning for 'Wiley and Gene'."

It was then that I decided to display my intelligent, inquiring nature. "Who are Wiley and Gene?"

The guide gave me a look of obvious disgust and replied in oh-so-low tones: "Wiley and Gene just happen to be the most popular <u>hillbilly</u> radio and record performers in this part of the world. They receive hundreds of fan letters per day!"

"I listen to them every morning while getting ready for school," breathed Jo Nell, of all people. "Aren't they sponsored by a grain company?"

The guide gave Jo Nell a gentle pat on the arm. "Right you are, <u>Sweetheart</u>! Wiley and Gene are, indeed, sponsored by Purina Mills!"

Then, Jo Nell moved her shapely frame closer to the tall, thin hunk, looked up at his bobbling Adam's-apple and cooed: "Do you announce on the radio, by chance?"

"No chance at all," laughed the proud one. "I am the <u>announcer</u> for Wiley and Gene!"

"God! I mean ... gosh! I <u>love</u> your voice!" She screamed. "It sounds so very mature! Oh, I mean ... it sounds so ... <u>manly</u>!"

"Thank you, sweet little lady!" He said. It was most evident that he had lowered his voice a couple of more octaves while responding to Jo Nell's compliments.

Jo Nell grabbed his arm, looked up again and moaned: "Would you mind if I walked with you while you show the <u>boys</u> and <u>girls</u> in my class the rest of the radio station? I've always admired you people in broadcasting!"

"I would be honored, Dear." He panted. "Hold to my arm if you would like ... and the rest of you <u>follow us</u>!"

While the rest of the group seemed to be sneering at my somewhat uncomfortable situation, I continued the drawn out tour of the WKY studios at the rear of the line with Jerry Berten. "Looks like you've lost ol' Jo Nell to that big shot radio announcer, Bill," he said.

"Bull! She's mine when I need her," I growled.

Finally, after touring the news room and witnessing the United Press ticking news-wire machine in action, the guide/host shook our hands individually, forced a big tooth-faced smile and said, "Anytime you are in the city, be sure to come back and see us here at WKY. Again ... I'm so sorry there wasn't much excitement here tonight."

Jo Nell purred: "I found it very exciting. I'm certainly going to come back, even if I have to hitch-hike."

The suave one kissed her on the cheek, to my disgust! "You are a Sweetheart," he blubbered. "And you'll never have to hitch a ride. Just telephone me when you're back in town and I will personally pick you up! Har! Har!"

Adding to my anger, my group laughed and applauded the host for making such a talented, funny statement to a commoner.

As we headed back toward the elevators to take us to our respective floors, I whispered to Jo Nell: "Midnight tonight? In the lobby?"

She stopped at the water fountain, twisted the knob, took a sincere slurp of water and replied: "Where's my damned ash tray you promised me?"

Before I could reply, she jumped aboard the overcrowded elevator just as the door closed, leaving me standing in the lobby beside Jerry Berten. "Are you meetin' ol' Jo Nell again tonight, Bill?" He asked.

"No." I replied in a low tone of voice. "I'm getting' some rest. She wore me out this morning!"

Next day, on the Greyhound bus whizzing back to Shamrock, Jo Nell displayed very little reaction to anything I had to say. As a matter of fact, there were obvious signs pointing toward frigidity as I whispered, "I'm going to forgive you for losing your pretty little head over that stupid radio announcer last night."

"Who asked you to forgive me?" She growled, secretly lighting a Camel cigarette under the green and white blanket. Then, staring out the window of the bus, she said, as if to herself, "I think he was the classiest dude I've ever met. And his voice! God, what a beautiful, deep voice. I'll never forget that voice."

Taking another deep drag from her cigarette, she continued to look out the window as she asked in a somewhat nonchalant manner, "By the way. Where's th' damned ash tray you promised me?"

It was at that moment that I realized I had lost Jo Nell forever.

It was also at that moment that I realized there was something special about radio.

CHAPTER SEVEN

After graduating from high school, the next obvious subject was college, a word seldom heard anymore. Today, it is <u>university</u>, which seems to have a more dramatic ring to it. Certainly, it sounds more intellectual.

I had no great desire to go to college, but since most of my pals were heading to the higher school of learning, my parents decided I should do the same. It was more a matter of "keeping up with the Joneses", rather than adding to your intellect back then. It was also something that required a fair sum of money. Dad was willing to borrow from the bank in order to get me that special amount of education. He was forced to drop out of school after the eighth grade in order to help with the family funds. He seldom referred to his restricted schooling, but he was determined his sons would get all the education possible.

Finally, I decided I would make my mark at West Texas State College in Canyon, Texas, which was located just a few miles out of Amarillo, near Palo Duro Canyon State Park.

In Canyon, I took up residence at Stafford Hall, the men's dorm, and my first day there was a bit sad. Sitting in my room, alone, I looked out the window at the traffic whizzing on the Amarillo highway, wondering why I was there. This was my first setting away from home.

I will never forget walking out of my room, headed for the coke machine, and hearing Hank Thompson singing, "*WHOA SAILOR*", from a room down the hall. As I punched the nickel into the machine, I heard a strange voice yelling, "Hey! Come on down here!"

Looking up, I saw this dude with a big smile on his face waving me to his room. As I approached him, he stuck out his hand and said, "I'm Bugs! Bugs Clements!" Over the loud music from his record player, he yelled, "I hope you like Hank Thompson's music, because you're gonna be hearin' a hell of a lot of it!"

Bugs was also a big fan of Floyd Tillman and Roy Acuff. He was to become my best pal at Stafford Hall.

My heart wasn't in it during my stay at West Texas State. My mind was on radio. Therefore, I majored in "speech".

In speech class, the professor caught my attention by emphasizing the fact that although radio was a very important avenue of communications, it was in the hands of "very idiotic personalities." He then went on to state how Arthur Godfrey was a "low caliber person who insulted the 'king's language' on a daily basis."

He really caught my attention when he grumbled, "Anyone who considers Arthur Godfrey special is an idiot … just like the absurd Mr. Godfrey."

I had read that CBS was paying Godfrey over one-million dollars per year, extremely big bucks back then, while the learned professor was taking home a very small percentage of what Arthur was making. I also liked the idea of working only 8 hours per week, as Arthur was doing, while the learned professor was putting in five times that amount of hours behind his desk at WTS.

I dropped out of speech class that day, never to return.

I will always regret the fact that my dad was sending me money for books while I was skipping class and spending the weekly checks for fun. Having my mind on radio, I took part of Pop's loot and rented a reel-to-reel audio-tape recorder at one of the record shops near the campus. I utilized the heavy machine to practice the art of broadcasting. Honestly, I was attempting to copy the voice and radio style of Arthur Godfrey.

Laying out of class one day, which had become a common practice, I set up the recorder and put together what I considered to be the perfect joke. Using my record player, I recorded, on tape, back-to-back music by such singers as Frank Sinatra, Ella Fitzgerald, Vaughn Monroe, Bing Crosby and the likes.

Every once in a while, on the tape, I would break in with my fake radio voice:"You're listening to 'Platter Palace', your favorite music, over KGNC, The Globe-News Station, in Amarillo!"

Since my Stafford Hall pals used my room nightly to play poker, I decided I would have some fun. I placed a towel over the recorder and then placed my radio on top of the towel, completely hiding the recording device and leaving the impression the sound they would hear was coming from the radio.

After the bunch had pulled up their chairs to the two card tables, had lit their cigarettes and had begun dealing the cards, I sneaked over to the recorder and gently pushed the button. Soon, Sinatra, Bing, Ella and the others were filling the room with music from what was announced to be KGNC's "Platter Palace". Even my phony voice, which was heard every few minutes stating, "This is KGNC, the Globe-News station, in Amarillo", was never detected by the high-rollers in my smoky room.

Watching them nonchalantly moving their feet to the music was an indication they believed they were hearing the mighty sound of KGNC, although paying it no special mind.

Close to the end of the tape, my recorded fake voice shouted: "We interrupt this program with this bulletin! According to the Associated Press, the Russians have bombed Oak Ridge, Tennessee! Once again ... we have just received the news that the Russians have bombed Oak Ridge, Tennessee! It has been reported that the bombs have hit one of the manufacturing plants for the atomic bomb, located in Oak Ridge!" Utilizing a few seconds of complete quiet, I added the somber words: "Ladies and gentlemen ... America is now at war! Stay tuned to KGNC for more details!"

These words caught the attention of my poker-dealing goofys. Without hesitation, they jumped up from their chairs yelling, "Did you hear that? America is at war!"

Then, they ran from my room, leaving their burning cigarettes smoking on my rug.

Before I could inform them it was all a joke, they had separated in various directions, most of them on the telephones, calling their respective homes.

Within a couple of hours, Professor Tolliver, who was in charge of Stafford Hall, had me in his parlor. Wearing his droopy robe and sucking on an unlit pipe, he said, "Bill, what you did tonight was an embarrassment to Stafford Hall." Coughing, and obviously attempting to collect the appropriate words, he continued: "Do you realize that most of the boys who heard your cute little radio announcement telephoned their parents, telling their folks that they were going to volunteer for the service, since America was at war?" A short pause, and then,"Bill, you have been responsible for a terrible rumor getting started! I've even had people call me during the past hour asking if I had heard the terrible news that America is at war!"

To emphasize his anger, Professor Tolliver arose from his easy chair, walked around the room for a moment and then growled, "My wife, Mrs. Tolliver, is in a high state of nerves because of what you have done. I've had to give her an extra dose of her nerve medicine."

The professor then ordered me to go to my room while he gave the serious situation more thought.

Before I could exit his room, he said, "I can't tell you what the outcome of all this will be. I will have to consult with the Dean and others. This could be very serious."

Just before closing the door, Prof Tolliver made one more statement. "I will expect you to get that recording gear out of your room, even if it takes all day tomorrow!"

I was happy to hear his "if it takes all day tomorrow", an indication he would expect me to lay out of my classes for another day.

Halloween rolled around and my good pal, Bugs, and I decided to have some fun. We went into the Stafford Hall laundry room and found a pair of coveralls belonging to E. G. Mitchell in one of the dryers. We went to my room and stuffed two pillows into the coveralls, making a dummy which, except for lacking a head, hands and feet, looked like a little man. Then, we found a broom and wrapped a heavy towel around the brushes. In no time at all, we had everything that was needed for our gimmicks. All we needed now was for the sun to set.

It was around 8:00 p.m. when we took the dummy and broom into a deep ditch, located near the 4-way stop sign just outside Stafford Hall. Bugs and I would watch the cars as they slowed down while approaching the stop-sign. Before they reached it, I would sneak out of the ditch and smack the toweled broom into the side of the car. It was so dark; the driver couldn't see what was going on. He could only hear the loud "bump!" Then, Bugs would toss the dummy on to the hood of the car, causing the person behind the wheel to believe he had hit someone.

The driver would stop the car, jump out and, after noticing it was only a joke ... and being relieved he, or she, hadn't caused a death or serious injury ... would nervously get back inside the vehicle and drive away. Several folks let us know they saw absolutely no humor in what we were doing for laughs. One big dude, a member of the WTS football team, jumped into the ditch and threatened to kick our butts. His girl friend, holding a beer can, talked him out of it.

After pulling the dummy prank for about an hour, we decided to take the dummy and broom to my room and go looking for girls at Bob's Hamburgers. Just as we were stepping out of the ditch, we saw this big, black vehicle approaching us, traveling very slowly. We couldn't ignore the temptation. We decided to give it one more whack.

As the car got in perfect position, I jumped out of the ditch and gave my hardest punch of the night to its' side. Immediately, Bugs made a perfect toss of the dummy on to the hood, where it remained as the driver smashed on his brakes and opened the door. As he stepped out, we heard a lady's loud, piercing scream, the loudest I had ever heard. As I started to step out of the ditch, I heard Bugs' voice yell, "Get back!"

"What?" I shouted.

"Get back in this damned ditch and keep your head down!" Ordered Bugs. Then, in a loud whisper, he said, "That's Prof Tolliver ... and that's his old lady doin' th' hollerin'!"

By this time, there were several people around the car as Mrs. Tolliver kept screaming her head off while the good professor was attempting to calm her. Prof said, "It's all right, darlin', just a little Halloween joke by some youngsters, I presume." However, his soothing words didn't stop his wife's loud screaming.

We heard Prof Tolliver tell one of the people standing near him, "I was just bringing my wife back from seeing her nerve specialist in Amarillo! I wish I could get my hands on whoever did this!"

Bugs and I crawled rapidly away from the scene, still in the ditch, as the uncontrollable screams of Mrs. Tolliver continued in the background, the perfect sound for Halloween.

Next day, there was a note tacked to the laundry room door

reading: *"Mrs. Lambert will be in charge of the hall today. I have been forced to take Mrs. Tolliver back to her doctor in Amarillo for a treatment. I am sure we will return tonight, unless there are complications."*

The note was signed: *"Professor Tolliver."*

Immediately below that note was another one, in bolder print, which read: *"Someone stole a pair of my coveralls out of the dryer. I will expect to have them returned immediately, no questions asked."*

Signed: *"E. G. Mitchell."*

It was inevitable: The Dean called me into his office for a meeting.

Utilizing his thick glasses while looking down at notations on his big desk, he asked, "Why have you been missing so many of your classes, Bill?"

I lied: "I've had an ear infection."

"Have you seen a doctor?

"Yes, sir."

"What did the doctor tell you?" He asked, giving me a gaze of deep study.

"He says I'm healed."

The Dean gave me another serious stare, indicating areas of doubt, leaned back in his big chair and looked upward at the ceiling. He coughed and informed me that I might be asked to leave West Texas State if I missed any more classes. Looking me square in the eyes, he grunted, "Now, you wouldn't want that to happen, would you?"

"No, sir," I replied, looking out his window at a pretty girl walking toward Bob's Hamburger Shop.

After visiting the Dean, I made several attempts at attending classes, finding all of them dull, except in Miss Marsh's English class.

Miss Marsh was beautiful, even though she wore glasses.

She was addressing us one day, explaining a subject I have long forgotten. As a matter of fact, I wasn't listening. Instead, I was studying her perfect body shape.

She caught my attention when she asked the class, "Are there any questions?"

For some reason I'll never be able to explain, I raised my hand. "Yes, Bill?"

My question: "Miss Marsh, are you married?"

Miss Marsh released a phony, embarrassed laugh and replied, "What does my being married have to do with the subject?"

"Because," I laughed, "as far as I'm concerned, you <u>are</u> the subject!"

Miss Marsh paused for a moment. There was a frown as she managed: "What do you mean?"

"I mean … when you are standing there, I can't absorb a thing you're talking about. Can't keep my eyes off of you!"

Miss Marsh remained completely silent for what seemed an eternity. The class was also quiet, leaving the impression I had really placed myself in one hell of a predicament. She walked to her desk and seemed to be in a very serious state of thought before she said, "Class is dismissed. That'll be all for today."

I expected Miss Marsh to ask me to remain in the room for awhile, giving her the opportunity to explode to me because of my stupid remarks. Instead, she turned her back on me as I walked out the door.

Later that afternoon, Jim Bledsoe, who had a room close to mine at Stafford Hall, knocked on my door and informed me I was wanted on the wall-phone. I picked up the hanging receiver and blurted, "Yeah?"

It was a calm, female voice: "Bill?"

"Yeah."

There was hesitancy before she continued. "This is Donna Marsh."

It then struck me that Miss Marsh was on the line. It also struck me that I never realized her first name was Donna. It was a perfect name for the beauty, I thought.

I managed a somewhat shaky "Yes?"

Without explaining the reason, she asked, "Bill, would you please meet me at the little café on the corner?"

"Do you mean, 'Bob's'?"

"No. 'Bob's' is too crowded. I mean the little café closer to downtown."

I agreed to meet Miss Marsh in one hour. Inside my mind was the fact she would probably inform me that she had talked with the Dean and that I was going to be kicked out of WTS. After all, I was already on the Dean's heathen list and had probably just added to his dislike for me by making a fool of Miss Marsh in front of a packed classroom; an inexcusable act if ever there was one. The fact I had also made a fool of myself had never entered my mind.

In order to make a respectful appearance, I put on a white shirt and tie. As I walked into the coffee shop at least ten minutes earlier than had been set as our meeting time, I noticed Miss Marsh was already seated in a booth and was sipping from a cup of hot tea, looking younger and more beautiful than ever. As I slowly approached the table, she removed her glasses, gave me a serious study from head to foot and said, "Sit down."

Seated, I ordered a coke from the only waitress on duty. Outside of the waitress and a man behind the counter, we were the only people in the tiny spot.

Miss Marsh wasted no time. She set her cup on the saucer and said, "You know I was mad as hell at you in class today, don't you? What you did was the most idiotic happening I've experienced since I've been teaching! It made me look like a fool! It was totally disgraceful!"

Even though she was most noticeably angry, she managed to utter her words in a loud whisper. I jumped in with, "I'm really sorry, Miss Marsh. I've been feeling bad about what I said to you." I added, "I really am sorry and I'm asking you to please forgive me. And you might be interested to know that the entire class is mad at me. Everybody walking out of the class told me I was a fool for making such a disrespectful statement to you."

Miss Marsh seemed to be ignoring my apology. She growled, "Do you realize I could most likely have you expelled from here?"

"Yes, ma'am."

Unexpected, she took my hand and said, "You'd have your little butt back toward … what's your hometown?"

"Shamrock. Shamrock, Texas."

Suddenly, there seemed to be a complete change in her attitude toward me. She managed a smile and her voice was very calm. "Well, you'd have your little butt back in Shamrock if you didn't look so damned much like my big brother."

I was confused and couldn't secure the words as she pulled a napkin out of the container and began wiping obvious tears. I managed, "I'm really sorry I hurt you like I did, Miss Marsh."

Adding to the confusion, she tightened her grip on my hand and smiled, "Well, I should have taken your stupid remarks as a compliment. And I would have if there hadn't been all of those others in the classroom!"

Now, I was completely dumbfounded. I couldn't react. Miss Marsh said, "I'm from a small town in Iowa. I moved to Canyon because my brother worked in Amarillo. He was the spittin' image of you! He also acted crazy like you! He had no sense at all!"

Before I could ask what was bringing on the tears, she spoke in the saddest tone, "He died a few weeks back. He was the closest thing to me, and he died. Got his little butt drunk and died in a stupid car wreck less than a mile from his duplex apartment in Amarillo!"

Clumsily, I said, "I'm sorry. God, I'm sorry. Will you please forgive me for adding to your hurt?"

There was a long pause as she regained her composure. Then, she really surprised me with, "You were forgiven before you ever came in this little dump. I just wanted to see you and talk with you."

I squeezed her hand and asked, "Would I be out of line if I asked you to let me buy your supper?"

She wadded the napkin and placed it in an ashtray. "No, but if you'll come to my place, I'll fix us both something special, as long as it's Italian food."

She laughed and added, "Would you do that for me?"

Donna Marsh fixed us spaghetti and meatballs. Her cooking wasn't anything special, but the conversation was. We talked until after midnight. As I sat next to her, she became younger, although she was only 24 years old at the time. There was a warmth about her that I hadn't felt before, but she kept a certain distance between us, letting it be known ours was simply a "friendly visit".

After a bit of silence, she volunteered: "I wish I wasn't a teacher, sometimes." Pause, and then, "Being a teacher puts a limit on true feelings."

We listened to some of her favorite records, most of them by Perry Como. It was very noticeable that she wanted my company because she was hurting over the recent loss of her brother.

"He was my best friend," she said. "God, he was special to me. And I've got to go to his stupid apartment, put it up-for-sale and gather his things within the next week or so. It's going to be tough.

"Why ... why did he have to get his silly butt drunk? The dummy!"

Before allowing herself to fall into another set of tears, she faked a laugh and said, "You had better go, now! You have to be in class tomorrow!" Pausing again, she added, "I <u>know</u> you have to be in class tomorrow because I received a note saying you had missed too many classes and I was to make a special notation if you failed to show up in mine!"

"Are you sure you want me to go?" I asked, hoping she would ask me to stay longer, which was obviously what she also wanted.

Without replying, she walked me to the door, pulled my head down and gave me a very serious kiss. Then, she held me very close and kissed me several times as I had never been kissed before. It may have been my youth or perhaps it was because she was the 'older woman', but I felt true love from this beautiful lady, a lady I hardly knew. She said, "I suppose I just needed a little attention. You were kind enough to give it to me." Kissing me one more time, she whispered, "Now, go get some rest."

Walking down the hallway from her apartment, I could feel her watching me before I heard her door close gently.

Next day, Miss Marsh handled the class in her normal dignified fashion, never giving me a glance. As I exited the room after class had ended, she made it a point to turn her back to me and converse with another student, completely ignoring me as I passed by. I attempted to talk with her, but she always seemed to maintain her distance. She would be friendly, but left the impression I was strictly a pupil, never allowing me any private moments with her. It seemed to me that she would always become lost in the crowd when I made an effort to strike up any conversation with her. However, I could feel her looking at me when my back was to her.

She projected the attitude that our visit in her apartment had never happened and it was really causing me some confusion. After all, we had only chatted and eaten her spaghetti! We hadn't even sipped wine!

Of course, there were the kisses.

To be honest, I was a bit "taken" by the beautiful lady. She seemed to understand me and my somewhat complex thoughts toward life when we were together that evening. Now, as I look back, she may have been barricading anything between us that might eventually develop into a state of realism by pretending I wasn't around.

I will always wonder about a telephone call to me, taken by Jim

Bledsoe on the dorm wall-phone. Jim said, "There's a lady who wants to talk with you, Bill!" I picked up the hanging receiver and answered, but there was no response. After about fifteen seconds of silence, there was a disconnecting "click". This took place while Donna Marsh seemed to be evading me in class.

Only a few weeks after striking up a relationship of sorts with Donna Marsh, she was found dead in a duplex apartment in Amarillo. Rumor had it she had taken an overdose of sleeping pills. The reason, according to her closest friend, who was also a teacher, "She was beautiful. She was also very lonely. She was hiding something that finally devoured her."

A couple of weeks following her suicide, her friend revealed the shocking news that the brother Donna Marsh kept referring to was, in reality, her boyfriend. They had moved from Iowa to Amarillo. They were waiting for his divorce to become final in order for them to get married. They had purchased a duplex apartment in Amarillo, where she spent her weekends and holidays with him. It was also mentioned that another woman, a waitress from an Amarillo nightclub, also died in the car with Donna's boyfriend.

Adding to the hurt, Donna was pregnant with the dead man's child.

Her friend said, "Donna would want me to tell you this, Bill. She thought the world of you. She just didn't know how to handle things."

I am certain Donna Marsh cared for me. I could feel her warmth, even when she was pretending I was of no importance to her in the classroom. She may have given thought to the fact that she was the older woman and I was that foolish young flirt. She may have also thought, as I did, that we had already started a small flame between us. Then, there was the fact that she was pregnant. During that era, this just wasn't the common happening among single women; especially teachers. What will always stand strong in my memory is that Miss Marsh was a loving individual. I will always believe she just couldn't stand her hidden hurt. When I was with her that one night in her little apartment, I had the feeling she "wanted to tell me something".

Now, I wish she had.

The passing of Donna Marsh was a tough stroke for me, and simply added cause for me to drop out of West Texas State College.

Also adding to my decision to leave WTS was a phone call from my mother, informing me a radio station was being built in my hometown, Shamrock, Texas!

CHAPTER EIGHT

The fact that Shamrock would soon have its own radio station really grabbed my attention. It was my daily prayer to be a part of it.

In 1950, the builders were hammering the structure together. The building was to be located about one mile north of town. I was walking among the carpenters, bringing them water, running to the stores for cigarettes and sandwiches, <u>anything</u> to allow my presence to be known.

A short dude named John Kennedy was hired as the station manager and the Program Manager was a not-too-friendly chap by the name of Acton Tillery. Tillery was to be the first of several pompous clowns placed in the position of "programming" I was to become associated with down through the years. He was also married to the owner's niece. Hence, the job!

The call letters for the Shamrock radio outlet were to be <u>KEVA</u>, honoring the owner's mother, whose name was *Eva* Cooper. There was a huge picture of Eva in the studio and regardless of where I walked in the room, while vacuuming the carpet (an extra assignment), it seemed her eyes were following me. I would pray to God that I would be allowed to keep my job. I would also pray to Eva Cooper, as a backup.

The owner's name was Albert Cooper. Mr. Cooper also owned the weekly newspaper, *The Shamrock Texan.*

KEVA was to be spotted at 1580 on the AM dial, about as far as you can go on the right side of the Philco, and it would broadcast from sunrise to sunset with 250 watts, allowing the facility to be heard for about 30 miles in all directions from the transmitter tower before turning into static.

While broadcast equipment was being moved into the building, I was literally begging John Kennedy for a chance to be an announcer on KEVA. It didn't matter what I was required to do, I was game. And I wasn't worried about the salary. I even told John I was willing to "work for nothing" in order to get some experience.

A few days before the little station was set to go on-the-air, Kennedy gave me the good news. "I'm gonna give you a chance," he said. "I don't know what I'll have you do, but you'll be doing something. And I'm not going to ask you to work for nothing. I'm gonna pay you $12.50 a week to start off. O. K.?"

"Thank God! I'm gonna be on the radio!" I yelled to my mother on the phone that memorable day. *"I got the job!"*

Before KEVA could go on the air, there was to be a "test period". This would give the engineers time to make certain everything met with the rules specified by the Federal Communications Commission (FCC) out of Washington D. C. The test period was to take place shortly after midnight, when the broadcast signal could be checked best, while most stations were off the air. The engineers would station themselves at various spots within the assigned KEVA coverage area and check the sound quality. Since I wasn't a licensed radio engineer, my job was to sit at the microphone and, every ten minutes, announce, "This is KEVA, broadcasting at 1580 kilocycles on your radio dial out of Shamrock, Texas with a power of 250 watts. This is a test."

Although this certainly wasn't anything that would grab heavy ratings, to me it was the most exciting assignment I had ever had in my life!

When the time arrived for me to go to the radio station and make the announcements, my mother telephoned all of our friends and relatives, saying, "Be sure and listen to the radio starting at midnight tonight! Set your radio dials at the 1580 spot."

When someone would ask, "Why?", Mom would say, "Just dial it in! It's going to be a <u>real</u> <u>surprise</u> that you won't want to miss!"

Most of our friends and relatives were working at day jobs ... and being asked to stay up until midnight to listen to the radio set some curiosity into action.

I arrived at the station around ten o'clock that night, nervous as all get-out. John Kennedy gave me the final instructions and then I was left alone behind the microphone. I wasn't to play any music. All I had to do was open the mike and say, "This is KEVA, broadcasting at 1580 kilocycles on your radio dial out of Shamrock, Texas with a power of 250 watts. This is a test." I was to make this simple announcement every ten minutes for at least three hours, giving the engineers time to move to different locales within the assigned listening pattern.

It was during this special assignment that I put every effort into sounding great! While making the first few announcements, I stated them in a normal tone, nothing special. Then, I decided to insert "personality" into the repetitious statements. I clicked on the microphone and, lowering my voice to almost a growl, blabbed, "This ... is KEVA (pause) ... broadcasting at (pause) ... fifteen (pause) ... eighty (pause) ... kilocycles (pause) ... on your (pause) ... radio dial ... out of (pause) ... Shamrock ... (long pause) ... Texas." Then, I really laid on the hesitancy before the "dynamic" close: "This ... is ... a ... test!"

My mother telephoned saying, "You sound so good! I'm so proud of you!"

Then, John Kennedy telephoned, breaking down my ego with, "What 'n hell is wrong with your voice? Have you got a cold or something? Are you falling off to sleep? My God! Speak up so we can hear you out here in the field!"

Around two o'clock that morning, my mother telephoned my Uncle John in Wellington, Texas, located 28 miles south of Shamrock, waking him up. "Are you listening to the radio?" She asked.

"I listened for awhile, but all I was getting was some weird sounding creature announcing something about a radio station there in Shamrock. Just kept saying the same thing over and over. No music, just the same old thing. I thought I probably had the wrong spot on the dial and decided to go to sleep."

Mother was quick to inform him, "That 'weird sounding creature' was Billy!"

"Billy? Billy, who?" Asked Uncle John.

"My son, Billy! Your little nephew, Billy."

Uncle John yawned and said, "Well … I'll be." He then dozed off to sleep with the telephone receiver still in his hand, he would tell me years later.

Finally, the date was set for KEVA to hit the airwaves and it was the main topic of conversation on the streets of Shamrock. Albert Cooper had placed big ads in his *Shamrock Texan*, including pictures of all of the "on-the-air personalities" that would be heard on the "Mighty 1580 Spot on Your Radio Dial!"

There, along with the others, was my picture with a strong underline which read: Bill Mac Smith, "Announcer". It was my first claim to fame and, as I remember, my mother purchased at least 20 copies of that edition of the "*Texan*".

Right up to the morning we signed on the air, John Kennedy had been undecided in what my first announcing duties would be. Finally, about an hour before the assignment was to hit the air, he grumbled to me, "Your job will be to read the markets". He wasn't referring to the "stock market reports"; I was to read the "livestock" market report and, since I didn't know a damned thing about hogs, cows, goats and horses, I was in a complete state of shock! I approached Bob Beller, one of the engineer/announcers (back then, they hired engineers who could also "announce", in order to cut down on the payroll) and asked him what I was to do, since I wasn't up on livestock. He slurped from his cup of instant-coffee, looked at me and said, "Just <u>read</u> th' damned thing!"

This was to be my first bit of advice in the field of broadcasting and, to be honest, things haven't changed much during the past half-century in radio. You don't have to know a damned thing about what you're saying as long as you can read.

Just think about it for a moment. Those big marquee news people you hear on radio and absorb on television, are doing exactly the same thing you do with the morning newspaper. They are simply <u>reading</u> the news to you. In radio, it's from a typed script. On television, it is read from a teleprompter, an expensive gadget locked underneath the lens of the television camera.

Of course, it helps if the men are handsome and the girls are good-looking while they deliver the news on television. Good voices on TV are not of extreme importance, since the viewer is "watching", while paying secondary attention to the sounds of the voices.

It was during the *KEVA 7:00 A.M. NEWS* that Bob Beller

announced: "Now, let's check the livestock report. Here is Bill Smith".

I've wished so many times that some type of recording had been made of my "first" professional sound on radio. I know it must have been much below the norm as a presentation, but my memories can only recollect the fact that I didn't mispronounce a word, didn't slur what I was reading and, all-in-all, I did a hell of a good job.

Might add: I was more than a little proud of myself.

Shortly after finishing my initiation into the proud world of broadcasting, which took about two minutes, I received the supreme compliment: Jerry Berten, who's parents owned Berten Drug, rushed into the radio station with a platter of ham, eggs and toast. He also had a big pot of fresh coffee for the rest of the folks on duty.

I'll never forget Jerry shouting, "Damned, Bill, you sounded good!"

The telephones were ringing with so many encouraging messages to me and all of the rest of the crew.

To the present time, that memorable morning in that small building in my hometown will always be that special period of importance in my life.

God had answered my prayers.

The second day of KEVA's gigantic arrival to the airwaves, John Kennedy approached me with an idea. He took me aside and said, "You have a pretty good voice." Then, he quickly attached, "It's not the best voice, but it could get the job done with a little training."

"Now ... I have this idea. Why don't we let you do a little daily show? Are you interested?"

After having so many compliments from the local listeners after hearing my livestock report the preceding morning, I chose my words carefully. It took me about five seconds to say, "Man! I'd love it!"

I had been a fan of Bill Sharpe and his terrific show on KWFT out of Wichita Falls for a couple of years. Bill played the top hits of the day by such giants as Sinatra, Ella Fitzgerald, Bing Crosby and the likes and I was especially fond of his theme song, *"OPUS ONE"* by Tommy Dorsey. So what did I do? I opened my new daily radio show titled, *"The Fifteen-Eighty Club"*, with *"OPUS ONE"* by Tommy Dorsey.

Needless to say, there was very little originality in my first productions on KEVA. Since Arthur Godfrey was my radio hero, I attempted to sound like Arthur after the second or third day I was on the air, and after I had sucked in some courage. After hitting my theme, *"OPUS ONE"*, I went into what I thought was the laid-back Godfrey approach by almost yawning into the microphone, saying, "Hello! Hello! Hello! And ... how ... are ... you? This is ... Bill ... Smith with ... your 'Fifteen ... Eighty ... Club'! Har! Har! Har!"

Before the last "Har!" had been released, John Kennedy stuck his head into the control room and, waiting until I had closed the mike, growled, "What in th' hell are you doing? You sound like you're takin' a slow crap!"

I'll never forget those words from John and will always remember them as the first bit of coaching I was to receive from a professional. He was a bit tough, but he was attempting to instill "originality" into my juvenile styling.

The *"Fifteen-Eighty Club"* caught on pretty good in Shamrock and, before long, I was trotting around town with more than my share of ego. The Shamrock girls seemed to like what I was doing on the radio and were either calling the radio station, requesting songs, or they would drop by after school and watch me through the glass window as I proudly "did my thing". In no time, I was beginning to feel like a "star"! I was also attempting to act like a big-shot. After all, only my bosses were aware of my fizzy $12.50 weekly salary.

I noticed the program director was becoming a bit jealous over my rapid success and he decided to go into action. Acton Tillery took me aside one afternoon and said, "You are being given another important assignment."

Thinking they might be giving me an additional bit of radio time, I said, "Oh! What is it going to be?"

He smiled and replied: "You are to clean the john and vacuum the carpet in the studio every morning!"

KEVA had only one "john", restroom, and there was only one studio. The additional duties weren't difficult, but I thought they were terrible insults to toss on KEVA's biggest "star"!

One day, Jackie decided to bring a girl friend and surprise me at the radio station. Surprise me, they did. The door to the restroom was open and the two caught me there, on my knees, cleaning the toilet with a brush. Since my back was to them, they attempted to rush out of the building to save me some embarrassment. However, old Acton had different ideas. Before they could get to the door, he rushed out of the control room and yelled, "When you finish with cleaning the toilet, rip me some news, John Boy!"

John Boy was a nickname he would hang on me reflecting my humiliating assignment of cleaning the 'john'.

Rising from the restroom floor, and noticing Jackie and her friend looking at me with some pity as I held the toilet bowl cleaning brush in my hand, lit a fuse of strong hatred in me for the program director.

I was finally given the job as *"Man On The Street"*, a thirty-minute program that had me interviewing people on Main Street in downtown Shamrock. It was aired between 12:30 and 1:00 p.m., Monday through Friday, and was a job I hated because very few people living in the town were anxious to get on-the-air with me.

I was to have one of the most exciting half-hours of my professional life one afternoon while doing the *"Man On The Street"* program. The night before, Bob Wills and his Texas Playboys had made an appearance in Shamrock, playing to a packed house. Although I wasn't a real fan of Western Swing music at the time, I took Jackie to watch the great entertainer and his band in action, a performance I will never forget.

As I was doing my *"Man On The Street"* show next day, I noticed Bob and several members of his band were having lunch in the Corner Café, where I set up my broadcast equipment for the radio program. Shortly after I hit the air, I walked over to Bob and, without having the courtesy to ask his permission, sat down beside him on a stool at the counter where he was seated.

I'll always remember Bob was munching on liver and onions for his meal as I put the mike to my mouth and said, "Ladies and gentlemen, I'm happy to be visiting with the 'King of Western Swing', Mr. Bob Wills!"

I'll also never forget Bob's reaction. He simply kept on picking at his food, apparently ignoring me ... and my statement. Watching some of the people in the restaurant laughing over my humiliating situation, I started to walk away from the scene. However, Bob grabbed my arm and pulled me back to my stool. He said, "My boy, you've got it a bit wrong. Spade Cooley is called 'The King of Western Swing'." Then, he laughed and said,

"Of course, I'm <u>really</u> th' King, just like you said!"

I then said, "Mr. Wills, I want to apologize for intruding on your meal."

Bob pushed his plate away and said, "I was just finishing, my boy." Pausing for a split second, he said the words that will live in my mind forever. "Now, let's you and me talk a while."

Bob Wills spent the entire half-hour with me, talking about his music and the fact that he had been raised less than fifty miles from Shamrock, in the Lelia Lake and Turkey, Texas area, making a living by "pickin' cotton and cuttin' hair, as a barber".

I will never forget the kindness Bob displayed to me that day, allowing me to do my first radio interview with a star. He even commented on my limited talent, saying, "You do a good job with that microphone, my boy. If I ever need an announcer, I'll know to come to Shamrock."

He then shook my hand and left the Corner Café with those who were with him.

A waitress ran up to me and said, "You're wanted on the phone, Bill."

It was Bob Beller, bragging on the job I had done with Bob Wills and informing me he had taped the show. "I'll leave the tape in your drawer here at the radio station," He said.

I put all of the broadcast equipment in my car and rushed to KEVA, anxious to get my tape of the Wills interview. On arrival, I walked to my drawer but noticed there was no tape. Before I could ask the receptionist what might have happened to the reel, she said, "That bastard, Tillery, has your tape."

I walked into the studio where Tillery was talking on the telephone. He ordered me to wait outside. "Can't you see I'm on the phone, John Boy?" He shouted.

After about ten minutes, he waved me inside. "What do you want, John Boy?"

I replied: "I want my tape. The tape of my interview with Bob Wills. I was told you had it."

Tillery smiled and said, "Oh, was that a tape of your interview with the fiddle player? I'm so sorry. We ran short on tape and I had to record over it. I needed to record a couple of commercials that we <u>may be selling</u>."

For the first time, I lost all control and was about to hit the goon. Bob Beller had walked into the radio station, without me noticing, and had listened to part of Tillery's crap. Bob stepped between us and said, "You go have lunch, Bill." Then, turning to Tillery, he yelled, "And you go to hell, Nephew!"

I was to meet another very important person in my life, while doing my bit with KEVA.

One afternoon after finishing my radio show, a pretty lady walked into the radio station and told the receptionist she wanted to speak to me. We walked into the studio, where we kept our coffee, and sat down.

"You are so good on the air, Honey," She said, a big, sincere smile on her face. "I'm a school teacher in Oklahoma and am headed for Amarillo. I just had to find you and let you know you have a new fan!

"You're gonna go a long way in this business," she added, kissing me on the cheek.

The sweet lady was to become one of my best friends. Everywhere there was a function for me in Nashville, Fort Worth, Dallas ... it didn't matter where ... she was always there, always giving me that wonderful, loving support.

She was also a great songwriter and would one-day help Elvis Presley hit the big time with one of her compositions, "Heartbreak Hotel"!

Her son, Hoyt Axton, was to become a good singer, songwriter and movie actor.

God, how I miss Mae Boren Axton!

"The *Man On The Street*" program was failing, because no one wanted to go on the air. Our astute program director informed me, "You are the problem, John Boy. You are simply not professional at your craft!" He added, "Tomorrow, I will take over the program until we can find someone else to do the show."

Next day, true to his word, Tillery set up for the job on the street. He had suggested I "listen carefully" to him, growling, "Perhaps you can learn something, John Boy."

After he had stood on the street corner for about ten minutes, blabbing ad-libs without anyone volunteering to stop and talk with him, Tillery was about to end the show early. Then, he noticed Mr. Pike, who was in his late 80s, had stopped and seemed ready to talk. Smiling, Acton put the mike toward Mr. Pike's face and said, "Well, well! We have a gentleman here who looks like he's ready to talk! What is your name, Sir?"

Mr. Pike, obviously unaware of a microphone, said, "My name is Pike. Where's th' nearest restroom around here? I need to take a crap!"

The door to every store in downtown Shamrock opened with people laughing hysterically as they stepped out to see the action they had just heard on the radio.

That evening, there was a big sign posted on the bulletin board in the KEVA control room reading:
"BECAUSE OF LACK OF REACTION, THE "MAN ON THE STREET" PROGRAM IS BEING CANCELLED. BEGINNING TOMORROW, WE WILL PROGRAM MUSIC BY THE BIG BANDS *BETWEEN 12:30 P.M. AND 1:00 P.M."*
-A. TILLERY, DIRECTOR OF PROGRAMMING FOR KEVA.

It was obvious my days with KEVA were limited.

Tillery had made it a point to inform me that he never had to read the news ahead of time. "I always read it 'cold'," he would say. "It's called 'talent', John Boy. Something you will never have."

One day as I was getting up from the floor of the restroom after cleaning the toilet bowl, I heard the shout from the control room I had become so accustomed to hearing: "Rip me the news, John Boy ... and make it fast!"

Instead of ripping the news from the machine, I decided it was time I delivered some news that I had been saving for this special occasion.

Utilizing the yellow paper we kept next to the newswire unit, I had typed several bits that I had hidden in my desk drawer. The type looked very similar to the regular news copy. Rushing into the control room, I handed the "news" to Tillery as he sat behind the microphone with the musical news intro blasting in the background. Before opening his mike, he yelled, "Now, get th' hell out of here and go back to cleaning the john, John Boy!"

Instead, I ran to my Chevy, started the engine and turned on my radio in time to hear *Acton Tillery* with the *Noon News!*

I crossed my fingers, hoping he wouldn't notice he was about to deliver news that I had taken a lot of time in creating for this special occasion. I heard: "Time now for the *KEVA Noon News* ... Acton Tillery reporting!"

It began with Tillery delivering the usual stuff you expected to hear about the Korean War in its beginning stages and then came the big news of the day: "Premier Joseph Stalin had emergency surgery for piles ... er ... uh ... I believe that should read hemorrhoids ... in Moscow today (there was a nervous laugh, here). Mr. Stalin seems to be recovering very well." There was a pause, but he undoubtedly hadn't caught on to the scheme. He continued, "*Metro-Goldwyn-Mayer* super stars, Mickey Rooney and Lana Turner have eloped and are ... honeymooning in Texas! Rumor has it they were spotted going into the honeymoon suite at the *Twenty-Trees Tourist Court* in ... in Shamrock?"

After hearing this big bit of news out of Hollywood, dozens of cars converged on the Twenty-Trees Tourist Court in our town ... just in time to see one of Shamrock's leading businessmen and his pretty secretary leaving one of the rooms.

Acton finally realized he had been taken. Ending the news ten minutes ahead of the normal time, he growled, "That's all of the Noon News. Now, we present music from the KEVA transcription library."

I never returned to KEVA, forfeiting a few days pay.

CHAPTER NINE

Even though I had gone through some difficult times with the program director at KEVA, I will always be grateful to those at the little radio station in my hometown who had the confidence in me, allowing me to get my foot in the difficult door of broadcasting.

Back in those days, it was necessary to have experience before most radio stations would even give you a chance. It was good having college diplomas, but they were of little benefit when attempting to get a job in radio. In the early 50s, it was almost impossible to get an audition with radio affiliates unless you had been "on mike" at some outlet somewhere.

KEVA in Shamrock might have been limited in power, but I could now announce to all concerned "I had worked in radio!"

Mr. Edward Burkhalter came to my rescue again. He had a college chum who was one of the chief honchos at KGNC in Amarillo, the NBC affiliate. Mr. "B" telephoned his friend and told him of my situation, saying I wanted to get into a bigger market. Unfortunately, there was nothing available at KGNC. However, the friend had recently talked with the manager of the CBS affiliate in Amarillo, stating that KLYN was looking for some help. He said he would attempt to set up an audition for me there, if the job was still open.

Within a couple of hours, the friend telephoned Mr. Burkhalter, informing him that I was set for an audition at KLYN but would need to get there ASAP.

Another prayer had been answered.

Mr. "B" had a suggestion and he handled it with caution. He said, "I know you're proud of your family name, Smith, as you should be. But I believe you need to have a radio name and Bill Smith is fairly common. Why don't you utilize your first and middle names as your professional handle? *'Bill Mack'* has a good ring to it."

It all came together nicely: "New name ... new town ... new job."

I don't know of anything more nerve-racking than making that first "audition" at a radio station located in a big market.

Jabbo Watson was the epitome of good management. He looked me square in the eyes and said, "Well, I've listened to your audition. You sound good ... at least, better than what I've been hearing on those tapes the people in programming have been bringing me for the past few days."

I felt relieved and grateful.

"Are you sure you want to get in this business?" He asked with a stare of honesty.

"Yes, sir. I really do."

"The money's a hell of a lot better in other jobs," he laughed.

"I still want to give it a whirl," I said.

"Can you get by on seventy-five dollars a week?"

Without hesitating: "Yes, sir."

"You'll be required to work six days a week, Sundays off." He was still in a state of inquiry. "That's a lot of work for very little loot."

"I want the job," was my reaction.

Jabbo: "Don't you even want to know what you'll be doing? The hours you'll be working?"

I said, "I'll leave that up to you."

Jabbo smiled and said, "You're going to be our *News Chief!* You'll do the *Noon News*, the *Six O'clock News* and The *Ten O'clock News*. Saturdays, we only have the *Noon News* and the *Ten O'clock News*." Giving it one more punch, he asked, "Think you can handle it?"

"Yes, sir."

Jabbo stood up, shook my hand and said, "Welcome to KLYN. Glad to have you. You start in one week!"

Jabbo was a taskmaster when it came to news. Over and over, he would roar to me, "Dammit, I don't want to hear you rip and read any news! Re-write it! Put it in your own terminology! I don't want our news department sounding like a two-bit outfit!"

He was pinpointing me to get the job done, as he wanted it done. "It's very important that we get all of the news first," he would emphasize, even though KGNC, the giant, had a big, well-organized news team. KFDA and KAMQ, both in Amarillo, also had very good newsmen on duty.

My involvement in "News" was destined to change drastically one Saturday afternoon in the early 50s when a couple of brothers broke out of the Potter County Jail in Amarillo, stole a car and headed for the back woods. Running out of gasoline and having no funds, they came upon the KLYN transmitter, which was located in the rural area. There was one engineer on duty at the time. The brothers jumped out of their stolen heap and held up our engineer. After taking his wallet, they ripped the telephone wires loose so he couldn't notify the police, bound his arms and legs with some rope, took his car, and hit the dirt road.

It was a lazy Saturday afternoon and I was working the radio control board as a favor to Cecil Boykin, who normally worked the dull weekend afternoon shifts at KLYN. I was on the telephone with Darlene Wakefield, making plans for what I hoped would be a big night with the pretty blonde when, suddenly, Jabbo Watson approached me in the control room and asked, "Are you having a nice time on the phone?"

"Sure am," I smiled. Then realizing the manager seldom came on the scene on Saturday, I asked, "What are you doing here, Jabbo?"

Before I could bid Darlene farewell, my boss yanked the phone out of my hand and shouted, "Our transmitter has been held up!"

"Gee," I replied. "Where did you hear that?"

There was foam in Jabbo's mouth as he yelled, "I heard it on KGNC, KFDA and KAMQ! Our damned transmitter has been held up and we've been scooped by every radio station in Amarillo!"

This takes a little explanation: Our engineer finally managed to free himself from the rope and being some sort of genius, as most radio engineers are, figured out a technological way to take the wires from the telephone and attach them to our transmitter wiring. Then, using the telephone as a microphone, he began yelling, "Send help to the KLYN transmitter! I've been held up! I repeat! Send help to the KLYN radio transmitter! I've been held up!"

The announcements were going out loud and clear to everyone who had their radios set to KLYN. Trouble was, I had the speakers in the control room turned down in order to carry on a sizzling conversation with Darlene Wakefield. KLYN was carrying a long *CBS* radio program at the time and I only had to open the mike every half-hour to give the station identification, "You're listening to KLYN … CBS in Amarillo."

In other words: My timing was wrong that day.

I will never understand why Jabbo didn't fire me after the transmitter hold-up … and my foul-up. Instead, he simply removed me from the news department and assigned me to the late-night shift where I would do a program titled, "*INSOMNIA*". Beginning at 11:00 p.m. and running until 1:00 a.m., Monday through Friday, I was allowed to play the big pop hits of the day … but no "hillbilly" music.

An exception to the rule was made when "Tennessee" Ernie Ford paid a surprise visit to KLYN and I was given the honorable assignment of driving him around town in order for him to visit record shops and competitive radio stations, plugging his *Capitol* records.

At the time, I was driving a '50 *Studebaker*. As Ernie positioned himself in the passenger seat and we struck out to visit the record shops and radio stations, the car stalled; out of gas. Luckily, there was a *Phillips 66* station on the corner. Ernie helped me push the heap on to the driveway.

Think about this: Here is a great star who had recently enjoyed a Number One hit with "*Mule Train*" …helping me push my dirty Studebaker, in the heat of the day …in downtown Amarillo!

Ford pushin' a Studebaker!

Now comes the real embarrassment: I only had fifty cents on me! I asked Ernie Ford if he would loan me a couple of dollars!

Ern roared with laughter and said, "Let's just fill that little gem up! We'll charge th' gas to Capitol Records!"

After visiting the record shops and a couple of radio stations, Ernie said, "Now, let's go have some lunch. And guess who's buying!"

Ernie Ford was such a nice guy. As we munched on hamburgers, he told me how grateful he was "to make it in this business".

Even Jabbo was a fan of "Tennessee" Ernie Ford. He said, "He's not a hillbilly singer. You can put him on your show if you want to."

Ernie came on the "*INSOMNIA*" program with me, staying until it shut down at 1:00 a.m. During those two hours, I saw the man in action. The phones were ringing off the hook! Ol' Ern took the time to talk to everyone who was fortunate enough to get through. He was extremely kind ... and <u>real</u>!

I'll always be grateful to Ernie Ford for helping me get into the country music scene on radio. After his appearance on my show, I began inserting more of the "hillbilly" recordings by such artists as Red Foley and my idol, Hank Williams, on "INSOMNIA" without any negative comments from the radio station manager.

"Tennessee" Ernie Ford, now in our Country Music Hall-of-Fame, died in 1991.

Jabbo Watson accepted a better job in Dallas. He was replaced by a wild, whiskey-drinking nomad from Waco, Texas named Ron Litteral. Ron was the complete opposite of Jabbo. Although a professional all the way, he was much more lenient and more giving ... except with the dollar. When I would approach him pertaining to a raise in pay, which was every payday, Ron would dig into his desk drawer, pull out a fifth of *Seagram's 7* and say, "Let's have a drink! Who 'n hell wants to talk about money on such a beautiful day as this?"

Ron was also a dyed-in-the wool country music fan. At one time, he was Hank Thompson's radio announcer while working on W-A-C-O in Waco, Texas. He was allowing me to feature lots of 'hillbilly' music on my radio show, changing the name of the program from *"INSOMNIA"* to *THE BILL MACK SHOW"*. Reaction from the listeners was so encouraging that Litteral decided it would be better to move my two-hour show to 5:00 a.m. "That way, you'll catch the 'rural' audience," he said. "The <u>real</u> listeners to 'hillbilly' music, th' farmers, don't stay up until eleven o'clock at night. I'm gonna move your show to 5:00 a.m. so you can grab the good folks before they head for the barns!"

Although it was a drag getting out of bed at 3:30 in the mornings, it was worth it. Ron gave me a raise in salary and I was having my share of fun, not allowing the early morning hours to interfere with my nightlife.

I was beginning to spend a lot of time with a cute little girl named Ella. Like me, she was a fan of Hank Williams. She would cook meals for me and then we would sing along with Hank after she had placed a stack of his *M-G-M* records on her big *Zenith* radio/phono combo.

When Hank sang, *"I'm So Lonesome I Could Cry"*, Ella would begin sobbing loudly. She informed me that it was her late husband's favorite song. The poor guy had recently been killed in action in Korea. A picture of the big man, in full Army dress, was setting on top of the radio/phono combo, making me feel a little sad. His big eyes seemed to be staring at Ella and me throughout the many cozy hours we were together.

"We were childhood sweethearts in Muleshoe, Texas," she purred. "His name was Horace. I miss him ... but life must go on, I'm told."

Indeed, life went on for Ella and she seemed to be handling the tragic loss of Horace very well. I was happy that I could be of assistance in easing some of her pain.

One morning after finishing my radio show, I was going through the new hillbilly records that had arrived in the mail and sipping on coffee. While I was listening to one of the new releases, Ron Litteral stuck his head into the record room and said, "Somebody out here is asking to see you. Says he wants to meet you."

I casually strolled into the reception area and noticed the only person seated on the long couch was a big dude in an Army uniform. As I approached him, I said, "I'm Bill Mack."

He stood up and looked down at me, remaining silent. He made me think of John Wayne.

"I understand you wanted to meet me," I smiled.

"That's right," he said.

I stuck out my hand and he took hold of it saying, "I'm from Muleshoe, Texas."

Without thinking, I said, "Really? A friend of mine is also from Muleshoe, Texas!"

The giant wasn't shaking my hand, just *holding* it firmly as he growled: "Yes ... I also know your 'friend' from Muleshoe."

"You know Ella?" I managed to ask.

"Yep," he replied, the grip on my hand a little more noticeable. "Ella is my wife!"

It then dawned on me that the huge hunk didn't look so much

like John Wayne. He looked more like the guy whose picture was on Ella's radio!

Before I could respond, he grumbled, "I don't want to hear of you messin' around Ella anymore." There was a pause. "Do you understand me, boy?"

Feeling very patriotic, I mumbled: "Yes, sir."

The mighty one then placed his cap on his head and, without any more commentary, walked out the door.

The receptionist noticed I was a little nervous. Handing me a cup of coffee, she asked, "Who was that, Bill?"

"Just another big fan of mine," I lied.

For some reason, KLYN had been set to broadcast a remote from *Club Royale* in Amarillo, featuring *Harry James and his Orchestra* ... and I was to be the announcer. The program was aired on *CBS Radio*. This was back when "live bands" were aired late at night on the network.

"And now ... from the beautiful Club Royale ... overlooking beautiful downtown Amarillo ... it's music by Harry James and his orchestra!

"Your announcer is ... Bill Mack!"

Harry James had one of the top orchestras in the nation and was married to the beautiful Betty Grable, at the time. Betty was the shining light at *Twentieth Century Fox* studios in Hollywood, and I had this hidden crush on her.

Before the broadcast was to get underway, I approached Harry, wanting to introduce myself and inform him that I was set as his "announcer".

After shaking his hand, I said: "I can't believe I'm shaking the hand that *touches* Betty Grable almost every night!"

I meant to insert a compliment, but had somehow chosen the wrong words, which was obvious from Harry James' hard stare into my eyes.

Harry hissed: "Keep the conversation short, boy."

The broadcast went very well on *CBS*, that night. Harry's music was beautiful. He tooted a *mean* horn, but he paid little attention to his *announcer*.

After the half-hour broadcast was over, he looked at me and growled, "You may go."

It was while working at KLYN and frequenting the honky-tonks that I began composing country songs in a serious manner. I began making the nightclub scene a common practice, hanging out regularly at the *Clover Club* and watching some of the country stars in action, peddling my songs. Hank Thompson was a special favorite. When Hank and his "Brazos Valley Boys" hit the stage at the *Clover Club*, I was always there.

As I write this, Hank and his beautiful wife, Ann, are very close friends. They live in the Fort Worth area. When Hank was inducted into our Country Music Hall-of-Fame in 1989, it was a special happening, personally. One of my real thrills was hearing Thompson's recording of my composition, "I'LL STILL BE HERE TOMORROW". I composed the song for him in the 50s. Over 30 years later, he recorded it ... and it was worth waiting for!

Things seemed to be moving in my direction as a would-be singer and songwriter.

KGNC in Amarillo presented a daily radio show featuring *Billy Briggs and The XIT Boys*, made up of Billy and two other musicians. Briggs played steel-guitar, Weldon Allard was on the bass-fiddle and Jess Williams played rhythm guitar. All three were very good singers and they had a terrific following. Billy also had a contract with *Imperial Records* out of Hollywood, California and was enjoying a mediocre hit titled, *"CHEW TOBACCO RAG"*, a song he had written.

Briggs was sold on a song I had composed titled, *"MAMA DON'T LOCK THE DOOR"*, and after hearing me sing the song a few times at the *Clover Club*, connected me with Lew Chudd, the owner of *Imperial Records*. Surprisingly, I was given a four-year contract with the label. I was also signed as an exclusive songwriter for Chudd's music publishing firm, *Commodore Music*, also located in Hollywood.

I was to find out it was a common practice for people such as Chudd to sign songwriters as singers on their record labels in order to latch them in as writers for their publishing houses, where the real money was. Songwriters have tremendous egos, most of them wanting to be singers.

I recorded *"MAMA DON'T LOCK THE DOOR"* and another song I had written, *"I'M MISSIN' LOTS OF LOVIN'"* in the studios of KAMQ, in Amarillo. KLYN didn't have the equipment to record music sessions. I utilized the best musicians I could find in the area.

When my first record was released on *Imperial*, I was excited beyond words. However, public reaction to the recording was minimal. I've often given thought to the fact that if I hadn't been a disk jockey at the time, that first release might never have been played on radio!

I played both sides of the record on a daily basis, whether I was getting requests for it or not.

Shortly after my *Imperial Records* release of *"I'M MISSIN' LOTS OF LOVIN'"* had a dismal run, Lew Chudd telephoned, informing me that Capitol Records had decided to have one of their new artists, Terry Preston, record the song! Of course, it was great hearing the good news that one of my compositions would soon be recorded on a major record label, although Terry Preston wasn't exactly a household word in entertainment.

The Preston version of *"I'M MISSIN' LOTS OF LOVIN'"* was a destructive bomb! When it came time for Terry's next *Capitol Records* release, his name was changed to Ferlin Husky. I had heard of artists changing record labels because of poor sales, but this was the first time I had heard of one changing his name because a recording flopped so badly.

Everytime I see Ferlin, I remind him of the fact that had it not been for me and one of my compositions, he might still be struggling under the name of Terry Preston.

Also making the *Clover Club* scene from time to time were the Maddox Brothers and Rose, billed as *"America's Most Colorful Hillbilly Band"*. They were based in the Modesto, California area and although they weren't outstanding musicians, their showmanship was unforgettable. They were the best-dressed group I've ever seen on stage, wearing blazing colors and bright sequins. There were four brothers: Fred, Henry, Cal and Don. Rose was the sister, a great singer. Bing Crosby once said, "Rose Maddox is the greatest of the female country singers!" Their mother was their manager and was one tough individual to deal with! Although she was a tiny lady, she was extremely demanding. It didn't matter at all that her sons were grown and married, Mama Maddox would take a belt to their butts if they "didn't behave".

Rose told me: "One time, Henry was sitting in the backseat of a car with a pretty little blonde. They were kissin' and huggin'. Henry was married and just doin' a little slippin' around. Well,

Mama saw them kissin', got her belt and jumped in the car with them, whippin' them both!"

When the Maddox Brothers and Rose hit town, they would be driving five brand new Cadillacs … with Mama riding with the one she chose to travel with to that particular gig.

The Maddox Brothers and Rose were the second act in country music to record my material. My song, *"WEDDING BLUES"*, written when I was still single, was their first release on *Columbia Records*, after leaving the lousy *4-Star* label. Later, they recorded my *"WHEN THE SUN GOES DOWN"*, also on the giant *Columbia* label. Although they weren't hits, I was very proud of the way the bunch handled my compositions. The Maddox Brothers and Rose supplied me with that much needed ingredient — hope. I'll always remember them in a special way.

After splitting with her brothers, Rose recorded "WHEN THE SUN GOES DOWN" on Capitol Records in the 60s. It wasn't a hit, but it's a personal treasure.

There was another nightspot about a mile from The Clover Club called, *"KILROY'S"*. *"KILROY'S"* was a real "dive". It was a life threatening beer joint-dance hall combination. Rumor had it that an ambulance from *Boxwell Brothers Funeral Home* would stay parked across the street from *"KILROY'S"* every Saturday night, saving some time. It was certain they would be called several times before the dance was finished, hauling various patrons to the nearby hospital or, in extreme cases, to the morgue!

Cowboy Copas often told the story about his "first and only booking at *'KILROY'S'"*.

Copas had purchased a new pair of boots at Amarillo's leading western wear store and was a little late in arriving at the dance hall for rehearsals. After entering the club, he was introduced to Kilroy, the owner. "He was about the biggest hunk I ever saw," said Copas. "I mean, he had to be seven feet tall and must have weighed three-hundred-and-fifty pounds! Big man!"

Copas asked Kilroy: "Where's th' dressing room?"

"Ain't got a dressin' room," growled the giant. "Ever'body changes their clothes in 'th' backstage crapper'!"

Cowboy said he went through the rehearsals with Kilroy's band and then went into the backstage restroom until time for him to hit the stage for his first "set".

"When it came time for me to go on stage, I noticed they had lowered a curtain of chicken wire! I asked the guitar picker what the wire was for and he said, 'It's for protection! Th' crowd gits a little drunk and when they do, they throw th' beer bottles at whoever is singin'!'"

Copas lit into his first song and, sure enough, the longneck bottles began hitting the chicken wire, sticking through the netting. "I'd a been a <u>goner</u> if that curtain of chicken wire hadn't been there! It was the roughest joint I ever played."

Cowboy made it through the first set then went back to the restroom and waited for the band to introduce him for his second and final show. As he walked out onstage, he noticed the chicken wire had been lifted. After asking the guitar man why the wire was no longer there, he was told: "Th' folks are tame, now. They're all too drunk to throw anything."

Copas did his usual patter and after finishing the first song of his final set, was approached by an innocent looking cowboy who mumbled, "Sing th' *'Lovesick Blues'*."

Cowboy informed him, "I don't sing *'Lovesick Blues'*. That's Hank Williams' old song." Attempting to be friendly, he added, "You go on out there and get you a girl to dance with an' I'll sing you something special."

"You mean … you ain't gonna sing th' *'Lovesick Blues?'*" Burped the cowhand.

Copas: "I told you … I don't sing 'Lovesick Blues'. Now go find yourself a girl … and dance!"

"You … you sure you won't sing th' *'Lovesick Blues'* for me?" Asked the persistent patron.

Copas faked a smile and repeated: "No!"

Cowboy said the drunk wobbled away.

About ten minutes later, he noticed the cowboy approaching the stage again, this time holding a Folger's Coffee can. "I just ignored him as he stood there holding the can," said Copas. "I was singing *'Filipino Baby'*, my big hit, when I noticed this dude was pouring something out of the coffee can onto my new boots! I thought it must have been either pee or water. I just kept on singin', thinkin' he'd finally go away if I didn't pay him any attention."

Cowboy laughed and said, "It was then I noticed him striking a match, just as I smelled the gasoline fumes! He set my new boots on fire! I had to run to the restroom and push both boots in the toilet to put out the flames! Ruined my brand- new boots!"

When the dance was finished, Copas approached Kilroy for his pay. The big man said, "You'll have to <u>whup</u> me for your money."

"What do you mean?" Asked Cowboy. "I <u>did</u> th' dance!"

Kilroy growled: "Yeah, but you wouldn't sing th' *'Lovesick Blues'* for one of my customers. If you don't please th' customers, you don't git paid <u>nothin'</u>! That is … unless you want to fight me for it!"

The Grand Ole Opry star picked up his guitar and headed for the exit. "All things considered, I was lucky to get out of that place alive!" He laughed. "Although I wasn't paid a dime for my appearance at *'Kilroy's'*, I realized I was one fortunate hillbilly by being able to walk out without any wounds."

As Copas was getting in the cab to go to his hotel, he heard Kilroy yell, "Let me know when you're back in Amarillo an' I'll book you back here!"

Sad note: Cowboy Copas lost his life in the plane crash that also took the lives of Patsy Cline, Hawkshaw Hawkins and their manager, Randy Hughes, on March 5, 1963. He was 49 years old.

My early morning country music radio show was going very well on KLYN. Naturally, I was very proud and was beginning to feel a bit important.

One morning in September, I noticed a big ad in the Amarillo Globe News announcing the upcoming Tri-State Fair, always a big happening in the Panhandle. There was also the big tag reading: "This year, see <u>IN</u> <u>PERSON</u> … Stars of Nashville's *'GRAND OLE OPRY'*! Ernest Tubb and his Texas Troubadours —- Cousin Minnie Pearl —Little Jimmy Dickens — Annie Lou and Danny — and SPECIAL GUEST, Hank Williams and his Drifting Cowboys!"

Immediately, I set my plans to have all of those scheduled to be in Amarillo on my radio show. I could hardly wait for their arrival. I had been tipped that they would be staying at the Herring Hotel. I was also told they would be getting into town Monday morning, the first day of the fair.

That Monday, I set the alarm about an hour earlier than usual in order to get to KLYN by 4:00 o'clock. I was anxious to call th' stars!

Around 4:00 a.m., I placed my first telephone call to the Herring Hotel, asking to speak to Ernest Tubb. The hotel rep informed me, "Mr. Tubb has left instructions to not be disturbed before ten o'clock."

"Ring his room," I said. "He'll want to talk with me since I am with CBS Radio."

I must insert here the fact that I was with CBS, but only through an __affiliated__ radio station. It's exactly as if I told someone I was with The Dallas Morning News or Fort Worth Star-Telegram when, in reality, I was simply delivering the newspaper.

In other words, I was misrepresenting the facts.

The guy at the Herring Hotel was probably tired after being on duty since midnight. Anyway, he took me at my flimsy word and began buzzing Ernest's room.

After about seven or eight rings, I heard a very sleepy, "Hello."

"Is this Mister Ernest Tubb? The Texas Troubadour?" I gushed in a very excited tone.

"Yes. Yes it is," came the reply.

"Mr. Tubb," I shouted, "My name is Bill Mack. I'm with the CBS radio station here in Amarillo. I wanted to take this time (remember, it's around 4:00 a. m.) to welcome you to our fine city!"

Ernest replied: "Thank you, son. That's awfully nice of you."

Feeling an avenue of progress opening, I drove right in. "Mr. Tubb, I do a radio show that will begin at five o'clock this morning. I would love to have you with me as a guest."

Then, to assure a positive reply, I added, "We'll play a bunch of your records if you will come on the air with me."

There was a friendly pause before Ernest said, "Son, I would love to visit with you this morning but we just barely got in town and I'm pretty well passed out." He released a little laugh and then continued, "Tell you what I'll do. I'll come by and visit with you tomorrow morning if the invitation is still open."

I said, "I guess it'll have to do, since you can't make it this morning."

Incidentally, Ernest Tubb did visit my show the next morning. Through the years, he would visit me many times. He was to become one of the most loved friends I've ever had ... in or out of entertainment. We lost him in 1984. He was 70 years old. Cause of death: Emphysema.

Next, I decided to telephone my idol, Hank Williams, who was also booked to stay at the Herring. The same individual who had answered my call to Ernest Tubb said, "Mr. Williams has left <u>strict</u> instructions to not disturb him until eleven o'clock this morning."

I gave him the same bit I had presented in order to disturb Ernest, stating I was "with CBS". And, again, he began ringing the room of the Drifting Cowboy.

This time, the telephone rang at least a dozen times before an exhausted voice came on with, "Yeah?"

Nervous, I asked: "Is this Hank Williams? The Drifting Cowboy?"

The strange voice spoke: "No. Hank is asleep. I'm Don Helms. What do you want?"

I said, "I'm Bill Mack. I'm with CBS. I need to talk with Mr. Williams."

Don said, "I can't disturb Hank. We didn't check in here until a couple of hours ago. His back is hurtin' him and he had to take pain pills in order to drop off to sleep."

I was persistent: "I don't believe you heard me. I'm with <u>CBS</u>! It's urgent I speak with Mr. Williams <u>now</u>!"

Don, Hank's great steel-guitar man, told me years later that he was afraid he would put Hank in a bad situation with the giant network if he didn't awaken him.

After about five minutes on hold, I heard a growl. "Yeah?"

"Is this Mr. Hank Williams? The Drifting Cowboy?" I asked, my approach full of excitement.

"Who wants to know?"

I coughed, catching the lack of excitement on the other end. "My name is Bill Mack ..."

Before I could release more, Hank inserted, "That's <u>your</u> problem. What 'n hell do you want with me at this hour of the morning?"

Again, I attempted to insert strength. "I'm with CBS in Amarillo and I will be doing a radio show at five o'clock. I'd like to have you as my <u>special</u> guest."

There was this very long minute of nothingness before I heard, "Do you mean five o'clock <u>AM</u> or five o'clock <u>PM</u>?"

By now, there was some fear in replying, "Five o'clock AM. Five o'clock this morning."

Another long, long pause added to the discomfort of the early hour. Then, the top country music star in the world released his true feeling pertaining to the matter.

"Boy, have you lost your stupid, damned, ignorant mind?"

(I can't recall the <u>exact</u> words, of course, but I did get the message.)

After Hank's words had been delivered loud and clear, there was the sound of an abnormally loud click ... followed by the buzz of a disconnected telephone.

Ron Litteral approached me one day informing me that I would be announcing a half-hour show that would be presented at 12:30 p.m. Monday through Friday. It would feature a new trio in town that was headlined by Leon Rusk, a singer/songwriter out of California who had decided to move to Amarillo. What caught my immediate attention was the fact Leon recorded for *King Records,* a company out of Cincinnati, Ohio that had produced such hits as, *"BLUES STAY AWAY FROM ME",* by the Delmore Brothers and Wayne Raney and Moon Mullican's *"I'LL SAIL MY SHIP ALONE".* Cowboy Copas, the singer whose new boots had been set on fire at *KILROY'S* Club, was also a *King* artist.

Leon's recording on *King Records* was a song titled, *"A Petal From A Faded Rose",* a beautiful ballad he had co-written with his friend, Merle Travis.

Rusk's band was made up of two other people; his girlfriend, who played steel-guitar and a tall, skinny dude who played lead-guitar. Leon was the singer. He also played rhythm guitar.

I found it a bit out-of-whack when I discovered there was no bass-fiddle in the group. I also questioned Leon's move from Los Angeles to Amarillo, considering it quite a drop.

"L. A. ain't th' town to be in unless you're a damned movie star," he growled.

Leon walked with a noticeable limp and I was told he had been involved in an accident in California that was caused by his driving while boozing. I also heard the rumor that he was "on the run from the law." He never discussed anything of this sort with me. As a matter of fact, he seldom discussed <u>anything</u> with me outside of the daily radio show.

It wasn't long before Leon Rusk and I got on a friendlier set with each other. We would go to *Gathwright's Café* and have lunch every day after doing the radio show. While sitting in the booth, Leon would pull a pint of whiskey out of his coat pocket and ease a bit of the contents into his coffee, making certain no one was watching except me. When he'd offer me a share from his bottle, I would kindly refuse it.

"This stuff will make you sing, you little 'sumbitch'!" He would laugh.

One day while having lunch, he said, "You can sing a pretty good song. I've heard them damned Imperial records of yours. Nothin' extra, of course, but enough to 'git by'." Laughing, he asked, "Do you know how to play th' guitar?"

"No," I replied.

Leon said, "Well, if you don't pick th' guitar while you sing, you're a damned freak! That's what's wrong with Governor Jimmie Davis! He stands up there and sings '*You Are My Sunshine*' and don't know what 'n hell to do with his hands, since he don't play th' guitar. He looks like a Methodist preacher without a pulpit! Looks stupid!"

One day he asked me to walk with him to his car after exiting *Gathwright's*. Opening the trunk, he pulled out an old guitar and handed it to me. "Here's you a 'starvation kit'," he laughed. "It ain't much to look at, but it's got good strings on it and I'm gonna personally teach you to pick th' thang!"

Leon had lots of patience when it came to teaching me chords on the old Kay guitar. He laughed and said, "Look at those pretty little hands. They're softer than a woman's! First thing we're gonna do is put some calluses on those dainty little fingers!"

In practically no time, the calluses were there. Within a few weeks, Leon had taught me the basic keys and I was proud of myself. The first song I learned to pick 'n sing was *"The Philadelphia Lawyer"*.

Even though I had known Leon for months, I could never figure out what part his "special lady", his pretty steel-guitar picker, actually played in his life. When I would visit their apartment, she seldom spoke. She was friendly, very sweet, but there was a sadness in her silence.

The lead-guitar man, Lloyd, also lived in the same apartment and he, too, was very quiet. He was a loner. The only time I heard him talk at all was during rehearsals for the radio show, when he would ask Leon what songs they were going to do.

Leon was drinking heavily, but never missed a radio show.

Even when he was drunk, he always sounded sober as a judge when performing.

One night when we were at *Gathwright's* having a meal, Leon took his bottle out of his jacket and poured some whiskey into his iced tea, something I had never seen before! I whispered, "You drink whiskey in your iced tea?"

He replied: "Billy boy, when you're a drunk, you drink your whiskey anyway you can get it down." He looked me square in the eyes and said, "You're lookin' at a hopeless drunk. I can write songs, I can sing songs, but that's it. No life to speak of, just the whiskey. And I know it'll kill me some day."

Then, he rapidly changed the subject and began laughing like a mad man.

Leon asked me: "How would you like to pick up twenty-five dollars come Saturday night?"

"What do I have to do?" I replied.

He said, "We're booked in Plainview, Texas and I thought it would be a good chance to get your skinny little butt on stage and let you show off a bit for all of them sexy little Plainview gals! Want to come with us?"

Leon had made my day. At last, I would be performing my first gig for pay! I gave him a rapid, "Yes!"

Even though my first professional appearance was only going to pay twenty-five dollars, I spent most of my meager savings to purchase a tan western suit and a pair of matching cowboy boots. I was determined to look the part.

Leon told me to meet him at the KLYN studios at 2:00 o'clock Saturday afternoon, where we would take his big Packard to Plainview. At exactly that scheduled time, I heard the honking of the horn. Sticking my head out the door of the station, I heard Leon yell, "Hurry up an' git in here you little sumbitch!"

I walked to the Packard as Leon raised the trunk in order to put the Kay guitar and my new cowboy suit and boots inside. After slamming the trunk, we got inside the car. I was seated next to Lloyd while the lady steel picker sat next to Leon, who was set to drive. There was a trailer attached to the rear of the Packard, containing the instruments and public address system. Because of the trailer, Leon had to ease out carefully.

Just before we had completely pulled away from the curb, the radio station bookkeeper opened the door and yelled something that we couldn't make out. Rolling the window down, we heard him repeat: "Bill! Your mother is on the phone! Says she needs to talk with you!"

I mumbled a few choice words as Leon said, "Go talk to your mommie, but make it fast."

I said, "Let's pull on out. I'll call her when we get to Plainview."

Leon growled, "Dammit, it's your mama on the phone! Go talk with her!"

Reluctantly, I walked inside the radio station and picked up the telephone at the bookkeeper's desk, wondering why he was working on Saturday. "Hello", I growled into the phone.

My mother gave me the usual words of love and then said, "I'm looking forward to seeing you tonight."

I was flabbergasted. "Tonight? Mom, I'm going to be in Plainview tonight. We're playing a dance over there! I'll see you next week."

Mom: "But tomorrow is Mother's Day! You've got to come home for Mother's Day!" Then, to make the conversation even more uncomfortable, she added, "Besides, I don't like to see you playing those old dance halls. You come home!"

I said, "Mother, I can't help it if it is Mother's Day. I'm going to Plainview with Leon!"

Before anything else could be spoken, I heard: "You're goin' home, Billy Boy!" It was Leon. He had come in to rush me and had picked up my end of the conversation with my mother.

"What?" I shouted. "I'm not going to Shamrock, I'm going with you to Plainview!"

Leon walked over and grabbed the phone from my hand. Speaking into it, he said, "Mrs. Smith, your boy will be with you tomorrow. My name is Leon Rusk and I want to wish you a Happy Mother's Day."

Highly ticked, I didn't hear the rest of Leon's commentary to my mother. I had walked back outside to the Packard. When Leon finally managed to get back to the car he said, "Next week I'm playing in Pampa, Texas. I'll take you with me there and pay you thirty-dollars. You're goin' home to your mother! Tomorrow is Mother's Day, for Christ's sake!"

"I may not be going with you to Plainview, but I'm damned sure not going home to my mama," I said.

Leon put his arm on my shoulder and said, "Billy Boy, you'll never know how much you'll miss your mama until she's gone …

like mine is. She ain't askin' much from you … and by God, you're gonna do as she says!"

He then opened the trunk of the car and handed me my guitar, suit and boots. I was mad! I didn't have anything to say to Leon. However, he was determined to make it easier as he limped beside me to my Studebaker, carrying the Kay guitar. After I had opened my car door and tossed my stuff inside, Leon put his arms around me and hugged me, something he had never done.

"I know you're a little hacked off, but I'll make it up to you in Pampa next Saturday night," he said, utilizing a voice of comfort I had never heard him use before.

I started up the engine on my little car, shoved it into gear and wheeled away from the curb. Looking in the mirror, I could see Leon leaning against his Packard, waving at me as I drove farther and faster away from him.

I drove to Shamrock that night but, still angry at my mother for fouling up my Plainview gig, I didn't go home. Instead, I picked up Jackie and we went to the movies and hung around the regular Shamrock haunts until everything had closed down. Then, I went home and crawled into bed, around two o'clock in the morning.

I didn't accompany my mother, dad and brother to church Sunday morning, even though it was Mother's Day. It was another way of letting Mom know that I was still ticked off because she had screwed up what would have been my first professional appearance. Also, I needed the sleep, having stayed out for the better part of the morning.

I finally jumped out of bed, showered and put on my new western suit and boots. I wanted to be out of the house before my folks returned from church. I picked up Jackie and we went to *Fry's Drug* for a sandwich and malt before heading to the Texas Theater. Aaron Fry, the owner of the drugstore, seemed happy to see me. He joined us at our booth, giving me an opportunity to praise my "tremendous success in radio" in Amarillo. As the waitress was placing our tuna sandwiches and malts on the table, she asked, "Did you know any of the folks killed in th' wreck this morning?"

"What wreck?" I asked, not giving any serious thought to her question.

"A western swing band had a big wreck out near Amarillo. Thought you might have known them." She said, catching my attention.

It dawned on me that it might have been Roy Terry's band, since his Panhandle Playboys were, indeed, western swing. Before diving into my food, I decided I would telephone Ron Litteral and ask him about what I had just heard.

Using Aaron Fry's office, I made the call to Ron. Before I could say anything past "Hello", he broke the news to me.

"Guess you're callin' about the wreck. Right?" He asked in a tone of extreme sorrow.

"Was it Roy Terry?" I asked.

"No," he replied. "It was Leon."

"Leon? Leon Rusk? What happened?" I shouted.

"The girl was driving and it sounds like she must have gone to sleep behind the wheel. Anyway, she crashed head-on into another car. Killed 'em all ... instantly." Ron moaned.

"Wait a minute! You said ... it killed them all?"

Ron: "Killed everybody in both cars! Leon, his girl and Lloyd. All dead."

After hearing this terrible news, I went home to see my mother.

I received a telephone call from Blaine Cornwell, the Program Director at KWFT in Wichita Falls, Texas. Blaine had heard I was ready to make a move from Amarillo and advance to a more powerful radio station in North Texas. I had admired Blaine's air work for several years. He had the perfect radio voice ... and was to become a very important guiding force for me after I accepted his offer and began packing things into my car for the move from Amarillo to Wichita Falls.

CHAPTER TEN

KWFT, located in the air-conditioned Kemp, Hotel in Wichita Falls, Texas was to be my university in broadcasting and Blaine Cornwell, the Program Director, became my first guiding force. Blaine had been my idol on radio for years via his *"Blaine Cornwell's Top Ten"* radio show on KWFT, a radio station that beamed into the Panhandle area of Texas like a local. He was one of the few Program Directors I worked with who had a great voice, tremendous talent and the brains to project how it was to be done.

I was hired as both, a disk jockey and emcee, on KWFT. I did an early morning d. j. bit, beginning at 4:30 a.m., and was also the singing host of the *"Hadacol Western Barn Dance"*, a daily half-hour program that was fed to several radio stations throughout the Southwest.

Hadacol was a bottled concoction that claimed to "cure all ills, giving you that bright, happy day feeling!" We were receiving lots of unsolicited testimonials, especially from the elderly, saying such things as, *"Hadacol* makes me feel better, more spirited, than I've ever felt in my life!" and *"Hadacol* makes me feel young again!"

Hadacol was finally taken off the market when it was discovered it contained more than the normal flow of alcohol! Some of the elders who had made such glowing remarks about the benefits of taking *Hadacol* were literally splashed when they were praising the product.

I eventually formed my own band in Wichita Falls. We were billed as *Bill Mack and his Blue Sage Boys* and, I'm very proud to say, it was a very good outfit.

Included in my band was a tremendous piano man named Buck White. He was also outstanding on the mandolin and, after leaving Wichita Falls, he became a member of Emmylou Harris' touring group. Later, with his talented daughters, Buck formed a group known as The Whites, now outstanding members of Nashville's *Grand Ole Opry*. His son-in-law is also a pretty good hand at the mandolin and with vocals. His name is Ricky Skaggs.

Also in my band was Elmer Lawrence on steel-guitar, still considered one of the best, and a 14-year-old fiddle player named Bobby Boatright, now with the most respected Texas Playboys western swing group. Also playing fiddle with me occasionally was "Pee-Wee" Stewart, a master with the bow.

On bass-fiddle was "Pappy" Stapp and playing lead guitar was Bill Adams.

Bill Davis, now living in Ardmore, Oklahoma, was my five-string banjo man. Many said he was on the same level as Earl Scruggs ... and I would have to agree.

Plugging the personal appearances on our daily radio show on KWFT, we were booked several nights per week throughout Texas and Oklahoma. We played movie theaters, high school gymnasiums and auditoriums.

We didn't perform at clubs or for dances.

Shortly after moving to Wichita Falls, I married my high school sweetheart. As I have already mentioned, Jackie Briggs and I began dating when we were both in our early teens. She was beautiful and was also outstanding at the piano and accordion. Jackie appeared on my various shows and presented some great work on several of my recordings. If you have ever heard my original *Starday* recording of my song, *"BLUE"*, the perfect piano work was performed by Jackie.

I had a very unique agreement with KWFT. I was given complete freedom to book country music acts into the Wichita Falls Municipal Auditorium and other locations throughout the Texas-Oklahoma area and could promote them on my daily radio shows. This gave me the opportunity to meet numerous entertainers during the beginning of their careers, several of whom would become super stars.

Some names that come to mind: Ray Price, Jim Reeves, Johnny Cash, Carl Perkins, Little Jimmy Dickens, Johnny and Jack, Kitty Wells, Slim Whitman, Roy Acuff, Marty Robbins, Porter Wagoner, The Wilburn Brothers, and many more.

(As soon as this book is put into print, several names I failed to mention will come to mind. And to those special friends: I apologize.)

Back then, it was the custom of the stars to visit the disk jockeys. Because of this custom, most all of the stars I met while at KWFT became close, personal friends.

One morning, as I was unlocking the doors at KWFT in order to do my 4:30 a.m. radio show, I noticed Tillman Franks and Johnny Horton sitting on the steps. Johnny had a big smile on his face and was holding a copy of his first recording for *Columbia Records*. He wanted me to be the first to play his "Honky Tonk Man", which I did.

Johnny died at age 35 in a head-on auto collision near Austin, Texas in 1960, after playing the Starlight Club. He was married to Hank Williiams' widow, Billie Jean, at the time of his death. Coincidentally, the last nightclub appearance made by Hank Williams was the same honky tonk, the Starlight Club, in Austin, in December of 1952.

One hot August night in the mid-50s, I presented a show at Spudder Park, an outdoor ballpark in Wichita Falls. It was a super special occasion for me, since my first baby, my daughter, Debbie, was born the day before. Jackie and I had prayed for a baby and God answered those special prayers when my darlin' Debbie arrived on the scene.

Tillman Franks had put the show package together, consisting of stars from *"The Louisiana Hayride"*. The bill featured Johnny Horton, along with several lesser names. Spudder Park was filled to capacity because one of the "lesser" names was a newcomer on Sun Records named Elvis Presley, who was kicking up some action via his first recordings.

It was my first chance to meet Elvis. He walked up to me as I stood near my car, parked in the rear of the stadium, and said, "Hi, Mr. Mack. I wanted to introduce myself. My name is Elvis Presley, Sir."

Since I was barely in my twenties, I found his approach a bit unusual. Elvis was very cordial, very gentle and oh-so-humble. To me, he seemed to be almost <u>overly</u> <u>humble</u>. I'll never forget watching this same calm, gentle dude, totin' the long sideburns, as he jumped on stage and the gentleness turned into near-rage! I have never witnessed fan "riot" as I saw it that night. Certainly, the Beatles caused craziness and, years before them, there was Sinatra. However, none could approach the magnetic style of Elvis Presley.

You've got to remember: This was when "Big E" was working for $125.00 per night, which included the cost of his two musicians, Scotty and Bill. Of more importance, this was before he had an entourage of protection. There were no police officers ushering him off stage to a waiting limousine on that blazing August night.

My mother and mother-in-law were in town to see their new granddaughter. Both of them were seated in the stadium that night.

Their review of Elvis: "Vulgar!"

Honestly, everyone in the ballpark that sizzling summer evening was watching an <u>event</u>. It was a preview of the greatest act ever to hit the stage.

It was a prelude.

Elvis was so proud as he showed me his pink and black, slightly used Cadillac.

After telling the Hayride gang goodnight and settling up the loot with Tillman Franks, I got into my car, anxious to head to the Wichita Falls General Hospital to see my new daughter. Before I could back out of my parking spot, Joe Carson, one of the area's better singers, asked if he could ride with me.

"Sure! Hop in," I said.

Elvis, who had been standing nearby, asked: "Can I go, too? I'd like to see your baby."

After viewing my seven pounds of joy through the nursery window, Elvis said, "You sure have a beautiful, baby. I'm proud for you."

Shortly after the August show, Elvis became an act in the Hank Snow Enterprises "Stable of Stars" and was set to make some appearances with Snow. Hank's manager was a robust character who had been Eddy Arnold's general rep before hooking up with Snow. The character's name was Tom Parker. Eventually, he let the world know he was to be referred to as <u>Colonel</u> Tom Parker. A native of Holland, his real name was Andreas Cornelis van Kuijk. He was born in the Dutch village of Breda on June 28, 1909. He illegally entered the United States in 1929.

Colonel Tom was a self-propelled sideshow specialist. Watching him in action was a study of the old bush league carnival days. He was a "hawker", and would do anything to <u>make</u> a buck; anything to <u>save</u> a buck. Before the show started, Colonel Tom would go out into the lobby and sell pictures, programs, key-chains — anything that could be peddled for a few extra coins. Even though he was in command of the acts, he preferred to do the sideshow style "hawking" himself. The Colonel didn't trust anyone when it came to handling the loot.

Before moving to Nashville, Colonel Tom was, indeed, a circus/carnival nomad, following the tents and Ferris wheels. He shouted ticket sales for "girlie" and "freak" shows for years.

At one time, the Colonel had a "Dancing Chickens" act, which he said originated in his native Holland. Hiring a single fiddle player to accompany them after the tent was filled with the "suckers" who had bought tickets, the chickens would dance like mad when the fiddler struck into "Chicken Reel".

It was a sight to behold — and a simple feat to perform.

Actually, the chickens were standing on a hot-plate that had been painted brown and covered with heavy dust, causing the audience to believe it was a small dirt floor under their tiny clawed feet. As the fiddle man got hot with *"Chicken Reel",* the Colonel, standing behind a curtain, eased up the electric heat control on the hot-plate.

It was either dance or die for the hapless chicks.

When the jig was finished, the Colonel would raise a little door and the chickens would "dance" off stage and into an adjoining box to cool off!

Gabe Tucker, who worked with Colonel Tom for years and was to learn his tricks of the trade, told me, "There wasn't a thing the Colonel wouldn't do to make a buck! And he came up with some of the most weird ideas imaginable!"

Some said it was because of Col. Parker's "freak show" approach that Eddy Arnold, who was considered a class act, fired him. Tucker said, "Eddy couldn't put up with Colonel Tom's carnival and sideshow ideas."

Evidently, he was becoming an embarrassment to Arnold.

Hank Snow, however, appreciated the fact Tom Parker knew how to showcase the stars and hired him as his general manager.

I witnessed part of the eventual breakup of Col. Tom and Snow in Wichita Falls.

It was in early 1956 that Colonel Parker gave me the opportunity to book Hank Snow and his Rainbow Ranch Boys into the Wichita Falls Municipal Auditorium. Snow was big marquee at the time and, as an "added attraction", Elvis Presley would be the opening act for "The Singing Ranger".

I was to receive 20% of door sales and 25% of the advance ticket income. Tickets sold for $1.25 in advance; $1.50 at the door. By telephone, Colonel Tom told me to lay heavy on advertising, especially on radio. He shouted: "Advertise! Advertise! Advertise! Plug th' show 'til they're sick of it and, just before they 'throw up', sell 'em a ticket!"

Naturally, the show was sold out in no time.

The Wichita Falls Municipal Auditorium was packed with well over 3,000 anxious fans, seated and anxiously awaiting the raising of the curtain. There was a problem, however. It seems the opening act had not arrived on the scene and it was almost showtime. Hank Snow, who was the "star", was raising all kinds of hell backstage,

"Where is that little basta'd?" He yelled. "It's time for the damned show to start, my fans are going crazy — and our little 'opening act' isn't here! Where 'n hell is he, Tom?"

Tom Parker, who had just walked into Snow's dressing room after selling pictures and programs in the lobby, replied, "I don't have any idea of where th' boy is, Hank! He's never been late before! I just hope he's all right!"

Snow's reaction was, "He's not gonna be all right after I get finished with him!"

It was fifteen or twenty minutes past show time and the crowd was going nuts! Since Elvis still hadn't made the scene, Colonel Tom approached me and grumbled, "Go on out there and bring Hank and th' boys on. We can't wait any longer for th' boy."

You must remember, this was an Elvis crowd, although Hank Snow would be the last to admit it. Being forced to "go on first" was the premium insult to The Singing Ranger.

I walked on stage and stood before the drawn curtain while the crowd began screaming, "We want Elvis! We want Elvis!"

It was impossible for me to calm them in order to make the necessary welcome and introduce the first act.

Then came the gruesome quiet.

I stepped to the center microphone, welcomed all of the kind folks to the show, and then announced, "Let's give a big hand to that fabulous star of R.C.A. Victor Records ...."

(Note here that Elvis also recorded for R.C.A. Victor —-)

I finished the announcement: "Here is America's most popular country music star ... The Singing Ranger ... Hank Snow and the Rainbow Ranch Boys!"

As the band struck up with Hank's signature song, *"I'm Movin' On",* you could have heard a pin drop in the audience.

Then came the joint crescendo ... "Boo!"

Before the obviously shaken "star" could sing the first bit of lyrics to *"I'm Movin' On",* came the rude reaction of the crowd, in unison, "We want Elvis! We want Elvis!"

It was bedlam! I can honestly say, I have never seen anyone in show business situated in such a horrible predicament as the normally ego inflated Hank Snow had been placed while he tried like hell to get some small bit of encouragement from the audience.

Finally, he managed a smile with something similar to, "Hello friends and neighbors. I'm so glad you came out to see <u>me</u>. Here's one of my best selling R.C.A. Victor recordings, a song titled, *'I Don't Hurt Anymore'!"*

As fiddle man Chubby Wise struck the introductory instrumental notes that normally brought the house down for Hank, the pennies started hitting the stage! This was the final straw for Snow. After he finished the song, he rushed off stage, his face reflecting both hatred and shock!

As a coincidence, seemingly from out of nowhere, Elvis walked to the opposite side of the stage at about the same time Snow was fuming off at the other side. He wasn't dressed in his normal show gear. As I recall, he was wearing a red baseball warm-up jacket. Even over the screams and "boos" from the audience, I could hear Colonel Tom tell Elvis, in a calm voice: "You can go on now."

Elvis asked, "You don't want me to dress?"

Colonel Tom simply replied, "Go on now!"

No introduction from me was needed. As Scotty Moore and Bill Black, his two musicians, rushed to their respective microphones, Elvis walked slowly to center mike with that "dare you" expression, while the crowd went crazy! Some of the young girls, seated on the front rows, were faking fainting spells!

Come to think of it, they may have actually been fainting. It was that kind of night.

While Elvis was blowing the minds of those who had been able to purchase a seat in the big auditorium, Hank Snow was literally super flushed with anger in his dressing room. I attempted to calm him, but it was of no use. He wasn't hearing a word I said as he charged back and forth in the room growling, "That basta'd! That little basta'd!"

Colonel Tom Parker walked into the room and was immediately face-to-face with The Singing Ranger, witnessing him at his angriest.

These words I witnessed from Hank to the Colonel: "Fire th' little basta'd!"

Colonel Tom Parker responded with: "No problem."

After watching and hearing the action that took place that night in Wichita Falls, I'm almost certain that everything was pre-planned by Colonel Tom Parker. There are several who agree. As far as I know, Elvis never missed a concert or was ever late for one. The Colonel was a stickler for image and detail. Even though his university had been the carnival, he learned well; even picking up some of the teachings handed down to him by the con artists in the various tents of the sideshow jungles.

Hank Snow was a master at the microphone on stage and inside recording studios, but he was no match for the former "girlie show" and "freak tent" host.

Colonel Tom had also taken note of Snow's outrageous ego and decided to utilize that quirk in order to free Presley from the holding power of Hank Snow Enterprises.

When you consider the fact that Hank Snow owned Elvis Presley and allowed the most valuable commodity in show business to slide gently into the paws of Colonel Tom Parker, absolutely free-of-charge, you can understand why Snow developed an instant hatred toward Parker. I was told Hank Snow never spoke to Tom after that final tour and all references to the Colonel had extra phrasing attached when spoken by The Singing Ranger.

After Colonel Tom Parker had become the manager of Elvis, he telephoned me in Wichita Falls in late 1956, wanting to bring "th' boy" back to town.

"You know, th' boy don't work as cheap as he used to," he said. "How much do you think you can afford to pay him if I git him your way?"

Realizing Elvis had made five-hundred dollars when he appeared with Hank Snow earlier in the year, I thought I would make the Colonel's day by telling him I thought I could afford to fork over seven-hundred dollars, no questions asked.

Colonel Tom's reply: "That's fine for me ... but how about 'th' boy'?"

To show you how times had changed in a matter of months, I arranged for Elvis to be paid $3,000 for his next appearance. The price of admission was also increased to $2.00 in advance; $2.50 at the door, considered "extra-high" for tickets back then.

The show was sold out within hours after the first announcement was made on radio that "Elvis is coming back to town!"

Elvis would telephone me from time to time when I was living in Wichita Falls. One day, he came to the radio station in the company of Faron Young and Teddy and Doyle, the Wilburn Brothers. Hubert Long, Faron's manager, was also there. I remember the shyness of Elvis, even though he was super hot at the time. He had little to say, preferring to listen to the goofy chatter between Faron and the Wilburns. He seemed to be in awe of them, resembling a little boy watching a merry-go-round in action.

In the early 70s I would be with Elvis for the last time. He was in Fort Worth for five consecutive nights and I had the opportunity to spend some time with him. He was grossly overweight and his attitude seemed to be dressed in a façade of realism. He was still quiet and, to a degree, humble. Perhaps he associated me with those days when he was crying out for stardom and the opportunity to be recognized. That day in Fort Worth, he seemed to be crying out for a chance to be alone. And really, he was alone. His entourage was made up of people who were obviously "out-for-grabs". They were mooching all they could off of "The King".

From what I've been told, I believe Elvis died of loneliness.

While still working for KWFT, Wichita Falls, in the 50s, I was approached by Mead's Fine Bread about possibly doing a jingle for them. In practically no time, I came up with a ditty.

I telephoned Elmer Laurence, the steel-guitar wizard, and "Pappy" Stapp, who played bass-fiddle, and asked them to join me at Nesman Recording Studios in Wichita Falls, where we would cut an audition of the jingle.

Lewis and Sally Nesman set up the old Ampex reel-to-reel recorder and, after a couple of "takes", we had completed the audition for the bread company.

The lyrics:

"Mead's Fine Bread is soft twisted, makes for better flavor—

Get Mead's Fine Bread at your store today and do yourself a favor.

That's what I said —- Mead's Fine Bread!"

The Mead's Bread advertising agency heard the jingle and, after giving it some thought, decided to take a chance on it. They were willing to fork over $200 to me for the simple little creation. This included the costs of the two musicians, studio time at Nesman Recordings and my vocals, accompanied by my guitar.

The $200 talent fee also included the copyright ownership for my jingle.

When I asked them if they wanted me to go back into the studios and make a more professional recording of the jingle, they said, "No. We're not going to put out any more loot on th' thing. We'll ship it out 'as-is' to a few radio stations and check the reaction."

Within a couple of weeks, the Mead's Fine Bread jingle had become the hottest little song in Texas! Since it was so hot on radio, Mead's Bread thought it might be a good idea to have the jingle placed on television.

Lewis and Sally Nesman were retained to create video animation of a skinny cowboy riding a skinny horse across the screen while strumming a big guitar, singing: *"Mead's Fine Bread is soft twisted, makes for better flavor. Get Mead's Fine Bread at your store today and do yourself a favor! That's what I said ... Mead's Fine Bread!"*

The television spot, utilizing the same audio track that was used for radio, was to become a tremendous success.

I received no extra reciprocation for the transfer of the jingle from radio to television. I wasn't concerned about the money. The little radio/television hit was making me a star!

Later on, of course, I would realize this was a big mistake brought on by not having an agent.

My *Mead's Fine Bread* creation was voted the Number One Jingle in the Great Southwest. The bakery even had small booklets, complete with a color picture of the animated cowboy on his horse, available in spots where the bread was sold throughout the Southwest. When you bought a loaf of Mead's Fine Bread, you were given the booklet, consisting of printed lyrics and sheet music to the popular jingle.

My trio would make dozens of Mead's jingles, changing the lyrics a bit, but there would be very little increase in the pay scale.

Then came the inevitable. The advertising agency representing the baking firm came up with the notion my singing, with only two additional instruments besides my guitar strumming, might be a little "outdated". It was at this time that they hired a "pop-style" singer and orchestra to replace Elmer, Pappy and me.

When the new approach to the jingle hit the television tubes and radios, there was chaos! Radio and TV stations began calling the Mead's Fine Bread people informing them that the listeners and viewers were in a rage.

Within a few days, the advertising agency approached me, asking me to please make some more jingles. Sally Nesman also telephoned, pleading with me to "help rescue the Mead's account!"

After a bit of discussion pertaining to the pay, I agreed to get Elmer and "Pappy" and go back into the recording studios.

There was a little more *dough* in the bread deal this time, though.

Because of the success of the Mead's Fine Bread ditty, my credentials as a jingle composer and producer had taken hold. Several big ad agencies contacted me pertaining to creating jingles for such products as trading stamps ("Well … the news is "buzzin' … squaws by th' dozen save *Big Chief Stamps*!")

There were jingles for super markets ("You'll really enjoy your shopping at *Piggly Wiggly* … more people shop there every single day, So always shop the *Piggly Wiggly* way!")

A few politicians running for office tracked me down, wanting jingles for their campaign. One dude's name was Victor Wickersham. Old Vic's jingle took some serious thinking. I finally came up with a musical doozy that began with:

"Vote for Victor Wickersham,

He's th' greatest man 'what am'!"

I can't remember if Wickersham won the election or not.

One star I first met while working in Wichita Falls would become a very special friend. He would cuss like a sailor and then put his arms around me and say, "I love you, Bill Mack." He was, in some ways, a wayfaring stranger from Shreveport, Louisiana who was destined to become a super star.

His name was Faron Young.

Faron Young was an exceptional pal. He told music promoter Billy Deaton: "If I loved Bill Mack any more than I do, I'd have to be a 'queer'!"

Although it was an odd statement, it was, nonetheless, a supreme compliment ... delivered *Faron Young* style!

Faron and I became pals at the very beginning. I was just starting out in radio while he was enjoying his first hit on Capitol Records, *"Goin' Steady"*.

Faron's choice of words could be an embarrassment. Utilizing profanity to make a point was a habit he couldn't control. However, Faron had a warm heart, even though he attempted to conceal that fact most of the time.

When Faron came to my town, he would stay at my house. And when Jackie and I went to Nashville, he would insist that we stay at his place.

In the 50s, I had written a jingle for a Texas politician named Bill Blakely. (*"For a good man in the Senate ... Let's put Bill Blakely in it ...etc.!"*) The jingle caught on big and the political contender decided to make an appearance in Wichita Falls in an attempt to attract voters. He also thought it would be a good idea for me and my band to be on stage with him, since I was singing his jingle. As an added thought, Blakely decided to have me book one of Nashville's hot stars to add importance to the blowout and I thought my pal Faron Young would be perfect for the grand occasion.

I called Faron, told him what the prospective senator was willing to pay him for the gig, and he accepted the offer.

When the night for Blakely's big show arrived, so did Faron. Realizing there were a bunch of the singer's fans in the audience, Blakely insisted that Faron be seated on the platform with him while he made his speech.

Faron took it on himself to "pull applause" during the senator-to-be's speech by waving his arms at the appropriate times, when Blakely made a statement of importance.

In my mind, I had a feeling something dreadful was in the making.

Sure enough, when the politician started speaking, I noticed my pal waving his arms at the wrong times. Blakely would make a simple fizz of a statement, such as: "Well, the weather is nice ..." and Faron would jump to his feet, waving his arms, leading the audience into applause. Then, when Blakely would say something similar to: "I promise to lower taxes and make certain everyone has a good, well paying job ..." Faron would simply lay back in his seat, fold his arms and yawn. Blakely, of course, never saw this, since the "star" was sitting behind him.

After the speech, Bill Blakely wanted pictures taken for the press, with Faron on one side of him and me on the other. There were blinding flashes from the cameras with various poses: Blakely's arms around us, shaking hands with Faron, shaking hands with me, etc.

It was quite a night.

Early next morning, I received a telephone call from someone with *The Wichita Falls Record-News*, our newspaper. He asked me to rush to the newspaper office because he had something he wanted to show me.

Immediately after walking into his office, he handed me several photos. "Take a look at these and see if you notice anything unusual," he growled.

I studied the pictures, nothing catching my attention for a few seconds. Suddenly, I caught what the newspaperman was referring to. In every picture, Bill Blakely was smiling, I was smiling and Faron was displaying an <u>extra</u> big smile ... while nonchalantly shooting the "finger"!

"Have you seen this morning's paper?" Asked the newsman.

Replying I hadn't had a chance to read it yet, he then handed me a copy. On the front page of the *Record-News* was a huge picture of Bill Blakely, Faron, and me. Faron's arm was around the politician's neck; his hand with "the finger" was very visible.

The news chief said, "I don't know why our people didn't catch that! I guess they were just noticing the big smiles —- and not the 'finger'!"

Sad to say: Bill Blakely lost the election.

In my opinion, Faron Young was the <u>original</u> country music outlaw, even before Willie Nelson. As a matter of fact, Faron's recording of Willie's composition, "HELLO WALLS", released in 1961, lit a career fuse for Willie.

Over thirty years later, Willie returned the kind favor by presenting Faron with a $30,000 prize bull for his Nashville ranch!

There was never a guess as to how you stood with the "Sheriff", as he was called.

Faron was known as "The Young Sheriff" in his beginning

years, stemming from several "B" western movies that he had starred in.

If you asked Faron's opinion about something, you could expect an honest answer; never a reaction doctored up or cosmetically applied in order to ease any discomfort. And there were many times he <u>volunteered</u> opinions, most times causing flushed faces.

If Faron liked you or found something you had done deserved it, he issued praise, often times backing it with a favor —- especially if you were a newcomer to country music or weren't in the mainstream of popularity in Nashville.

For some reason we will never know, Faron Young, at age 64, took his own life, with bullets, on December 10, 1996.

Yes, I said "bullets". He shot himself, grazing his head with the first bullet. Then, he cocked the gun again and finished the job.

When I received the "Song of the Year" award for "BLUE" from the Academy of Country Music in Los Angeles in 1997 (on the ABC Television Network), I dedicated my trophy to some special people in my life who had recently passed on.

I mentioned Dewey Groom, owner of The Longhorn Ballroom in Dallas, a dear friend who had helped so many country artists when they were down on their luck.

I acknowledged Mae Axton ... the great lady who represented our industry so well and was there with the praises when she heard me doing my first broadcasts in my hometown.

Then, I mentioned Faron Young ... a talented pal who will never be replaced on stage or in my memories of brotherly love.

There was another nominee in Oklahoma who hired me to compose a jingle for him. He liked what I had created and paid me 50% of my cost, promising to pay the remainder "after the election".

He won the election, but I was never to get the rest of my loot from him. He had his attorneys write me with a photocopy of the deposited check he had given me as half-payment on the jingle, claiming he had paid me <u>in full</u>. Unfortunately, I had failed to mark anywhere on the check that it was for "partial payment". I had also failed to make up a contract for my services for him when I handed him the completed jingle. Therefore, as is the case with many political figures, it was my word against the "Great Representative of the Proud State of Oklahoma".

All was not totally lost, though. Several years later, when my radio show out of Fort Worth-Dallas caught on, I was making an appearance with Conway Twitty, promoting one of his companies operating out of Oklahoma. Guess who had to set the deal with me. That's right, it was the former politician from the Sooner State.

Conway, a good pal, had insisted I be hired to emcee the function, which the political genius had to pay for out of his own pocket. My price was $3000, when the normal cost for my hosting duties would have been about one-third that amount.

I demanded my pay in advance ... and in <u>cash</u>. And even though the hot-air specialist wasn't overly friendly while doing so, he wet his fat thumb with his tongue and counted out the loot to me, most of it in twenty-dollar bills.

Incidentally, I told Conway why I had jumped my price a bit for the dude.

Conway's laughing reaction was: "Lay it on him!"

It wasn't long before Conway informed me that he, too, had encountered some questionable acts from the ex-politician and had severed all business ties with him.

Conway Twitty was a very special friend. I lived near him while working in Oklahoma City for a short while and we spent quite a bit of time together. He was one of the kindest people I have ever known in a business that can sometimes be a bit confusing when you attempt to measure reality in friendships. Many times, especially if you are put in a position where you can either <u>help</u> or <u>hinder</u> an artist or individual, as is the case with disk jockeys, you seldom know how the individuals really feel toward you.

It was during this period that Conway became closest to me. I will always remember how he went out of his way to telephone me regularly and, as mentioned, hired me as his emcee at various times.

When I began my radio show out of Fort Worth-Dallas (much more on this, later) Conway would telephone me from his airplane, <u>The Twitty Bird</u>, when flying near the radio station and we would chitchat on the air. This happened many times and were to become very important "happenings" on my program. Back then, it was an exciting event when you heard a disk jockey talking with a super star while the singer and his band were up in the clouds!

Conway recorded my song, "Clinging To A Saving Hand", telling me it was his "favorite gospel song". To add to the compliment, his album was titled, "Clinging To A Saving Hand".

*One night when Conway was appearing at "Cowboy's", a big
country music nightclub in Dallas, I attempted to reach him by
telephone to invite him to drive over to Fort Worth and sit with me
on my radio show later that night.*

*Whoever took my call wasn't too encouraging about my invita-
tion. He said, "Conway doesn't like to do radio interviews. And,
besides, when he finishes his show here in Dallas, it will be too late
for him to drive to Fort Worth to be with you on the air."*

I accepted these as the final words.

*I had been on the air for about two hours when I noticed the guard
at the radio station heading for the front door. Then, I saw the smiling face of Conway as he entered the door to the control room. And
although it was about two o'clock in the morning, we had a great
time together for a couple of hours before he had to "hit the road to
the next gig".*

*Before he left the microphone, I said: "I was told you didn't like
to do radio interviews! What persuaded you to change your mind
and come over here in the middle of the night?"*

*I'll never forget Conway's reply: "You asked me to come over.
You ought to know by now that we're good friends ... and there's
not a thing I wouldn't do for Bill Mack."*

*Cindy had a surprise birthday party for me June 4, '93, and
nobody wanted to dampen my happiness by telling me Conway
had been rushed to a hospital in Springfield, Missouri immediately after playing a show in nearby Branson. Besides, there were no
details on why he was admitted or his condition.*

*Early the next morning, June 5, 1993, Conway died of an
abdominal aneurysm at the age of 59.*

I was to have my first taste of television when KWFT signed on
the air, affiliated with CBS-TV, in the mid-50s.

Blaine Cornwell, always there in my corner, arranged for me to
do a "live" show on KWFT-TV, Channel 6, every Saturday night.
Everything was "live" on television back then, before videotape
was being utilized.

Mine was a 90-minute program titled "The Big Six Jamboree". I
had my band on hand and, in order to fill that wad of time, I
allowed just about anybody who could sing a song, pick an
instrument, or dance a jig to be on the show.

You will never realize how tough it is to fill 90-minutes of time
on television.

This was when TV was a relatively new thing; the <u>most</u> <u>exciting</u> new attraction! Anything seen 'on the tube' was considered <u>great</u>! And it was all in black-and-white.

I'll never forget how everyone, without exception, would sit around the television set listening to that agitating whistle and watching a motionless "test pattern", waiting for <u>anything</u> to come on the screen.

Such TV features as "Industry On Parade" and "The Carpenter's Helper" were considered "must-see" programs, even if you had no interest in 'industry' or 'hammers and nails'.

"The Big Six Jamboree" caught on in a big way, even though the talent wasn't exactly big marquee.

I did have some big name guests drop in.

Marty Robbins came by "to sing a song or two" and ended up doing over a half hour because the audience in the big studio absolutely refused to let him leave! It didn't bother Marty, though. He loved every minute of it.

Slim Whitman was a guest, even though he acted frightened when he saw the tiny light beam on the camera, leaving the impression he, too, was unfamiliar with television.

Roger Miller would come by from time to time, playing his fiddle and singing his songs. He was beginning to spark in a big way, developing that 'I'm gonna do it <u>my</u> <u>way</u>' attitude that would eventually become his multi-million dollar trademark.

Tillman Franks brought a new singer into town, asking me if he "might do a song on the television show" and, certainly, I was glad to have him. His name was David Houston and the minute I first heard him, I knew he was headed for stardom.

"The Big Six Jamboree" was the hottest local show on television, running for several years, filled with happy sponsors.

Our ratings took a big drop, though, when an accordion player and his troupe decided to make the television scene.

I lost over half of my audience to Lawrence Welk and his bubbly crew.

It wasn't long before "Five-Star Wrestling" took the place once occupied by "The Big Six Jamboree" and, honestly, I was happy to leave the scene. I was beginning to feel very tired from all of the radio-television activity that was taking so much of my time and energy.

In the late 50s, Ken Brown sold KWFT to a group out of

Manhatten, Kansas. Ken moved to the Los Angeles area, where he was operating radio stations with his business partner, Bing Crosby. Blaine Cornwell, who had been such a guiding force through his encouragement to me, also moved west with Ken.

The new owners were very good to me, making it as easy as possible for me to continue with the radio station I have always referred to as my <u>alma</u> <u>mater</u>. They even built a small studio in my home, allowing me to do my early morning broadcast in my pajamas.

Even though I attempted to present my radio shows with excitement, the atmosphere had changed drastically. I had lost the "feel" and was suffering from what many would categorize as "burn-out".

Without a doubt, it was time to make a move.

Bill and Faron Young

The Entertainers

Bill and good friend Willie Nelson

Bill and Conway Twitty

Doing a photo shoot at Monument Valley

Bill and Tex Ritter. KWFT Wichita Falls, Texas

Left to right: Joe Poovey; Bill; Billy Deaton; Faron Young; and Charley Pride

Photos M

Bill and actor
Ben Johnson

Bill with George and
Nancy Jones

Carl Smith, Roy
Drusky and Bill

Bill as M.C. of "The Buck
Owens Ranch" TV show in
Oklahoma City.

Ernest Tubb
and Bill

Photos N

Bill with Kitty Wells and
Johnny Wright

Bill and good pal "Big" John
Brigham (Stagecoach driver)

Bill and Bill Monroe
"The King of Bluegrass"

Bill with good friends
Charlotte Johnson,
Connie Smith and
Asa Johnson

Photos O

Bill and Harold Taft (Bill named him "The World's Greatest Weatherman")

Hosting Bob Hope's 80th birthday charity event in Port Arthur, Texas

Norm Alden, Ruta Lee and Bill

Buddy Van Horn, David Valdez, Bill and Clint Eastwood on the set of "A Perfect World" (Bill supplied period music for the movie)

Bill with Roy Acuff "The King of Country Music"

Photos P

Bill and actor Wilford Brimley
(Wilford's favorite song is
"Drinking Champagne")

Bill and Buck Owens

Bill and Cindy sing "Happy Trails"
with Roy Rogers and Dale Evans

Bill and June Carter Cash

Wes Rose, Bill
and Roy Acuff

Photos Q

Bill, Mike Curb
(of Curb Records),
and Hank Thompso

Bill and Ray
Price in the 50's

Bill and Roger Miller
(I really miss him)

The last
photo with
Waylon
Jennings

Photos R

Bill and Jerry Lee
Lewis, "The Killer"

Bill and Reba McEntire in
the early years of her career

Getting a kiss
from Tammy
Wynette

Johnny Rodriguez,
Willie Nelson, Janie
Fricke and Bill

Bill and
"Whisperin'"
Bill Anderson

11 year old LeAnn Rimes visiting Bill, promoting her independent album "All That" which included "Blue".

Bill and LeAnn at Mid-America Truck Show Louisville, Kentucky

Bill and 14 year old LeAnn

13 year old LeAnn and Bill in Austin, Texas during the filming of the video for "Blue"

Bill and Wilbur Rimes (LeAnn's Dad and producer)

Photos T

Bill & Jerry Clower interview Boxcar Willie on "Country Crossroads" TV (photo courtesy of FAMILY NET and COUNTRY CROSSROADS)

Tanya Tucker, Bill and Marty Rendleman

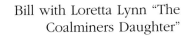

Bill with Loretta Lynn "The Coalminers Daughter"

Bill, "Country Crossroads" producer Jim Rupe, Gene Autry. I have been doing "Country Crossroads" since 1969. (Photo courtesy of FAMILY NET and COUNTRY CROSSROADS)

Photos U

Chill Wills and Bill

Mother Mabel
Carter and Bill

Marty Robbins,
Bill and "Little"
Jimmy Dickens

Bill reading
over script
during taping
of Country
Crossroads TV

Photos V

Bill and Slim
Pickens

Bill and Merle
Haggard

Jan Howard,
Bill, George
Jones and
Bill Monroe

Mel Tillis,
Connie
Francis
and Bill

Photos W

Kris Kristofferson
and Bill

Mel Tillis, Morgan
Fairchild and Bill

Ken and Jackie Johnson. Ken is
my producer on OPEN ROAD XM
SATELLITE RADIO (Channel 171 –
12:00 noon to 4:00 pm – Eastern)

Bill and Lee Abrams (Lee is Senior
VP and Chief Programming Officer
of XM Satellite Radio)

Bill and Tanya Tucker doing a live
broadcast from Louisville, Kentucky on
XM Satellite Radio, OPEN ROAD Channel 171

Photos X

CHAPTER ELEVEN

I accepted an offer from Dave Stone to join him at KDAV in Lubbock, Texas in the late 50s. Although it was a good radio station with lots of listeners, it was a totally different approach to broadcasting than I had experienced during the years I was associated with KWFT in Wichita Falls.

For one thing, it was a "daylight 'til dark" AM outlet. That is, it was limited in hours. Via its' licensing agreement with the Federal Communications Commission, KDAV could only broadcast from sunrise to sunset. Therefore, in order to make money, a heavy load of commercials was inserted in every program.

The mail and telephone response was unbelievable.

Dave Stone was from the "old school" of country music promoters. He was a disk jockey himself, giving every 'country' recording artist a fair share of airplay. He also gave all of his d.j.s a free hand in what they wanted to air.

Dave owned four radio stations, every one of them "all-country". He was the first to format a radio station totally country. Dave did this with all four of his outlets at a time when so-called "block-programming" was the norm. That is, a radio station might play one hour of country music, then one hour of "pop" or "rock", etc. Also, during this era, stations affiliated with networks such as *CBS, NBC, ABC* and *Mutual*, would carry a lot of uninteresting drab from the nets.

If anyone was ever dedicated to our brand of music, it was "Pappy" Dave Stone. Every record label, and many country artists, owe so much to this fine man. He was selling truckloads of records by steadily pushing our country music products and heavily promoting those singing the songs, when most radio outlets were totally ignoring the country sound.

I have long thought Dave Stone should have his spot in our Country Music Hall of Fame in Nashville.

Dave really rolled out the welcome wagon to me when I arrived in Lubbock. He rented a house for us and had everything set to go when Jackie and I arrived in the *Caprock City* with our baby daughter, Debbie.

As we were moving into the house, a tall gentleman walked up to me and introduced himself, saying he was our neighbor, living one house down the street from us. He stood around talking with me as the moving van people unloaded the furniture.

"We listened to your programs out of Wichita Falls," he said. "Glad to know you'll be with us on KDAV."

I told him I was glad to meet him, although most of my concentration was on the people hauling our mixture of stuff into the house we were seeing for the first time. Although Jackie didn't complain, it was a far cry from our house we had just vacated a few hours earlier in Wichita Falls.

My new neighbor said he had a son who was a singer, and who had performed on KDAV's *Sunday Afternoon Talent Search* program.

Silently, I thought: "Just what I need. Now, he'll be bringing his son over for me to listen to as he warbles some Hank Williams songs."

As Jackie walked up to us, I said, "Jackie, this is our new neighbor." Then, feeling a bit embarrassed, I added: "I forgot your name."

He said, "My name is Holley."

All of a sudden, it dawned on me.

"Are you related to Buddy Holly?" I asked.

"He's my son," replied the good man.

Incidentally, Buddy dropped the e̲ in Holley after signing a recording contract. From here on, I'll utilize the professional spelling.

Mr. Holly said, "My wife has some food prepared for you folks when you get time. I want you to meet her ... and she is looking forward to having you as neighbors, just as I am."

For some reason, I had never met Buddy Holly, but I was very impressed with his parents. Like Mr. Holly, Buddy's mother was a very special lady. They were to be good and caring neighbors; absolutely wonderful human beings.

They invited us to their church.

I had a morning radio show on KDAV but my heart wasn't in it. Dave and his people were so very nice, but the shoe didn't fit. I soon realized I had made a mistake in moving to Lubbock. Problem was I didn't admit to Jackie that I was unhappy with our move. Instead, I went through a tremendous mood change.

Also working as a D.J. at KDAV at the time was a skinny guy from Littlefield, Texas, just down the road from Lubbock. His name was Waylon Jennings. Before getting into radio, Waylon had worked with Buddy Holly for awhile as one of the "Crickets".

Although Waylon and I were friendly with each other, we didn't become close friends, partly because of my low frame of mind. I did see the talent in Jennings and realized he was far above the norm as a guitar-picker and singer. He was also a very good songwriter. However, his talent wouldn't be discovered until he moved to Arizona. Old friend, Bobby Bare, heard him and suggested Chet Atkins sign him with R.C.A. Records. The rest, of course, is history.

Also doing a D. J. shift was Arlie Duff, a very funny dude and a great songwriter. He composed, "Y'All Come", which has become a classic, and several other good songs. Arlie, like me, was unhappy while working at KDAV, and would eventually move to Austin, where he became a very important fixture in broadcasting.

Arlie died of a heart attack in 1996 ... while playing golf in Austin.

I hadn't been at KDAV long when I received a phone call from Blaine Cornwell, telling me the good news that I had a job in Long Beach, California at KFOX Radio if I wanted it! This was what I had prayed for!

I accepted the West Coast job and told Dave Stone I was pulling out for California. Blaine had the moving van set to come to Lubbock and pick up our furniture when, for some reason I still can't understand, I backed out, deciding I wanted to remain in Texas.

I telephoned Blaine and thanked him for the offer, telling him I had decided to stay where I was. He kindly accepted my weird decision, although he did inform me he thought I was making a mistake by not taking the radio job in the huge Los Angeles area.

He said: "Everybody's trying to get into the competitive Los Angeles market, Bill. I wish you'd give second thoughts to your decision."

I told him I had given it serious thought and my decision to remain in Lubbock was firm.

It wasn't long before I was feeling more depressed than ever, realizing I had made such a huge mistake in turning down the California offer. It wasn't an easy time for Jackie, either, since she had to witness my dark moods. She made every attempt to comfort me.

Adding to the hurt was when Jackie had a miscarriage.

Dave Stone set up a separate recording studio for me to do my jingles, which was a very successful venture, and I was given a lucrative deal with Channel 11 in Lubbock, doing a weekly television show with some very important guest stars. Working the floor, not on camera, was a funny dude named Don Bowman. Don eventually received his big break in entertainment, although not from me. A beautiful little lady from Lubbock named Rolna English would sing from time-to-time on my TV show and sang some of my jingles. She was a great talent and finally received her just reward by becoming a member of the Lawrence Welk show on ABC-TV.

It was while doing the television show that I first met my good friend, Jimmy Dean. Jimmy was from Plainview, Texas, not too far from Lubbock. While visiting his mother in Plainview, he decided to surprise me by coming on my TV show one night ... at no charge!

Without a doubt, this was the best television program I presented to the good folks in Lubbock.

Let me add something of importance, here: Jimmy Dean has done as much for the country music industry as any single individual I can think of. He was the first to boost the country product on nationwide television. Back in the 50s, he did a daily program on CBS-TV. In the 60s, Jimmy presented a program on ABC-TV, in prime time.

Jimmy was responsible for the blooming careers of Patsy Cline, Roger Miller, Roy Clark and many other super stars.

Help me figure this one out: Jimmy Dean is not in the *Country Music Hall of Fame*, as I write this!

I've discussed this issue with several people in Nashville and Los Angeles. The average response has been, "I thought Jimmy Dean was in the *Country Music Hall of Fame!*"

If Jim isn't placed in this hallowed spot, it will reflect absolute disgrace to our proud industry.

Even my television show was beginning to drag on me and I was rapidly losing interest. Really, I was losing my feel for all avenues in broadcasting for the first time in my life and, as I recall that era, I had reached a point to where I wanted to walk out of radio and TV altogether.

Making the problem more serious, I was still in my twenties when this attitude was overtaking me.

Let me stress again the fact that my unhappiness in Lubbock wasn't because of Dave Stone and his fine staff. It was simply a time when I was feeling very little happiness. Honestly, I believe I was suffering from emotional exhaustion. If I had approached my problem wisely, there would have been no need to leave Wichita Falls for Lubbock. I still question that move. I didn't need a different radio station. I needed rest! My weight had dropped to around 130 pounds and I was, literally, an emotional wreck.

Adding to my emotions was something that took place February 3, 1959 that will always rattle my mind.

I was doing my morning radio show when Wes Youngblood, the program director, walked into the control room and handed me a bulletin that he had just ripped from the newswire machine.

I announced: "Buddy Holly, J. P. Richardson, known as "The Big Bopper" and Richey Valens have been killed in a plane crash near Mason City, Iowa."

After a short pause, I added, "Stay tuned for more details."

I automatically thought of my neighbors, Laurence and Ella, Buddy's parents, realizing what a period of tragedy they must have been going through.

As I mentioned, I had never met Buddy Holly.

I was about to pick up the telephone and call Jackie, suggesting she go over to the Holly's house, when Wes rushed back into the control room and shouted, "My God! Mrs. Holly just telephoned the radio station asking if what she had just heard you announce was true! Nobody had notified Buddy's folks about the plane crash!"

I immediately jumped up from my chair at the control board and asked Wes to take over my radio show because I had to head to the Holly house!

It is not a law that the next of kin be notified before an announcement is made on radio or television of a death. It is a courtesy. However, if a person in the public eye dies, the various news associations attempt to beat each other to the wires.

Buddy Holly was certainly in the public eye. Therefore, no attempt was made to telephone his parents, telling them their 23 year-old son had died in a plane crash in the Midwest.

I was to find out Mrs. Holly was ironing when she heard me make the announcement on KDAV. I was told she was in such a state of shock that she finished ironing Laurence's shirt before it finally dawned on her she had, indeed, heard me tell my listeners that her son was dead. Then, she telephoned the radio station for a confirmation.

As I entered the Holly house, the press had already converged on the scene and the room was filled with people. Mrs. Holly was weeping, surrounded by loved ones. Mr. Holly, who was seated next to his wife, saw me standing by the door, got up from the couch, and approached me.

Of course, I was in a deep state of shock myself as Laurence placed his arm around me and whispered, "I know this has to be tough on you, Bill." Then, with tears rolling down his cheeks, he added, "We love you, Bill, and we certainly don't blame you for anything. You didn't know we hadn't been informed of this terrible news."

February 3 will always be a dark and depressing date to me.

It wasn't long after the Holly happening that I received a telephone call from Gabe Tucker in Houston informing me that a powerful radio station in San Antonio was about to go "all-country" and wanted me to be with them. I mentioned earlier that Gabe had, at one time, worked with Colonel Tom Parker. When he telephoned me, he was associated with H. W. Dailey, the most successful record distributor in the Southwest. "Pappy" Dailey also owned *D Records,* an independent record label that I was recording for at the time, and *Glad Music,* a music publishing house located in Houston that was handling my songs.

"Pappy" was also producing the works of a strong singer named George Jones.

I told Gabe that I was certainly interested in making the move and, within two hours, Herb Carl, the manager of KENS, San Antonio, Texas, hired me!

I was anxious to make the move.

Bill and Waylon Jennings clowning around. (Bill and Waylon were disk jockeys together in Lubbock, Texas in the 50's)

CHAPTER TWELVE

Leaving the dusty, but friendly, city of Lubbock, Texas was a bit sad because Dave Stone and the bunch at KDAV had made such a lasting impression on me as being authentic, caring people.

San Antonio, however, was a "paradise". I will always remember when I awoke one morning and discovered bananas growing in my back yard! And the aroma of the natural floral settings was something I had never encountered before. It was a big city, made up of a potpourri of people, many of them of Mexican heritage.

I will always consider San Antonio an exotic city.

On my arrival at KENS, *The Express News Station*, I realized I was in a terrific terrain for broadcasting. First of all, it boasted 50,000 watts and was on-the-air around-the-clock, something completely new to me. And after entering the hallways and chatting with Herb Carl and his crew, the energy re-entered my body! For the first time in months, I was feeling on top of the world, both physically and emotionally.

Herb revealed his plans to me:

KENS was set to become a 24-hour country music outlet with knowledgeable, professional disk jockeys behind the microphones.

The d. j. list included Charlie Walker, who had spent years hosting his country music radio shows at KMAC in San Antonio and was a Columbia Records recording artist. Charlie was running strong with hits at the time, including, "Pick Me Up On Your Way Down", Harlan Howard's great composition.

Also on the payroll was Neal Merritt, a former television weatherman-turned-country disk jockey, who had a terrific voice. (Several years later, Neal would write a Number One hit titled, "May The Bird Of Paradise Fly Up Your Nose", belted by country music hall-of-famer, Little Jimmy Dickens!).

Ray Baker, who would eventually become one of Nashville's outstanding record producers, was also assigned d. j. duties with KENS.

Joe Simpson, a skinny dude with a great talent, would charm the listeners with his honest approach to radio, as would Bill Shomette, another old pro.

I was assigned the early morning slot, from 6 a.m. until 9 a.m., Monday through Friday.

Immediately after hitting the airwaves in November, 1960, I realized I was associated with the country music "giant of the airwaves"! And I wasn't wrong in my belief. *The Express News,* San Antonio's leading newspaper, was owned by the same conglomerate that owned KENS, now claiming to be "the world's first full-time country music station, with 50,000 watts!"

Also on the scene was KENS-TV, which added to the heavy promotion of its' sister radio station.

I had never experienced response to radio as I did while doing the early morning bit on KENS. I was also happy over the fact that my show was *Number One* in the oh-so-important radio ratings in San Antonio!

Herb Carl, the station manager, approached me one day and said, "You're being moved to the 3:00 p.m. to 6:00 p.m. spot."

"Why?" I asked. "My show is Number One in ratings!"

Herb said, "Charlie Walker wants the early spot and, since we promised him we would do as he wished if he would exit KMAC and join us, I have no choice!"

I was really hacked off about this because Walker, who had pretty well controlled the country music radio scene for years in San Antonio, was revealing the fact he was jealous over my ratings and wanted to 'change positions'. I would have felt a hell of a lot better if he had asked me my feelings before running to Herb Carl's office.

Eventually, Charlie left San Antonio and joined Nashville's *Grand Ole Opry,* where he is still a member.

All of the disk jockeys were making good loot on personal appearances, in addition to the better than average radio salaries.

Radio salaries have always been below the norm, except in major markets ... with the advantage of high ratings.

Because of the popularity of my radio show, I was booked several nights a week at various nightclubs throughout the South Texas area, most of the time playing to full houses, because the air personalities were allowed to "plug" our appearances during our radio shows. Appearances were also good promotional advantages for the radio station.

After I had been with KENS for several months, Pappy Dailey arranged a contract for me with *M-G-M* Records, which was a very strong label at the time. One reason Pappy was able to swing a deal for me with the big outfit was because his company was the leading distributorship of its' kind in the Great Southwest, selling a tremendous amount of *M-G-M* records.

Pappy set up my first record session in Nashville. It would also be my first trip on an airplane, and I was a bit shaky. It wasn't the air flight that had made me nervous, but the idea that I would be recording at the Owen Bradley Studios and singing my songs to the accompaniment of some of Nashville's top musicians. And when Pappy informed me that the world famous Jordanaires, the group that did the backup singing on most of Elvis' recordings, would be singing backup for me, it almost did me in.

Pappy Dailey didn't do any producing to speak of. Instead, he handed the reins over to Buddy Killen, who also played bass-fiddle on the session.

Also set for the session were Pete Drake on steel-guitar, Buddy Harmen on drums, "Pig" Robbins playing piano, and Tommy Jackson on fiddle. This was, without a single doubt, the greatest conglomerate of musicians to be found in the city of Nashville.

While riding in the car toward the Owen Bradley Studios with The Jordanaires and Buddy Killen after having a meal at one of Nashville's better restaurants, Buddy asked, "Bill, would you like for me to stop and get a bottle of 'instant relaxer' for you before we begin the session?"

Although I told Buddy it wasn't necessary, I had my doubts.

I will always be grateful to Buddy Killen for his strong interest in me that night. Several years later, Buddy formed one of Nashville's most successful music publishing houses, *Tree Music*. After selling the firm to Sony, he became a Music City multimillionaire.

When I was recording my *M-G-M* stuff in Nashville, the average session ran three hours in length. Otherwise, there would be overtime costs for the studio and the musicians. Happy to say, I did my four songs in the allotted time and I was thrilled at the sound Buddy had produced.

I recorded *"You're Not The Kind (To Be True)", "Adding To My Misery", "Please Don't Let Her Know"* and *"Where Were You (When The Doorbell Rang)"*. These accounted for two 45-rpm M-G-M Records.

Only *"You're Not The Kind"* would peek-a-boo in the Billboard charts ... and then drop out. The others were bombs.

All was not lost, however. When M-G-M decided to drop me from their "Cradle Of Stars", Pappy arranged another deal for me. This time, it was with *United-Artists Records*, also a big label at that time. It was also a label that the Dailey company was distributing.

United Artists needed Pappy Daily ... and Pappy Daily was obliged to me for laying heavy on his products on KENS.

All in all, it was a playpen form of payola! "You scratch my back ... and I'll scratch yours!"

Pappy and I headed back to Nashville and, with the accompaniment of the same talented crew, Buddy Killen producing, we churned out four more forgettable songs.

I really don't have to go into details on the outcome of the second session, except to say it was similar to the first.

My record <u>sales</u> were also similar.

To summarize: It just dawned on me that both, *M-G-M* Records and *United-Artists Records*, have closed up shops.

Hubert Long, the manager of Faron Young and a bunch of others, telephoned me one day in the early 60s, offering to bring a super show to San Antonio. He wanted me to produce the country music extravaganza, which I agreed to do. In exchange for my production duties, I was to receive 20% of the intake after paying for the commercials purchased on *KENS, KENS-TV* and newspaper ads in our mother newspaper, *The San Antonio Express News*.

I discussed the agreement with Herb Carl and he was sold on the idea, since it would be a great promotion for the radio station.

There would be two separate shows. One would be in the afternoon and the second show would be presented that night. The cast included: Jim Reeves and The Blue Boys, Patsy Cline,

George Jones, Ernest Tubb and his Texas Troubadours, Ray Price and his Cherokee Cowboys, Faron Young and his Country Deputies, Grandpa Jones, The Wilburn Brothers, Sonny James, Roger Miller, Roy Drusky, Skeeter Davis, Bill Anderson and Claude Gray.

I'm sure there were some other acts on that show that have slipped my mind after 40 years.

I do remember I invited Ralph Emery to be our guest emcee, which he was happy to do. Ralph was married to Skeeter Davis at the time and was hosting the all night radio show on WSM.

Also with us was kingpin disk jockey Paul Kallinger, from XERF, Ciudad Acuna, Mexico! Paul was billed as: "Your good neighbor along the way!"

God, what a voice this man possessed! He was also a great human being.

Since the the huge country music fest was to be presented on Sunday, I booked most of the acts in various nightclubs in the San Antonio area on the preceding Friday and Saturday nights, in order for them to pick up some extra loot.

Grandpa Jones, one of the funniest men who ever lived and who specialized in picking the old banjo while singing ancient mountain songs, was mis-booked somehow. He was accidentally set to play *The Farmer's Daughter*, the leading country music nightspot in San Antonio, that Saturday night. This was a club that catered to the western-swing two-steppin' crowd who liked to belly-rub to bands such as Hank Thompson, Ernest Tubb, Bob Wills and the likes.

The Farmer's Daughter bunch wanted their music loud and with a heavy beat!

Grandpa hired three musicians to accompany him and his twanging banjo in the huge honky-tonk.

I received the news that the western-swing patrons didn't dig the banjo pickin' star, many walking out while he was pickin' and singin' such signature songs as *"Old Rattler"* and *"Good Ol' Mountain Dew"*, and I was very interested in finding out how Grandpa felt about the situation. Seeing him backstage at the auditorium Sunday afternoon, I asked: "Grandpa, how did it go for you at *The Farmer's Daughter* last night?"

Grandpa replied, "Bill, you'd have thought I was singin' 'Silent Night', th' way they reacted to me an' my ol' banjo!"

Grandpa had come to San Antonio after touring with an act

known for their pill popping antics. I asked him how the tour went.

Grandpa replied, "Bill, them boys would have swallered a button if you'd have give 'em a glass of water."

Of all the genuine, entertaining people I have ever known, nobody could outshine Grandpa Jones.

Both San Antonio shows were sold out well in advance. It was to be the greatest country music extravaganza I've ever participated in. It seemed there were almost as many people backstage as were seated in the audience. I have never seen as many super stars on one package.

I had just purchased a new Martin guitar and decided I would have the many artists, roaming around backstage, autograph it.

The first "star" I approached was Roger Miller. Handing him the Martin, I said, "Roger, sign my new guitar."

Without hesitation, Roger took the Marks-A-Lot pen I had handed him, laid my new guitar on his lap and scribbled: _BILL MACK SMITH_, underlining the name.

I shouted, "What are you doin'? You wrote my name!"

Roger looked up at me and said, "It's your guitar."

No more comment.

Another incident took place backstage that Sunday that was to grab some worldwide attention, many years later.

Patsy Cline was going strong in the early 60s and I had written a song a couple of years before that I thought she might be interested in hearing, believing it was the kind of material that fit her recording style.

Patsy was a class act, specializing in torch songs ("_I Fall To Pieces_", "_Crazy_", etc.). However, offstage she could release expletives like a seasoned sailor.

She grumbled, "Let me hear your damned ol' song!"

Taking my new Martin guitar in hand, I ushered Patsy into a secluded dressing room, closed the door, and began warbling,

"Blue, oooh, oooh, oooh ...

Oh, so lonesome for you...
Why can't you be blue over me?
Blue, oooh, oooh, oooh –
Oh, so lonesome for you –
Tears blind my eyes 'til I can't see ... "

And, of course, the lyrics went on.

Although I wasn't presenting my composition in the best environment, Patsy seemed interested. After finishing my singing, she patted me on the arm and said, "Put that damned thing on tape an' send it to me! I like it!"

A beautiful and very talented little San Antonio lady named Joanie Hall recorded a good demo of my song and I shipped it to Owen Bradley, Patsy Cline's record producer. I also sent a demo tape to Patsy.

Charlie Dick, Patsy's husband, said he can still remember her receiving my tape.

Tragically, Patsy died in the plane crash March 5, 1963 at age 30, never recording my tune.

Thirty-five years later, a child singer would record the song I had titled, "BLUE", and make it a super hit, winning me a Grammy.

I began making more and more personal appearances, mostly in the South Texas area. Because of my radio shows and the fact my recordings were being played frequently on various radio stations in Texas, I was receiving more offers to play the country music nightclubs than I could fulfill. And I was making more money than I had ever made in my life.

Since I was burning the proverbial candle at both ends, I began losing weight again, not realizing I was highly allergic to the smoke in the honky-tonks I was playing. I was also smoking cigarettes quite heavily back then, a habit it would take a long time to break.

Instead of cutting back on my overloaded schedule, I kept going; pushing myself.

Even though it was taking its' toll on me, I was enjoying the game.

Ask any male entertainer and most every one of them will tell you of one special danger: The super-charged female fan.

I was to meet a very special representative of this species while working in San Antonio.

In order to protect the innocent, we'll call her, 'Joyce'.

I was doing my show from 3:00 p.m. until 6:00 p.m. Monday through Friday, from the *North-Star Mall Shopping Center* in San Antonio. The radio station had built a nice little glass enclosed studio in the center of the huge shopping establishment, where

143

gobs of people would stand outside, listening to me on the exterior speakers.

A real live disk jockey in action!

I first met Joyce one day when she stopped outside my little booth and smiled at me through the glass. She was absolutely beautiful. She had long brown hair, matching brown eyes, and a perfect figure. Naturally, I made the mistake of sliding open the door and inviting her to step inside, which she did.

After entering, she informed me that she was my "biggest fan", and that she listened to my show every day, without exception.

First day, Joyce only stayed in the broadcast booth with me for about fifteen minutes, telling me she "had to run", but would see me again.

A few days went by and Joyce returned. This time, she was wearing brief shorts and a midriff. It was also obvious she had been sitting in the San Antonio sun, since she had a perfect tan. She had a couple of paper cups in her hand as she waited for me to unlatch the door.

"I brought you a little refresher," she giggled, handing me one of the drinks.

I can't remember what the drink consisted of. However, I do recall the fact that I began feeling very relaxed after drinking it.

Joyce was also sipping on hers. She spent a little more time with me that day, telling me some personal facts about her life. She said she was a divorcee, that her husband beat her regularly when he had been drinking, that she had no children ... and that she was going to move to Dallas in a few weeks where she would be modeling clothing at Neiman Marcus.

I was quite impressed.

She asked, "Are you coming to the Hawaiian Luau here at the mall tomorrow night?"

"I don't know," I replied. "Are you going to be here?"

"Yes," she purred. Then, she added, "I'll see you here!"

Next night, there was Joyce, dressed like a Hawaiian dancer, at the big get-together at *North-Star Mall*. She was drinking a special concoction with different fruit bits glowing in the glass. It was obvious she was a bit tipsy, asking me to dance with her to the music being provided by a Hawaiian band.

My wife, Jackie, was also at the mall with me that night, as were several associates from KENS. I introduced my new-found friend to all of them.

As we danced, Joyce whispered, "Is that your wife?"

"Yes."

Then: "I'm so sorry you're married."

Before the Hawaiian blowout was over, Joyce was wobbling around the mall, holding her liquid refreshment, completely out of control.

The next day, Joyce came back to my broadcast booth, looking a bit worn. It was obvious she was still suffering from a heavy hangover. I unlatched my door and she walked in, sitting down in the guest chair.

It was then that she told me she was in love with me!

I told her she was simply lonely after going through her divorce. I also said I wanted to be her friend, but that was it.

She began to weep.

Undoubtedly, the people looking through the glass were wondering what was going on. Finally, I told her she should go home, get some food in her stomach and rest up.

"You'll feel much better, tomorrow," I said.

Joyce patted my arm and told me goodbye.

A week or so went by, after Joyce had made her last visit to me in my booth, when I received a visit from a total stranger, wearing a dark suit and cowboy hat. He knocked gently on my door and, after I opened it, said: "I've got to talk with you."

"You'll have to wait until I'm finished with my show," I responded.

He was persistent. "No! You'll talk with me now!"

Realizing he meant business, I invited him in. He got right to the point.

"I came here to kill you," he said in a calm but serious tone of voice.

"What?" I asked, thinking I might need to call for a security officer.

"That's right," he said, tears filling his eyes. "My friends talked me out of it."

By this time, I was feeling threatened, to say the least. I asked the obvious question, "Why? What have I done to you?"

He said, "You know why. Joyce!"

It seems he was Joyce's husband, and there had been no divorce. According to him, they had been very happy together until I had come along. He also mentioned their three children.

"She told me about how you and her had shacked up together

145

followin' the Hawaiian party here at th' mall," he said, openly weeping.

I rapidly reacted, forcing an appearance of anger. He was a skinny dude and didn't leave the impression of being a fighter. A 'killer', maybe, but not a fighter.

"My wife was with me at the party," I said. "I danced with Joyce one time ... and that was it!"

He then said: "Well, I've got to be honest. It ain't just you I was concerned about. I found out she's been messin' around with a bunch of musicians. Even went out with one of my best friends. But she only <u>admitted</u> goin' out with you! She kinda bragged about it when she was drunk th' other night!"

He finally believed me. He was still sobbing as he shook my hand and apologized for being in such a frame of mind that he "could have made a bad mistake", if I hadn't assured him he was wrong.

He walked out of the broadcast booth and I watched him carefully as he headed toward the exit to the mall.

A few months after Joyce's husband had paid me the uncomfortable visit, I ran into a friend of mine from Bandera, Texas, located just out of San Antonio, who happened to be a deputy sheriff. It seems he knew Joyce's husband very well and was also aware of her "outside activities".

He said, "He shot his best friend over her! Didn't kill him, but put him in the hospital with a bullet in his arm."

Joyce never returned to my broadcast booth.

Herb Carl called the KENS bunch together and announced that a Houston, Texas group was buying the radio station. He assured us there was nothing to worry about, that since KENS was the Number One station in the market, the new bosses were determined to retain the same winning format, featuring <u>country music</u>.

The Houston people undoubtedly had different ideas. The rumor circulated that the new owners' wives hated "hillbilly" music and found it embarrassing!

Herb said, "Take my word for it! It's only going to get better for all of us! I'm having a meeting with the new bosses tomorrow and I'll lay heavy on the fact it's going to be 'country music or nothing at all'!"

One of the KENS sales reps attended the meeting next day

with Herb Carl and the gang from Houston. Seems the new owners also had their wives with them at the get-together. The sales rep told me, "Herb and I had just seated ourselves comfortably and I was anxious to hear Herb go to bat for the radio station and our country music format.

"Started off, one of the new owners simply stated, 'This country music is a little new for all of us. Our other radio stations program people like Frank Sinatra and Bing Crosby. We just wanted to see what you folks thought we should do in the future?'"

The salesman laughed and said, "Before the new owner had time to sit back in his chair, Herb volunteered the statement of doom. He said, 'I never did like country music.! I've always regretted we started playing the <u>stuff</u>!'"

Within a few weeks, it was announced that KENS was dropping its' country music format and going more into sports, news and 'popular' music.

Although I had lived in San Antonio for a few years, I didn't visit the world famous Alamo, located only a few blocks from KENS, until the week before moving to Fort Worth-Dallas ... where I was to enter a completely new avenue in broadcasting.

CHAPTER THIRTEEN

Leaving KENS and San Antonio was such a sad occasion. First, the radio station had been the most successful of any I had worked for. The salary was good, I genuinely liked the people I had worked with, and it seemed I was constantly busy, doing the things I really enjoyed doing.

Then, there was the city itself. As I mentioned, I will always consider San Antonio to be an 'exotic' city. The people had accepted me so very well and, all in all, I had enjoyed my stay in the Alamo City more than any other locale I had been placed.

When word was out that KENS had dropped the country music format, I immediately received job offers from various parts of the country. I wanted to stay in Texas and had whittled the proposals down to two markets, Houston and Fort Worth-Dallas. Finally, after being given a very good offer from a guy named John Buckley, I decided I would make the move to Radio Station KPCN, located in Grand Prairie, Texas, located in the Dallas area.

When old friend Arlie Duff, working in radio in Austin at the time, heard I was accepting Buckley's offer, he warned me: "Don't go to work for that weird dude!"

I should have listened!

KPCN was another daylight 'til dawn outlet, making me feel like I was drooping back in time. It was also located in a cow pasture,

149

south of Grand Prairie. However, it had a tremendous listening audience, ranking close to *Number One* in ratings in the gigantic and important Dallas radio game.

Since I had been nominated D. J. of the Year, was recently "Mr. D.J. USA" and had served on the Board-of-Directors with the Country Music Association in Nashville, those working as on-the-air personalities at the station must have felt a bit intimidated. My arrival at KPCN was less than cordial. When I first walked into the radio station and introduced myself, there were no handshakes or words of welcome. Instead, there was an obvious *chill* in the air.

The exception here was Jim Newton, an old pro. Laughing, he took me aside and said, "Man, welcome to the 'station of the star's! These dumb asses are jealous of anyone who can <u>read</u>! They think <u>ad-lib</u> stands for something you keep in the trunk of your car!"

A man named Giles Miller owned the radio station. He was a political figure in the Dallas area, deep into his personal attitudes toward national happenings, but was very nice to me. However, his son, Giles, Jr., didn't share his daddy's natural friendliness. He was very much wrapped up in the fact that he was the son of the owner and could do as he "damned well pleased!" He was also a d. j. of sorts, his mentor being Joe Poovey, another disk jockey on the KPCN payroll who left the easy-to-read impression to me that I wasn't wanted.

I walked up to Giles, Jr., stuck out my hand and said, "I'm Bill Mack."

He ignored my introduction and, being a bit on the heavy side, shuffled into the radio station control room where his pal, Poovey, was doing his radio show. I saw them look at me through the glassed window, laughing, and could almost read their lips: "We'll make life a livin' hell for him!"

The receptionist was a sweet lady who was taking note of the idiotic, child-like rudeness. She got me a cup of coffee and said, "They're jealous. Don't pay any attention to them. When they first heard you had been hired, they began making plans to make you miserable."

I was anxious to connect with the manager of the station, who was running late that morning. When he finally arrived, he strutted rapidly into his office, not slowing down for a greeting to either, the receptionist or me.

Jim Newton, who was standing near the coke machine, snarled and said, "There goes th' boss! He got to be boss by taking a mail order course in 'stupidity'!"

It didn't take long for me to realize Jim Newton was his own man! It was also easy to decipher the fact he was the only true professional I had met thus far in the broadcast facility.

After waiting around for about an hour, the manager opened his office door and growled to me, "Come in."

I walked into his abode and he slammed the door closed, leaving the impression he was 'setting the mood'. Then, without a word of welcome, he sat down at his desk and, picking up a fly swatter, began his spiel.

"I run a radio station here that I'm damned proud of!" He shouted. "We have managed to get good ratings and lots of listeners with our own little family here!"

Swatting his desk at an imaginary fly, with the swatter, he continued: "Now, we don't need any big shot, big time, big city disk jockey who thinks he's God's gift to radio, comin' in here upsetting things!

"And, I just might add, I damned sure won't allow any big time disk jockeys comin' in here and screwing up our happy little family!"

I was sitting in a state of shock. I noticed that every time he spoke the word, "big", he emphasized it with a heavy blast to his desk with the fly swatter.

He said, "Now ... I want you to know one thing, I ..."

Before he could crap any deeper into his oratory, I jumped up from my chair, jerked the fly swatter from the his hand and twisted it into several circles. I then tossed it to him, hitting his protruding belly, and shouted, "You swat that thing one more time ... or shout one more word of stupidity at me and I'm going to punch you! Do you hear me, you idiotic dumb-ass?"

The manager was literally shaking; his face had become a putrid pale. It was easy to see he had dethroned, rapidly.

As I stepped toward the door to exit, he said, "Please ... please wait just a minute."

Walking toward me in a state of gentleness, he extended his shaking hand and quivered, "Wel ... welcome to KPCN."

Ignoring his hand, I opened the door and walked out of his office.

The receptionist, who had obviously heard most of the conversation that had taken place 'behind closed doors', laughed and said: "That a boy, Bill! Welcome!"

Needless to say, KPCN wasn't to be my cup of tea. Although the attitudes of those on the premises changed to a friendlier setting after my discussion with the manager, who had decided to resign, there was still discomfort.

One thing I will always remember about KPCN is the fact that it was *unique*, breaking most accepted rules and regulations attached to broadcasting. To make the disk jockeys happy, there was a beer cooler in the control room that was always fully stocked with brew. Although the listening audience wasn't aware of it, most of the d.j.s were most likely holding a 45 rpm record in one hand and a Budweiser in the other while doing their daily thing!

As I look back on it, I wouldn't trade my short stay with the Grand Prairie outlet.

Another one of the air personalities on duty at KPCN was Horace Logan. Horace was the head honcho with the *Louisiana Hayride* during its' hay day and was a true professional. His knowledge of country music and radio approach made him a very important fixture at the radio station.

Horace, like Jim Newton, found the flaws at KPCN to be a little on the unbelievable side.

Again, considering the rough edges, KPCN was a very successful operation, playing what Dallas-Fort Worth wanted to hear! Even though it was a daytime-only spot on the AM dial, it was winning ratings over the big stations in town, including KRLD, WBAP and the likes.

I've often wondered: If there had not been the flaws, the beer coolers and "don't much give a damned" attitude in that radio station, located in a cow pasture near Dallas, would it have been so popular with the listeners?

That combination of oddness may well have been the secret of KPCN's success.

John Buckley, the person representing Giles Miller who had hired me, called me one morning after I had completed my air shift at KPCN, telling me to meet him at his motel room.

Buckley lived in Austin, where another of Miller's radio stations was located.

When I walked into the motel room, I noticed Buckley had one of his men-friends with him as he asked me to have a seat. Immediately, he let it be known that he had been listening to my program while driving into Dallas from his home in Austin and that he and his room mate, a nervous character named 'Lee', had not liked my way of doing a radio show.

"Therefore," he said, "I'm <u>firing</u> you."

I wasn't surprised in hearing this, since I had been told by one of Buckley's ex men-friends, that I would be axed in order for Buckley to give 'Lee' a chance as a disk jockey.

Without making any statement, I left the motel room. For some odd reason, I felt very tranquil, as if a tremendous load had been lifted from my back.

Before the day had ended, I was approached by KCUL in Fort Worth with a job offer, which I accepted. The good news here was that I wouldn't have to move the furniture. My home was in Cowtown.

John Buckley, a confirmed alcoholic, was found dead from a heart attack in a restroom at the Longhorn Ballroom in Dallas a few months later. He was a very strange and lonely individual.

CHAPTER FOURTEEN

When I was hired as Program Director of KCUL in Fort Worth in 1963, I was placed in charge of a radio station located at 1540 on the AM dial. Now, as most of you probably know, stations on the far-right side of the dial are a fizz when it comes to coverage. Even though KCUL boasted 50,000 watts of power, the outlet was assigned a strange coverage map by the Federal Communications Commission and the result was, you could hardly hear it in Dallas! You could hear it quite well in Amarillo, but not in Dallas, thirty miles to the east.

KCUL also had a weird format. It would broadcast anything to make money. This was obvious when, at 11:00 a.m. every day, it switched to Mexican/Hispanic for an hour and, unless you spoke the language, there was no reason to listen because it was strictly a "talk" program, featuring one of the most suave individuals I have met. The host's name was Oscar Argumedo. Oscar would arrive at the radio station at least an hour before his broadcast time every day, usually accompanied by one or two beautiful "senoritas". Always dressed in a tailored dark suit and tie, he would lay a heavy smile on me as he shouted, "Hello, Meester Beel Mack!"

Oscar would usually drop by for a visit with me as I did my daily radio show, which was aired just before his program, from 8:00 a.m. until 11:00 a.m. On the air, we would chat about everyday happenings. I loved Oscar's somewhat broken English approach. The ladies listening to my show informed me they thought Oscar was "darling"; "cute!"

One day, in my office, Oscar informed me I should invest in some cattle his cousin was importing from Old Mexico. "Meester Beel! You must eenvest in these cattle! They are so cheap een price! You weel make lots of dinero! Mucho money!"

I told Oscar the truth. I was almost broke. I had no money to invest.

"But Senor Beel! You must get the money! Borrow it! Steal! But get the money for these cows! You must, Meester Beel! I want to make you rich!"

Well, there was no way I could raise the loot, so I forgot about it. However, a couple of weeks later, Oscar came on my radio show and, after I had introduced him, he went on the open microphone exclaiming: "Folks, Meester Beel Mack is so very smart! He is so very wise!"

"How did you reach that decision, Oscar?" I asked, in a state of amazement.

"I'll tell you why, Meester Beel," he smiled. "Listen, folks! A few weeks ago, I found out my cousin was eemporting some cattle into Texas. I eenvested many dollars to buy a bunch of the cattle and I try to get Meester Beel Mack to eenvest, also. However, Senor Beel is wise! He keeps his money and doesn't eenvest in the cows. Now, we find out the cows I bought are worth nothing. They are sick! They need to be keeled!"

"Killed, Oscar? Why should the cows be killed?"

"Because, Senor Beel, we find out the cows all have *dicks* in them!"

Like a fool, being in a state of shock, I shouted: "What?"

Oscar repeated: "All the cows have *dicks* in them!"

By now, the radio station receptionist was picking up the telephone like mad. It appeared everyone was listening to the show, which was very unusual, and had caught me in one of my most embarrassing moments. I attempted to change the subject, but before I could, Oscar realized, by my flushed expression, that I couldn't believe what I was hearing. He said, "You never heard of *dicks?*"

Before I could say another word, he volunteered: "You know … *dicks!* The tiny little bugs!"

Relieved, I said, "You mean *ticks!*"

Oscar: "That's right, Meester Beel, *dicks*! The cows all have *dicks* in them!

KCUL, 1540 on the AM dial in Fort Worth, Texas, didn't have a heavy news department. As a matter of fact, there was <u>no</u> news department. Simply a newswire machine and who ever was working that day made up the bulk of the news sector. Other outlets in the Fort Worth/Dallas Metroplex, such as WBAP, WFAA and KRLD had huge, proud news departments and *the news* was a very important factor in grabbing a listening audience. It's still that way today.

The lack of strength in our KCUL news force was never more obvious than when Jackie, my wife at the time, and I were driving to one of our favorite Mexican restaurants for lunch on a November day in 1963. We were chatting while the car radio was set to WBAP, the NBC affiliate in Fort Worth. Suddenly, we heard the announcement: "We interrupt this program to announce that sounds similar to gunshots have been heard in Dallas where the parade is underway honoring President John Kennedy. That is all the news we have ... and, according to initial sources ... the sound could be fireworks."

I forgot who made the announcement, and when we first heard the interruption, there wasn't too much concern for about a minute. Then, we heard: "Here is more news from the presidential parade route in Dallas. The President may have been hit by gunfire!"

There was that pause, to grab your attention, and then, "Yes, it's official now, President Kennedy has been shot! Stay tuned for more details!"

As I remember, Jackie and I didn't say anything because of the shock in hearing the dreadful news. I turned the car around and headed back to the KCUL studios, located in South Fort Worth. I had driven only a minute, it seems, when we were told our Texas Governor, John Connally, had also been hit by gunfire. By the time I heard this, I was in the parking lot of *Seminary South Shopping Center*, where KCUL had studios in a spot called The South Arcade.

I rushed into the radio station lobby and shouted to the innocent receptionist, "Call for some extra help! We're going to need some more personnel here to handle the news!"

"What news?" She asked. I remember she was munching on a sandwich.

"My God! Haven't you heard? The President has been shot ... in Dallas!"

I had hardly released the words to the receptionist when the announcer on duty eased out of the control room and blabbed, "My wife just called on our hotline and said she'd heard President Kennedy had been shot. Guess I ought to check the newswire!"

Now, can you imagine how I felt toward KCUL, after finding out no announcement of the President's shooting had been made on the radio station I was presumably programming?

There were at least three or four people in the studios at the time, either air personalities or sales reps, but there was no one checking the newswire and the receptionist was too busy devouring her sandwich to answer what telephone lines may have been ringing, attempting to tell us the news or make inquiries.

By the time I ripped the news from the machine, President Kennedy was dead, although it had not been made official. The latest wire report stated that both, our President and our Governor, had been taken to Parkland Hospital in Dallas and that, reportedly, a Catholic priest was with John Kennedy.

I still have the yellowed news bulletins from that horrible day in my collection at home.

I had the receptionist telephone every air personality on the KCUL payroll, ordering them to get to the station as soon as possible. In the meantime, I was heading to Dallas with the tape recorder. Taking the tape recorder was quite a big deal. It was a heavy reel-to-reel job that took quite a bit of maneuvering to set up and place into action. Here, again, was a reflection of my combination of shock and stupidity at the time. It was literally impossible to get in or out of Big D. Most major roads were blocked. After all, no one had been arrested and the city had gone crazy! Fort Worth was in a similar state since President Kennedy had spent his final night in our city and had just finished a breakfast speech before flying to Dallas a few hours earlier. I remember how it had rained heavily the night before and there was some concern about how the crowd might be small "if the weather didn't brighten up", which it did. Had it continued to rain, I've always thought the President would have utilized the "bubble" on his car in the parade and might not have died. Of course, we'll never know. I do know a few old Fort Worth cowboys had let it be known via our now well-manned telephone lines at the radio station that they were "headin' to Dallas t' kill them bastards that shot our President!"

I still have my "Radio News" badge for admission to the Texas Hotel and "Breakfast With The President".

Might mention here that a great portion of Kennedy's personal "guards" had spent most of the night before in Fort Worth's popular 'Cellar', an underground honky-tonk where no holds were barred when it came to booze and pretty gals. It was reported that the presidential personnel had a hell of a good time until the wee hours of the morning. This, of course, had nothing to do with the killing of our leader; it was just noted that there might have been a few hangovers in the important crowd next day.

Before the weekend had ended, Dallas-Fort Worth had witnessed their saddest day in history, according to most folks. It was a most personal blow to everyone I knew. I have never seen tears and heard the sobbing I heard during those bad November days. As would be expected, KCUL wasn't attached to NBC, CBS or ABC. We did, however, have Mutual News and, as I remember, Mutual's news crew was just about as fizzy as KCUL's. Rumor had it that most of the Mutual bunch were people who had at one time been broadcast giants, but had seen their better days and were working for the minor radio network in order to pick up a few extra bucks and to keep a bit of ego on the marquees. It was also rumored that in order to strengthen their aged nerves, the reporters gulped liquid ad-lib from a handy little pub, conveniently located near their studios in New York, before hitting the microphones. There were times when it was noticeable. Our crew laughed about the "mangled Mutual News" many times, when you could almost detect hiccups. However, there was nothing to laugh about on that *Frightful Friday* and the days that were to come.

I continue to have my doubts about the shootings of John Kennedy and John Connally. I'm of the opinion Lee Harvey Oswald was, indeed, behind a gun, but I also have that hunch that at least one or two other hit-men would have had to be a part of the company in order to accomplish what was done with the rifle ... or rifles. My thoughts toward the matter are of very little importance, of course. Lee Harvey Oswald was captured, and everything was pointed against him. Here, again, I have some questions. There is not a thing on paper or on record pertaining to what was said while he was behind closed doors at the police station. It was simply stated by those in charge that Oswald was, undoubtedly, guilty and that he, alone, had done the shooting.

Among the few statements on record made by Lee Harvey Oswald was a yell to the television cameras shortly after exiting the closed doors at the Dallas Police Department: "I hope somebody will come forward and give me legal assistance!"

Dallas was in a complete state of disorder, embarrassment and shock. Really, there was fear in the air. I will never forget that the *Dallas Cowboys* were scheduled to play the *Washington Redskins*, two days after the killing of President Kennedy and, as luck would have it, the game was to be played in Washington, D.C. As the *Cowboys* ran out on to the field, there was booing as I had never heard ... and haven't heard since. Also, there were those huge signs held by some of the fans of the Redskins ... *"BEAT THE DALLAS ASSASSINS!"* Coach Tom Landry had extreme sadness in his eyes that afternoon as he paced the sidelines, and the *Dallas Cowboys* played *defensively*. They weren't afraid of the *Redskins*; they feared the fans! As I remember, the *Washington Redskins* won the game but, very important in my memories, they hugged the *Cowboys* after they had beaten them on the field. They showed compassion, realizing the Dallas team had gone through hell in the city that hated them so badly that day.

There is no need to recall the happenings pertaining to the shootings in Dallas. Lee Harvey Oswald was shot and killed on national television by nightclub owner, Jack Ruby, as he was being transferred to the county jail in Dallas. At one time, Ruby owned the *Bob Wills Ranch House* in Dallas after purchasing it from Bob, who didn't like running the club because it required too much of his time. Eventually, it became *Dewey Groom's Longhorn Ballroom*, and was known as the largest country music nightspot in the nation for several years.

I'll never forget a phone call I received from the owner of a small, smoky and smelly honky-tonk in Fort Worth the weekend Kennedy had been assassinated. I could hear the loud, bad band playing in the background as he yelled, "Do you thank we could git Jackie Kennedy to come here to my club if we wuz to do a benefit for th' Kennedy family? I'd be willin' to give her th' door receipts." Then, he added, "I'd pay th' band off what I made at th' bar!"

Jack Ruby was placed in the Dallas jail where he would die of cancer before ever standing trial for the shooting of Lee Harvey Oswald. Oswald was buried in Fort Worth, in the same cemetery where my dad is buried, only a mile or so from my home.

A few days after Oswald had been killed, I received a telephone call from Marguerite Oswald, Lee Harvey's mom, who lived near KCUL. She informed me that she listened to my radio show "almost every morning" and wanted to know if I would be interested in bringing a few people from the media to her house for an informal news conference. "I don't want a bunch of news people here," she said. "You pick out about a half dozen you can trust, bring them to my house and I'll tell you what I know is th' truth about my son."

I telephoned a few hombres I knew who worked in the news departments of a couple of radio stations, and two newspaper people, Jack Gordon and Tony Slaughter. Both of these dudes were connected with <u>entertainment</u>, not regular news people. However, they were personal friends and I thought they could get the job done.

We arrived at Marguerite's humble house in Fort Worth and she invited us in. As I recall, she served us coffee. Then, after everyone was relaxed, she made the expected statement that her son did not kill President Kennedy or wound our Texas Governor. "It was a framed situation," she said, displaying anger.

After talking for a few minutes about how Lee Harvey had been "set up", she invited our questions. I was the first to raise my hand and, after she nodded, I asked: "Do you mean to tell us you actually believe your son is innocent? Really, Mrs. Oswald! You must be as certain as everyone else seems to be that Lee did the shooting!"

Marguerite Oswald looked me square in the eye and said, "Out! Get out of my house, all of you!"

As we walked toward our vehicles, Jack Gordon put his arm around me and laughed: "Bill, you didn't waste any time! You got right to the point!"

Tony Slaughter agreed with Jack. He said, "That was the

shortest press conference I ever attended. Hell! My coffee was still hot when she threw us out!

Honestly, I considered KCUL to be the most ridiculous radio station I was ever attached to. There was no power, the programming was ho-hum, and it was a dreadful experience every day. I was Program Director, which made it even more embarrassing, since what was aired was presumed to be of my choosing. This was far from the truth, however. Kurt Meer, the owner, and George Faulder, the General Manager, were after one thing: Money. It didn't matter what was put on the air, as long as it brought in the loot. Also, my pay was pathetic. However, this was back in 1963 when almost all of the air personalities were being paid scum fees. Of course, New York, Chicago and Los Angeles were big-pay markets and, as I look back, I realize I had the opportunity to work in all three of those huge areas. However, my heart … and my parents … lived in Texas, and I simply didn't want to pull up stakes from the Lone Star State.

I still regret not giving New York (actually, it was Newark, New Jersey but, basically the same area), L.A. and Chicago a whack. I've done very well in Texas, but it was a long time coming, and I've been reminded many times by various entertainment figures and some of my peers of what a fool I was in not testing the super markets of broadcasting.

When WJRZ called, offering me the opportunity to do a country music show just across the bay from New York City, they assured me I would be loved by the people in an area that, supposedly, despised our country brand of music.

"Don't believe it!" They said. "New York is made up mostly by transplanted Texans, Okies, and Arkansawyers! You'll go over big!"

After seeing the dark shadows of New York, I chickened out. The tall buildings were, to me, monumental assurances that things wouldn't work well for me on Wall Street and Fifth Avenue.

Even though I hated every minute behind the microphone at KCUL, some of the greatest moments in my professional life occurred while I was attached to the flimsy outfit.

I received a telephone call early one morning from Bob Wills, the King of Western Swing. We had formed a most treasured friendship down through the years and he, like myself, lived in Fort Worth at the time. He said, "Remember me telling you about ten or fifteen years ago that if I ever needed an *announcer,* I would call you?"

Recalling Bob making that off-the-cuff statement to me in my hometown, Shamrock, Texas, after I had just completed an interview with him on KEVA, I laughed, "Yeah, Bob. I remember."

"Well," he said, "I need an 'announcer'."

It seems Carl Johnson, a fairly wealthy businessman from Fort Worth who was also a big fan and friend of Bob, had struck upon the idea of putting the money behind a daily Bob Wills radio show that would be aired over, of all radio affiliates, KCUL. Carl had approached George Faulder with the idea, and some loot, and Faulder had told Carl that I would be the radio host, hearing I was the reason Bob had agreed to hook up with KCUL. He had always liked my "announcing" and wanted me to be a part of his radio program.

It was agreed that we would record five 15-minute radio shows on tape every Monday morning, utilizing an audience in the *Town Hall* auditorium at *Seminary South Shopping Center* in Fort Worth. Bob wanted to work before a crowd in order to add the "live" excitement to the programs. The shows were set for airing during the noon hour every weekday on KCUL.

The auditorium where the programs were pre-recorded, seated about three-hundred people, as I recall. We were certain the place would be filled every Monday morning, since there was no admission charge to watch and hear Bob Wills and His Texas Playboys perform for approximately one and a half hours.

The first recording date was set, the announcements and promos were punched heavily on KCUL well in advance of the date:

"Be at Town Hall in Seminary South Shopping Center Monday and <u>see</u> and <u>hear</u> the King of Western Swing, Bob Wills and his Texas Playboys! Come early for a good seat ... because it's all <u>free</u>!"

We were set and ready for the biggest entertainment event to hit Fort Worth in years!

Monday morning rolled around and, as the time arrived to begin the recording of the first radio show, there were approximately twenty people in the auditorium. Now, this wasn't Bob Wills' fault. After all, he was still a very hot star. The small crowd simply reflected the embarrassing fact that only a puny few had caught the heavy plugs on KCUL. The radio station just didn't have any listeners to speak of!

I'll always remember how Bob peeked out at the limited crowd through the curtain, looked up at me from under his big white hat, pulled the cigar from his mouth and said, "Well, my boy, when you're hot, your hot!"

I noticed one thing, immediately, about Bob Wills. Ego was never a part of his makeup. A bit like Ernest Tubb, a fellow Texan, he always had time for his many fans and was the last to exit the hall after a performance. He signed autographs and shook hands until the place was empty.

Something else: He never took intermission after the dance began. It was four hours of non-stop western swing. If one of the Texas Playboys needed the rest room, he'd sneak off the bandstand, run into the john, do his thing, and then rush back on stage. Of course, Bob always knew who was running for the crapper and he would keep a pretty close watch on the time.

Luke Wills, Bob's brother and a member of the band from time to time, told me once, "Bob knew everybody had to take a pee every once in awhile, but if you stayed off stage too long, he'd take note and let you have it after the dance was over. Also, take more than two breaks during the four hour gig and Bob might dock you a bit."

Luke laughed and added, "Bob seldom took a break. I don't know how he did it! His bladder must have been th' size of a pumpkin!"

The crowds finally grew at the broadcast tapings for Bob and it wasn't because KCUL had picked up in listener ratings. Word-of-mouth let the good folks know that Bob Wills and his Texas Playboys were doing free shows on Monday mornings and, in all, we recorded 52 radio programs with the great man on reel-to-reel tape.

I'm proud to say that I wasn't paid a talent fee by the radio station or Bob for being the 'announcer'. I would have been proud and happy to do the shows without pay. However, I received the greatest reciprocation that could be imagined when it was understood by all concerned that I would be given complete ownership of the taped radio programs after they had been fully used on KCUL.

Shortly after Bob's death on May 13, 1975, at 70 years of age,

Capitol Records utilized the taped shows and released a double-sleeve album featuring *"Bob Wills and his Texas Playboys ... Live!"* It was a successful venture.

Really, the radio features didn't showcase Bob at his best, because he was working with a limited amount of musicians, about seven, and it was quite a letdown from the band he carried during his highlight days in the late 30s and into the 40s, when he proudly boasted having about 25 Texas Playboys with him while playing to sold-out crowds all across the United States. This included a big "horn" section, along with the regular fiddles, guitars, steel-guitar and the usual conglomerate of musicians. Also, Bob let it be known to all concerned that his music was not "country" nor was it "western".

"It's Western Swing!" he would emphasize.

Even when he was inducted into the Country Music Hall-of-Fame in Nashville in 1968, he pushed the point. "I don't know why they put me in th' Country Music Hall of Fame," he said to me as I stood backstage with him at Ryman Auditorium on that special October night.

"I'm proud to get it, but I'm not 'country' and I'm not 'western'!"

Bob Wills was one of the most humble men I've ever known and it was partly because of his Panhandle of Texas raising. He told me, "I've picked more cotton than the best of 'em." He was also proud of the fact that much of his musical styling was founded while listening to the black cotton pickers sing the sad blues while moving slowly on their knees, filling their long sacks with cotton bolls. He said, "We didn't pick cotton, we *pulled bolls*! And those 'dark' people would sing like I've never heard!

"I guess my favorite singer of th' bunch was Billie Holiday. She was th' first singer I paid admission to see, and that was back when the price of admission was about a day's work in the cotton fields."

I had the good fortune to work many shows with Bob. Several times, he would ride with me in my car while his band occupied the bus. I never failed to feel a bit nervous being in the company of "the ol' man", as he was called by those who worked with him. He loved to get my reaction after laying one of his beloved tales on me.

Bob had a reputation of being heavy on the booze at times, although I never saw him take a swig of liquor. By the time I was working with him regularly, he had "sworn off" all kinds of alcohol.

"Had my share of it," he told me. "More than my share, really. Never did any kind of drugs … but had my share of the whiskey."

I remember him adding, "I don't recommend it."

Bill hosting the weekly television program "Cowtown Jamboree" from Panther Hall in Fort Worth, Texas.

CHAPTER FIFTEEN

In 1964, Bill and Corky Kuykendall opened *Panther Hall Ballroom* on East Lancaster Street in Fort Worth, and they chose *Bob Wills and his Texas Playboys*, along with Dallas singer, Billy Gray, to headline the grand opening.

Panther Hall was destined to become the most popular country music nightclub in the nation. It had been built as a professional bowling alley. After failing badly, the alleys were ripped out, and a huge dance floor was installed. The big hall would accommodate over 2000 belly rubbing enthusiasts! It was a tremendous success. Everybody who was anybody in country music, made an appearance at *Panther Hall*. I was to become the host of the television show that was presented from there every Saturday night at 6:00 p.m. on *KTVT-TV* out of Fort Worth. The program was titled, *"Cowtown Jamboree"*. The TV show was one hour in length and in living black-and-white. Even though we were on television against the cute little dolphin, *"Flipper"*, which was in <u>color</u>, "Cowtown Jamboree" bagged top ratings in the Fort Worth-Dallas market.

Most of the visiting acts hated doing the television show because there was hardly any rehearsal time, and the sound was far below average. Also, since there were no rehearsals, the director had to guess which instruments were going to be featured during the instrumental breaks. Most times, when the fiddle was playing, the camera would be on the guitar ... and vice versa. Seldom was the camera in the right place at the right time! I believe this was one reason the show was so very popular. It was funny to everyone ... except the stars on stage!

One special bit that will always have a hot spot in my memory was the night George Jones made a tremendous scene! The stage at *Panther Hall* was over 5 feet off the main floor. It was a tall sucker! George's band, *The Jones Boys*, had played a couple of tunes, and it was time to bring on the star, who had been on his bus sipping on liquids of encouragement. George was weaving a bit on the side of the stage when I walked out into the spotlight and announced: "And now ... here he is! Let's give a big *Cowtown Jamboree* welcome to —George Jones!"

The band broke into the instrumental intro to George's signature song, *"White Lightning'"* and George strutted, a little wobbly, toward center stage. However, he didn't stop! On full camera, he took a 5-foot dive to the dance floor, with his guitar in hand! The band kept playing the instrumental intro as a sudden silence fell on the folks in the audience who had come to see the television show "live". Typical George Jones fans, they idolized the man, and were afraid he had broken some bones! Also typical of George, he wasn't wounded at all. With cameras still perfectly focussed on him, he arose with no noticeable damage. Still holding to his guitar, he simply walked to the floor entrance to the stage, followed the steps, walked back to center mike, and commenced singing *"White Lightning"* ... without missing a beat!

The crowd loved him.

During this important era, Porter Wagoner was a hot act because of his syndicated television show, which was the most successful of the bunch. He was booked to play *Panther Hall*. Included in his company was a cute little singer named Dolly Parton, who was becoming very popular for a couple of big reasons! Now, I've got to be honest. I hated to see Dolly's predecessor, *Pretty little Miss Norma Jean* leave the Wagoner bunch. Seems Norma Jean had married a wealthy furniture dealer in Oklahoma City, and he had laid down the law: She had to pull away from ol' Porter, which she did.

From time-to-time, I would grab my audio recorder and do interviews with the acts set at *Panther Hall*. Since Dolly was picking up a lot of attention, I arranged, through Porter, a get-together with the beauty at the motel where the band was staying. It was also understood that I would interview Porter, since he was the big star. I recorded the question and answer bit with Porter first, then Porter left me alone with Dolly, because he had some things to do before the dance got underway.

Dolly was an interviewer's dream-come-true. She giggled out her answers, and laughed and flirted like a silly little schoolgirl. Running out of questions, I couldn't help asking the obvious: "Tell me something, Dolly. Are *they* real?"

Without missing a beat, Dolly flashed herself for me! It was only a split-second happening, not giving my eyes time to focus. Sometimes, I think she may have only *pretended* to flash me.

Either way, she grabbed my attention

July 31, 1964 is a date I will always remember. I also recall that it was a Friday. The KCUL engineer telephoned about 5:00 a.m. to inform me no one had shown up to sign the radio station on-the-air. This was back when most radio stations, except the super powers, signed off at midnight (Are you old enough to remember the playing of "*The Star Spangled Banner*" when stations bid you a *"good night"?*). They would sign back on, around 5:00 a.m.

Since I was Program Director, it was my duty to toss on some clothes and rush to the radio station. I ran into the empty, dark control room, and signed on with the appropriate *"Good morning ... this is Radio Station KCUL in Fort Worth, Texas ... 1540 on your radio dial, with a daytime power of 50,000 watts ... as authorized by the Federal Communications Commission, Washington D.C."* Then, I hit the start button on the old reel-to-reel recorder, allowing a preacher to present his regular morning sermon.

While the preacher was preaching, asking for more money in order to keep his sermons on the air, I checked the overloaded news machine where typed yellow paper lay all over the floor. This mess consisted of the continuous bits that had been fed all night by The *Associated Press* newswire.

I was slurping some coffee when I noticed: *"Country music singing star Jim Reeves and his piano man, Dean Manual, are missing in an airplane flown by Reeves."*

I was doubly shocked, because I was scheduled to appear with Jim at *Panther Hall Ballroom* in Fort Worth August 8, just a little over a week later! Anytime Jim played a show or dance in the Fort Worth/Dallas area, he would telephone me and ask me to bring my guitar and join him and his band, *The Blue Boys*. The reason for this was because Jim and I had been good, personal friends for years, and he knew I would give his upcoming appearance some free, heavy plugs on my radio shows. He would also shell out a hundred and fifty dollars for my "talent". I had done the same for him while working in San Antonio with KENS. Now, as I look back, it might have been a form of "payola", since Reeves certainly didn't need me and my guitar to add enjoyment to his personal appearances.

Although the plane had not been found, it was presumed Jim and Dean had crashed somewhere. They had flown to look at some real estate Reeves was interested in purchasing.

Next night, while doing the television show at *Panther Hall*, the Kuykendall brothers had insisted I plug Jim's scheduled appearance the next Saturday night, making absolutely no mention of the missing plane. "We don't want to mention anything that might hinder ticket sales," Corky Kuykendall said. "Besides, until they find Jim's body, he's still gonna be here, as far as I'm concerned!"

I felt like a fool, but was in no position to argue. After all, the Kuykendalls owned the hall, and were my bosses. I kept saying, "Jim Reeves will be here next week!" … all through the hour-long mess.

After signing off the TV show at 7:00 p.m., I jumped in my car and headed for the house. It was only a few minutes after entering my Chevy that I heard the announcement on the radio: *"Country music star, Jim Reeves, and his piano man, Dean Manual, were found in their crashed airplane just inside the Nashville city limits. Both men were pronounced dead at the scene."*

I was devastated. I also felt like an even bigger fool by not making references to the fact that Jim and Dean were "missing", while doing *"Cowtown Jamboree"*, less than an hour before.

Jim Reeves was 39 years old at the time of his death. Sorry to say, I don't have information on Dean's age. He was a bit younger than Jim, and was such a nice guy. It seems the plane had crashed in the back yard of a family on vacation, and since it was in a heavily wooded area, the crash was hard to spot from the air. The plunge had taken place during a late afternoon thunderstorm.

Marty Robbins, who lived near Jim Reeves, told me that he was outside his house, shampooing his hair with rainwater from the passing storm, and actually *heard* the crash. He told me, "I was rinsing my hair and heard what sounded like a crash.

However, I passed it off as possibly being more thunder in the distance from the storm that had just passed through our area. Now, though, I know I heard Jim's plane crashing. I even told my wife it sounded like a crash."

A few days later, Jackie and I went to Jim's funeral in east Texas.

Something of interest: A few years ago, I was sent a copy of the contract Jim Reeves had signed with Panther Hall for the August 8, 1964 engagement. You must remember, Jim was among the best selling acts in country music at the time. His price on the signed contract: $1,500 ... which included his band and all expenses.

Jerry Lee Lewis held the attendance record at *Panther Hall Ballroom*. He was the wildest act going at the time. He was known to push the piano off stage, and crash it, if he had a hankerin' to do so. The fans thought this was simply a part of his act, but a lot of the "crash" scenes were brought on by fierce anger within *The Killer*, as he was called. One night, Jerry was doing a show that also featured *Little Richard*, another rockin' super-star, and there was a big argument. It seems *Little Richard* and his manager were determined that Jerry Lee should open the show because *Little Richard* "was the star!" Meanwhile, Jerry Lee's manager disagreed, believing his man should be in the featured spot, closing the show. The fury of *who was to go on first* and *who was to close the show* went on for a couple of hours in the hotel room, where both acts, and their crew, were staying. Finally, Jerry Lee announced, "Hell! Let Little Richard have his way! If he thinks he's th' star, I'll go on first! No problem!"

That night, Jerry did, indeed, go on first as was agreed. Not only did he open the show, he left the impression he was going to remain on stage until closing time! Although he was set to play for only an hour, after almost two hours, he was still beating the piano like a wild man, screaming his songs, and driving the fans crazy. They loved him, as usual. Meanwhile, *Little Richard* and his manager were "out of it" on the side of the stage, attempting to get Jerry Lee's attention and coax him to wind up his act, and allow *Little Richard* to do his thing.

After approximately two hours of super entertainment, the crowd stood up from their seats, screaming praises at *The Killer!* Jerry Lee waved at them, smiled, bowed, and then, before exiting the stage, reached over to the side of the piano, picked up a can of lighter-fluid, opened the lid on the piano, and sprayed the inside heavily with the fluid. Next, he struck a match and set the *Steinway* on fire!

Walking past *Little Richard* and his manager, Jerry pointed back at the burning piano and grumbled, *"I left you a hot act to follow, Brother!"*

Also hanging heavy in my memories was that eventful night Jerry Lee was playing *Panther Hall Ballroom*. He always filled the joint, and this night was no exception. He was going wild, doing his thing, when suddenly, a half-filled beer can came zooming from the crowd, hitting *The Killer* in the kisser! Jerry Lee looked down at the short dude wearing the cowboy hat, picked up the piano stool, tossed it at the culprit, and noticing he had missed him, jumped from the stage and proceeded to slug it out with the cowboy!

Finally, the security guards broke up the one-sided fight, pulling the badly beaten cowboy away from Jerry Lee and ushering him toward the *Panther Hall* office. Meanwhile, *The Killer* jumped back on stage, sat down on the piano stool that had been pushed back into position, and lit into *"Whole Lotta Shakin' Goin' On"* ... as if nothing had happened!

After completing his show that night, we met in his dressing room, and as he sipped from his glass, he looked at me and said, "Yeah. It takes all kinds to make th' night interesting."

Another interesting night with Jerry Lee occurred when two representatives from the Dallas District Attorney's Office approached him with a warrant for his arrest. It seems he had failed to show up in court over a contract dispute with a Dallas honky-tonk owner a couple of years before, and was heading for jail. They weren't going to allow Jerry to perform. "We've got to take you with us, now," they growled. I took one of the cops aside and said, "Would you please let him do his show? If not, there's going to be hell to pay with that full house out there. There'll also be a lot of unneeded publicity."

Fortunately, one of the lawmen was a fan of my radio show. He whispered something to the one that was with him, looked at me and said, "Alright, Bill. We'll let him do his show, but then he has to go with us to Dallas."

Jerry Lee finished his act, and as he was walking off stage, I did a little extra pushing. Turning to the two men who had presented the warrant, I asked, "Can he ride with me? I'll drive him to Dallas in my car. We'll follow you." Then, pushing a little extra energy into the matter at hand, I added, "I want to be with him through this. He is a very close friend. I promise you, I'll have him at the jail when you get there."

I'll always be thankful to those two guys. They took me at my word, and allowed me to drive Jerry Lee Lewis to the Dallas jail, where I remained with him until time for him to face the judge next morning.

Out of unexpected kindness, the jailer didn't lock the cell. Jerry chatted with fellow prisoners and various police people during our stay.

Next morning, Jerry was found "innocent of all charges".

Jerry Lee has never allowed me to forget that I, like him, am a "jailbird".

There was plenty of action, but 1967 was probably the saddest year of my life. Although I seemed to be doing well in the radio and entertainment business, my home life was crumbling.

My daughter, Debbie Lynn, was the one who suffered most during this time, something I will always regret.

Jackie was not the devoted *honky-tonk* follower. Neither was I, in reality, but my job was requiring that I spend more time at *Panther Hall*, and while Jackie was growing tired of the smoky environment, I was well adjusted to it by now, even having my share of fun in the company of the various artists who were in town to entertain.

I would do the television show, and then hang around for the dances, most times not driving back to the house until the wee hours.

I didn't make this a weekly habit, but was finding more time to be away from home. In the meantime, Jackie was letting me know she was getting tired of my "honky-tonk habits", insisting I spend more time at home with her and Debbie. Of course, she had every right to form this attitude, because we had both been raised in family backgrounds that looked down on "beer joints and rowdy crowds". We were having many arguments, caused by my easing away from those family teachings.

This was a period in my life when I was giving in to the scenario of, as the old song stated so well, *"dim lights, thick smoke, and loud, loud music."*

While working out of Wichita Falls and Lubbock, I had made it a point to restrict my personal appearances to shows. I mentioned earlier that I didn't play dances or appear at nightclubs with my band, turning down a lot of offers. And this was a decision I had made that I never regretted. I didn't enjoy the honky-tonk atmosphere during the Wichita Falls/Lubbock era.

Preceding Wichita Falls, when I was in Amarillo, I frequented the *Clover Club*, but did so to "see the stars ... live!" I was a kid just out on my own, still in my teens, who had made the move to the "big city"!

I was seeing some of the biggest names in entertainment for the first time. And, being in radio, I was also *meeting* the stars! It was a big deal!

As I look back on those beginning days, I didn't make the nightclub scene to dance or drink. I was the young punk who was given the opportunity to walk on stage and introduce such names as Hank Thompson, The Maddox Brothers and Rose, Lefty Frizzell and others!

After leaving Amarillo, though, I pushed the honky-tonk scene into the back of my mind. Wichita Falls had nightclubs such as the famous MB Corral, owned by the Miller Brothers, a great band, but I seldom went there unless I was hired as emcee.

I don't recall ever attending a dance during the short time I was in Lubbock. The *Caprock City* was "dry". Even though the population was around 100,000, it was "against the law" to sell intoxicating drinks in any form, when we were living there. Therefore, there were very few nighclubs in the city, in 1959 and 1960.

After moving to San Antonio, and signing with the major record labels, I began making appearances at honky-tonks on a regular basis. However, Jackie would travel with me while doing most of the gigs.

Fort Worth is a honky-tonk haven! More opportunities came knocking in Cowtown and Dallas than ever before, when it came to the clubs.

Jackie was a very good mother. We would occasionally hire the baby-sitters for Debbie, but Jackie was of the correct opinion that our daughter shouldn't be left at home with a sitter on a regular basis, in order for us "to go honky-tonkin'."

One night, after a big argument pertaining to my uneven nightlife, Jackie demanded I make the choice: It was to be the nightclub life ... or a home life.

I got in my station wagon and left home.

There was an effort to get back together, but I'm afraid I wasn't pushing hard enough, in order to make the marriage work. Finally, in 1967, it ended.

My divorce was the first in my family, something I would always regret. More important, I will never forgive myself for the hurt brought to Debbie, a beautiful and loving daughter.

It was also a very tough time for Jackie.

Again: This was a period in my life that was made up of more hurt than happiness. And it was taking its' toll on several very good individuals.

Every time I hear the Willie Nelson song, "Night Life", it takes me back to that tragic, inconsistent time in my life:

"The night life ... ain't no good life ... but it's my life!"

In 1967, KCUL made a deal with Panther Hall Ballroom to promote a *"Date with Glen Campbell!"* Glen had just started showing some action as a single artist on *Capitol Records* after working with The Champs, The Hondells and The Beach Boys. *Capitol* released the news that they had "signed an act worth keeping" and the Kuykendall Brothers, owners of *Panther Hall*, decided to book ol' Glen while his price was still relatively cheap. That's when it was decided to offer some lucky little gal from Fort Worth the chance to have a date with the good lookin' new singer.

It was required that all ladies interested in having a date with Glen Campbell, including dinner and accompanying him to his gig at Panther Hall Ballroom, needed to write a short note telling why they would like to have a date with him. It was also a requirement that a recent photo of all ladies accompany the note.

Definitely off the record, it was understood by *Panther Hall* and KCUL that "the prettiest of the lot" would be the winner, regardless of any "reasons". Therefore, the judges tossed all of the paper aside and fumbled for photos when the bits of mail arrived at KCUL. As I remember, the amount of mail received was very little, since KCUL had very few listeners and Glen Campbell wasn't exactly the hottest act "going" in the Summer of '67.

It was also made a matter of record that I, too, would be in the Campbell get-together with my "date". Jackie and I were divorced and I was miserably single. My date would be the KCUL receptionist, a get together that was decided on by the management of the radio station, and it was something neither of us looked forward to. The receptionist informed me, "I'm only going because I <u>have</u> to. Besides, there's a free meal and a table near the bandstand to see Glen Campbell involved." Then, giving me a look of complete disgust, she added, "So, don't think I'm just one of those cuties you're always flirtin' with on the radio! Besides that, I know you just went through a divorce and might have *other things* on your mind!"

The grand night finally arrived. A limousine was hired to take Campbell, his date, me and the uncomfortable KCUL receptionist to Fort Worth's *Italian Inn* for a good meal, and then we would all occupy a table next to the stage at *Panther Hall* while Campbell did his thing.

The receptionist and I met at KCUL where we were to enter the limo, go to the motel where Campbell was staying, pick him up and, then, all of us would be driven to the house of the "lucky one". There, Glen and I would go to the door, meet the "lucky one", usher her to the limousine and head to the *Italian Inn*. Well, all went per schedule. However, there was a change in expectancy when Glen and I knocked on the front door of the humble little house. Before I could make the second knock, the door opened and there were deafening screams: "Glen Campbell! Oh, my God! It's him!"

Looking back, there was not a single, "Bill Mack! Oh, my God! It's him!" to be heard.

The "lucky one's" mother let Campbell know immediately that she was the one he ought to be taking out for the evening. "I'm th' one who adores you!" She screamed. Then, she threw her bony arms around the star and shouted, "Hug me! Kiss me, you good lookin' singer!"

Suddenly, the expression on Campbell's face revealed the fact that he had rather be back in the studios at Capitol, singing harmony with Merle Haggard, than where fate ... and some dishonest judging ... had placed him for the evening. The small room was filled with bodies, mostly female, and all of the friends, neighbors and relatives of the "lucky one" were demanding turns in hugging and kissing the "*Gentle On My Mind*" star. Setting the situation into a more uncomfortable scenario was when the "lucky one's" daddy entered the room from out of nowhere and growled loudly: "What 'n hell is goin' on here?"

"It's Glen Campbell, Daddy! He's here to take our baby out on a date!" Replied the mother, still pawing at Campbell. "Ain't he good lookin'?"

Those were the very words needed to trigger the daddy's response. "Who 'n hell is Glen Campbell?"

"He just happens to be the hottest new act in th' business right now, he is! He's th' one who sings '*Gentle On My Mind*'!"

I can still hear Daddy's words: "I don't like th' damned song … an' I don't like th' damned singer! Ernest Tubb could put that crap-singer in th' shade … fast!"

Finally, we made the escape to the front porch, the "lucky-one" hanging on to Glen's arm while the picker/singer placed the Capitol smile on his face, as all professionals are forced to do from time to time. The three of us headed for the limousine at a fast pace! The limo driver and the radio station receptionist both had odd expressions on their faces, undoubtedly accompanied by some fear, after hearing the rage from inside the house that had held steady for about ten minutes. As the driver opened the door for Glen, the "lucky-one" and me to enter, we heard Daddy's voice. It was loud and resembled the sound of a ruptured gorilla: "Just one damned minute," he garbled, holding Campbell by the shoulder with his mighty hand. "I want you to know somethin', you big-time singer, you!" He paused for a moment to gather more strength in his voice. "Yeah! I've heard about you big-time hillbilly singers … an' I just want you to know that if my daughter ain't back home by midnight, there's gonna be hell to pay!"

Campbell looked speechless. I decided to intrude: "But Glen's show at Panther Hall isn't over until one o'clock, sir! We can't have your daughter back before close to two o'clock."

The daddy looked at me and moaned, "Th' hell you say. An' who might you be?"

I smiled and said, "I'm Bill Mack from KCUL."

The honest, snarling response: "Never heard of you."

We finally assured the unhappy father that his blessed daughter would be returned to the home in good health and without harm as soon as was possible, following Glen's gig at the hall. As the limo backed out of the drive, the daddy shot us the "finger".

We finally managed to make it through an uncomfortable dinner-for-four at the *Italian Inn*. Pictures were taken of the "happy duos" seated in a booth. After my miserable "date" had excused herself to the restroom for a few minutes, we went back to the limousine and were driven to *Panther Hall Ballroom*, less than a block away from the restaurant. There, Glen slid backstage and it was left up to me to accompany the two ladies to the table near the stage. By this time, the "lucky-one" had gulped down some wine and was allowing her emotions to be heard. "I miss Glen!" She screamed, looking at me with tear-filled eyes.

"We'll see him right after his show," I said, patting her shoulder, holding her clammy hand and attempting to place some verbal comfort on the matter at hand.

Might mention here that the lucky lady was nineteen years old, thin and not too bad looking, although she wasn't to be categorized as a "beauty". I remember she had brown hair, wore glasses and had an over-bite. Now, the reason I recall the <u>overbite</u> is because she snuck a few kisses from me when good ol' Glen was on stage and the receptionist, my "date", was staring around at the lighted beer signs throughout the huge hall. Little did Glen's lucky winner realize that the last person the receptionist was interested in at the time was me.

The "lucky-one" looked toward the radio station receptionist and, noticing her back was to us, pulled my face toward her and laid a ten pound kiss on my mouth, That's when I felt the over-bite for the first time. She whispered, "Do you love <u>her</u>?" as she motioned her head toward the receptionist, who was studying a glowing *Pearl Beer* sign.

"No. She works with me at the radio station. We're just good friends."

"Good!" Then, she planted another overbite to my lips. This time, though, the receptionist caught the action taking place. Her reaction? She nudged the "lucky-one" and said, "I need to go to th' rest room. Wanna join me?"

The most comforting words I had heard that evening were, "I believe I <u>will</u> go with you," spoken by the "lucky–one".

Glen Campbell finally went on stage and, honestly, I can't remember hearing a single song he laid on the packed house that night. The reason? All through every song the great singer performed, my ear was absolutely itching deep inside from the screams, "Sing it, Darlin'!", "Oh, my God, he's singin' that for me!" and assorted other releases of vocal energy from the "lucky-one". When Glen hit into *"Gentle On My Mind"*, his final song for the evening, his lucky "date" looked at me, her eyes went back into her head and she screamed, "God! I'm faintin'! God! I love that man!" Then, she fell back into her chair, threw her legs upon the table and finally rolled out of the chair on to the floor. Luckily, almost everyone was watching Campbell, including my "date", the receptionist, and it wasn't long before the lucky little lady was back on her feet, screaming, "Glen, Darlin'! I love you!"

After Campbell finished his act and rushed off stage, Bill Kuykendall, the co-owner of *Panther Hall*, approached our table with a serious expression on his face. The crowd was still applauding as he whispered loud into my ear, "Glen is feelin' bad. He said it must have been th' Italian food you folks had earlier. He wants to know if you'd mind taking the lucky little lady home." Then, Bill smiled and added, "Tell her Glen will mail her an autographed picture and a copy of his new album."

As the receptionist, the "lucky-one" and I entered the limousine and headed toward the house of the "winner", she sobbed loudly, "Oh my God! I miss Glen! I hope he don't die!"

"He'll be alright tomorrow, Honey." I said.

She continued to cry with great energy until we reached her house and the nervous limo driver opened the door for me to exit with the lucky little lady and accompany her to the awaiting parents. As she opened the door to enter, Daddy stepped outside, grabbed my arm and yelled, "What 'n hell did that hillbilly singer do to my baby? Why is she screamin' an' cryin' like this?"

"It's alright, Daddy," cried the darling one. "Glen is sick! He wouldn't hurt a fly!"

Old daddy wasn't so certain of things, though. As I walked toward the limousine, he yelled, "Listen! You tell that singin' hillbilly that he ain't welcome at this house, anymore! Tell him if he comes 'round my daughter again, I'll kick his butt!"

As the limo driver eased us back toward our cars, parked in the KCUL parking lot, the receptionist yelled at him: "Hurry! I need to use the rest room, bad!"

The long evening would soon be flushed into a simple memory.

I believe the most hilarious thing to take place during the *Cowtown Jamboree* television era involved the *One-Man-Band*. This was an old Fort Worth boy who wore a coonskin cap, picked the guitar, had an attachment around his neck that held a harmonica to his mouth, and a home made wooden foot pedal that was connected to a drum. He could sing, pick the guitar, blow the harmonica, and beat the drum with ease. It wasn't necessarily good, but it caught the attention. As I recall, the old boy was also a handyman at Panther Hall and, I suppose, worked at wages below union scale with the understanding that he would be allowed to appear on the television show from time-to-time, which he succeeded in doing.

One Saturday evening, I introduced the *One-Man-Band* on camera and he went into a song titled, "Old Rattler", that would allow him to shine as singer, picker, harmonica man and drummer, all-in-one. As he was shouting out,"Heah, Rattler! Whooie! Heah, Rattler, Whooie!", it was a bit obvious that he might have had a few energy slurps before coming on the set. Suddenly, he lost his balance, fell backward over his drums and ended up on his butt with his feet high in the air. There was a bit of laughter from the crowd and then, silence. Then, for all of those in the audience and the good people viewing the tube to hear, the voice of the One-Man-Band broke the silence of the hall with: "Shiiiit!"

It was to be his most memorable ... but final ... performance at Panther Hall.

CHAPTER SIXTEEN

Judy entered my life during this span of time. She was, and still is, a very good, beautiful lady. She was devoted to me and my attempts to exist in the different, somewhat thoughtless life I was living. I was hanging out at various honky-tonks almost every night. I did the gigs at Panther Hall every week as host of the television shows, and I was also booked at *Dewey Groom's Longhorn Ballroom* every once in a while, but these were paid appearances. I was now patronizing several of the not-too-classy fizz joints in the Fort Worth-Dallas metroplex on a regular basis. Being a disk jockey, almost everything was "on-the-house". I thought I was having a great time.

It was also in 1968 that things began to fizzle at KCUL. There was a new station manager, Roy Lemons, on the scene. Lemons was determined to become a radio star, although his talent in that direction was completely lacking. One day, I heard Lemons talking on the telephone with Lawton Williams, the songwriter and radio man who had written the hit, "*Fraulein*", and several others. At the time, Lawton pretty well controlled the Fort Worth country music market because of his strong association with radio. It seems Williams was telling Lemons he, old Roy, should be doing the morning radio show, the one I was doing five days a week. At the time, there was no love between Lawton and me and I was of the opinion he was attempting to get me off KCUL because I, too, was beginning to make a mark in the Fort Worth-Dallas radio/songwriting market. I had just written the song, "*Drinking Champagne*", which was beginning to show some action. Anyway, I knew my days were limited with the radio outlet and decided it was time to quit. However, I didn't walk into the manager's office and turn in my notice. Instead, I went on the air next morning and said, "Folks, you have always been there as my listeners and my friends. I place friendship far above radio station managers. Therefore, I want you all to be the first know that this will be my last day on KCUL. I haven't even told the station manager yet, but after the show ends this morning, I'm heading for greener pastures."

Telephones started ringing at the station like never before. The receptionist ran into my control room and yelled, "Are you really quitting ... or is this a joke? The phones are going crazy!"

I assured her I was leaving and as soon as I played my last recording that morning, I again told the listeners, "I'm gone!"

I walked into my office, picked up what few things were there, shook a hand or two, and left the building. Then, I got in my Ford and left the KCUL parking lot for the final time.

The news of my KCUL exit spread rapidly. I walked into my apartment and heard the phone ringing. It was Corky Kuykendall, the co-owner of *Panther Hall*. He had called to inform me that since I was no longer employed by KCUL, they were going to have to find a new host for the *Cowtown Jamboree*" television show. "Nothin' against you, personally," he said. "We just need to keep KCUL happy, since they give Panther Hall a lot of free plugs!"

Hanging up the phone, I realized I had no money in the bank to speak of, no radio show, no more television shows, no hopes and, honestly, no future. For the very first time in my life, I had no tomorrows to look forward to.

After a couple of days of wondering what lay ahead for me in broadcasting, I received a telephone call from Jack McFadden, Buck Owens' manager. He asked, "How would you like to go to work for Buck?"

"Love to! When do I start?" I asked. I didn't ask what I was to do. I simply needed a job and was willing to go to work for my old pal, Buck."

"Tell you what we need," said Jack. "We need you to be the emcee for Buck's television show."

"Great! When do I start?"

Jack McFadden was a very good friend. He realized that I might have been hurting for money. He had telephoned KCUL to reach me and had been informed, "Bill Mack doesn't work here anymore."

Jack laughed, "Now, the pay's not so good, but it will be a lot of fun … and your ugly face will be seen all over the country. See, the reason we're hirin' you to do th' show is because you're almost as ugly as Buck!"

Buck's television shows, "The Buck Owens Ranch", left the impression they were from his ranch in California. The programs were pretaped at the WKY-TV studios in Oklahoma City in order to save money. Costs of filming in Los Angeles, the area nearest to Bakersfield, Buck's home spot, were far beyond Buck's pocketbook. It was far cheaper to fly the Owens company to Oklahoma City than drive the hundred miles or so to L.A. Also, the price of known, professional emcees were much more expensive in Los Angeles. Thus, the reason for hiring Bill Mack, I suppose.

I was glad to receive the news from Jack, although I realized there wasn't going to be too much money involved after making the trips to Oklahoma City from Fort Worth. A few days later, I received a telephone call from Jack Beasley, a super pal who was owner of Radio Station KLPR in Oklahoma City. "What's this I hear that you're gonna be doin' that damned TV show with Buck?" He yelled.

"That's right, Jack."

He continued: "Hear you'll be startin' up with ol' Buck in a couple of weeks! Is that right?"

"Two weeks. You're right, Jack."

Jack: "Also hear you quit that piece of crap, KCUL. Is that right?"

"Right, Jack."

There was a big, loud laugh: "Welcome to Oklahoma City! You're gonna work with me!"

I well remember Beasley saying, " … work <u>with</u> me." It wasn't " … work <u>for</u> me."

Jack shot me a money figure he planned to pay me which was much more than I had made working at KCUL. Also, he was allowing me to live in a house he owned in Oklahoma City that was completely furnished. It was a very good, generous offer from a very special friend. I accepted it immediately.

Beasley hired me as Program Director at KLPR, although there was very little programming to do. I would also do a morning radio show running from 6:00 am till 9:00 am. It was an easy and enjoyable gig.

I had some enjoyable days while working in Oklahoma City. One of my neighbors was my good friend, Conway Twitty. Conway had an unusual gift, besides singing and songwriting. He could pick up on my feelings. Many times he would drive up to the radio station as I was walking out of the building after finishing one of my shows. Conway always had that special smile. He would roll the window down and yell, "Get in! Let's go have breakfast!"

There was a special spot we frequented for breakfast. One morning as we finished our eggs, he asked, "How long before you leave Buck and Jack and head back to Texas?"

"What makes you think I'm planning to leave?" I replied.

Conway laughed and said, "I know you're going to leave. My question is <u>when</u>?" He was reading the reality of my mind. I asked him how he had become aware of my feelings toward my Oklahoma City ventures.

I'll always remember Conway dropping his smile and giving me a very sincere stare. He said, "I read your heart. You're not happy with Buck, you're not happy working at KLPR ... and you miss Texas. You need to go back to Fort Worth an' Dallas."

Subject dropped.

Also living in Oklahoma City were singers Wanda Jackson and Norma Jean. Norma was Porter Wagoner's female singer before Dolly Parton on his popular syndicated television show. I thought Porter had lost his mind when he replaced *"Pretty Little Miss Norma Jean"* with Dolly.

Wrong again, of course.

Working at KLPR at the time was one of my Hollywood cowboy heroes, Tim Holt. Tim wasn't the run-of-the-mill Saturday afternoon matinee shoot 'em up film star. Most of those were found at *Republic Pictures* or, perhaps, attached to one of the poverty row outfits such as *Monogram* or *PRC* (Producers Releasing Corporation). No, Tim made westerns for *RKO*, one of the more respected studios.

In reality, Tim was a serious actor and made some very good movies. Remember *"Treasure Of Sierra Madre"*? It was a great motion picture, picking up several Academy Awards. It featured Humphrey Bogart, Walter Huston and Tim Holt as three greedy gold prospectors.

As I write this, Tim's movies are shown regularly on *The Westerns Channel* on TV.

Tim Holt was my hero.

My job with Buck Owens was not to be as much fun as expected. For several reasons, it was a very difficult show to do.

My assignment on *"The Buck Owens Ranch"* was as official master-of-ceremonies and I would be on camera throughout each 30-minute program. We would tape several shows every time Buck hit town. We would have special, big marquee guests and the format was simple. However, there would be the expected problems, most of them caused by Buck's moods and short temper. If a mistake was made that required a "re-take", he might go into a rage about "time" and "costs". Most verbal beatings were given to members of his band.

All syndicated shows back in the 60s were much more difficult to capture than now because of the equipment used and the fact that digital processing was not yet being utilized. Also, giving credit where it is due, Buck was the producer. All money spent came out of his pocket, since there was no central sponsor. Also, Owens demanded all shows be as close to perfection as possible. After all, he was Buck Owens and was about as "popular as they come" during that period in time and he wanted every program to reflect that fact.

Even though it was a good break for my career, doing the television shows with Buck was beginning to wear thin. Buck and I had been friends since 1960 but the pressure of the syndicated programs was having a tremendous affect on me. I was a very neurotic person during that time frame and Owen's attitude, while video taping the "ranch" shows, was lighting the short fuse within me on a frequent basis.

One day, Buck had given Tom Brumley, his very fine steel-guitar picker, a tough time because Tom had missed the mark on something quite incidental, and as Buck was walking beside me in the WKY-TV studios, I said: "You know, Buck, your bad attitude is beginning to get on my nerves." Then, I added something on the order of, "If I were Tom Brumley, I'd take that steel bar he holds in his hand and shove it into the appropriate place."

Buck didn't respond to my statement and, as I recall, everything went quite friendly between us for the rest of the session. I thought my comments to Buck might have done some good."

It was the last video recording session of *"The Buck Owens Ranch"* television series I was to do. Buck's office never called me again to inform me of the dates that had been set with WKY-TV to record. Instead, Buck's son took over the emcee duties, which was fine with me, and a few months later, the "ranch" show would be terminated because Buck had signed with CBS to co-host the show, "Hee-Haw!" with Roy Clark.

During its entire time span on CBS-TV and, eventually, in syndication, I was never to be a guest on *"Hee-Haw!"*. I was told Buck vetoed all suggestions that I participate.

The former Judy Cummings and I were married in Oklahoma City. As I mentioned, Judy was one of the most beautiful, caring people I have known. However, because I was so wrapped up in the Buck Owens Ranch television productions and my KLPR duties, it was an almost spur-of-the-moment marriage, I'm sorry to say. Judy was dedicated to me and let it be known by struggling to make things come together in both, my personal and professional life.

As I look back, this had to be a most troublesome time for this very kind, very caring lady. I realize I wasn't supplying much happiness.

Judy never complained.

On a cold February day in 1969, I received a telephone call at my home in Oklahoma City from Hal Chesnut, the manager of WBAP Radio in Fort Worth. He said, "We're thinking of turning our midnight to 5:00 a.m. slot to country music. Wanted to see if you might be interested in hosting it, should we decide to do so."

Since I had been praying to get back into Fort Worth for months, my reply was quick and simple: "Yeah, Hal! I'd love to talk with you!"

"When can you come here and discuss it?" He asked.

"How about this afternoon?"

"Get your butt down here," he laughed. "I'll wait for you."

As I remember, it was a three-hour drive from Oklahoma City to Fort Worth at that time, before the Interstate had been jazzed up. I arrived at the WBAP studios about an hour earlier than had been expected and it was to be the most important drive I had made during all of my years in broadcasting.

186

CHAPTER SEVENTEEN

My meeting with station manager, Hal Chesnut, and Mr. Jim Byron, who was the CEO at WBAP, was quite comfortable and went very well. It was late afternoon and they wasted no time in telling me their plans.

For years, the station had suffered in the ratings game because several outlets in the Fort Worth-Dallas market had grabbed the majority of the listening audience with high-powered disk jockeys playing rock music, the fad at the time. Meanwhile, WBAP had continued to play what was called "good music". The elder heads-of-state refused to allow their broadcast powerhouse to be "just another radio station". The main focus was news. Such giants as Sinatra, Ella Fitzgerald, Tony Bennett and the bunch supplied the music. True, the music was good … but the ratings were rotten!

Hal Chesnut was a true country music fan and his idea was to take the 12:00 midnight to 5:00 a.m. period, drop Sinatra and pick up Ernest Tubb. "Do you think it will work?" He asked.

"Without a doubt," I replied and I was being very honest. At the time, radio was in a similar situation that we find it today. The fans wanted the <u>real</u> article but most stations were presenting a façade while calling it *"Mod Country", "Pop Country", "Today's Country"* and related pieces of crap. The true followers of country music were turning off the phony outlets and turning on their record players! I was absolutely certain that the only things needed were the records and a telephone. My thought was: Toss away the music reporting charts, which most of the fizzy stations were utilizing to make up their play lists, pick up the telephone and listen to the people! This wasn't ingenious thinking. Everything pointed to the fact that the real fans were being ignored by radio and, as always happens, "country" was taking a big drop.

I'll always be grateful to Hal Chesnut and Jim Byron for their confidence in me. That day following the somewhat short meeting, they shot me a salary figure which was very good and I quickly accepted their offer.

I'll always treasure their handshakes and those beautiful words: "Welcome to WBAP."

My arrival at WBAP was met with mixed reactions. Most of the people on the scene were very encouraging, happy to have me aboard, believing my program might bring in some needed revenue. Then, there were those who considered my joining the company an insult. One heavy-set matron caught me in the hallway one day and growled: "Don't tell me what I hear is true! Don't tell me the radio station is going to start playing 'hillbilly' music!."

I tried to be friendly. "It's not 'hillbilly' music, ma'am, it's 'country'."

She wasn't satisfied with my reply. "Same junk!" She shouted as she wobbled toward her office.

My first program on WBAP, 820 on the AM dial, was on March 2, 1969. I was nervous as hell, realizing if I failed that night, the management might well change their minds about the new all-night country music format. Ads had been placed in The Fort Worth Star-Telegram and huge signs with my picture were stuck on the back of city cabs reading: "Bill Mack ... All Night Long ... WBAP 820". Hal Chesnut and Jim Byron had made certain that my "coming" was to be known. However, that first night was to be one of the most nerve-shattering events of my professional life. It seems Carl Smith, the great country singer, had been booked at Ray Chaney's Stagecoach Inn, a big honky-tonk that was going strong at the time. That night after I had just hit the airwaves with my first show, in walks Carl and Ray. Carl was wearing Ray Chaney's wig and they were attempting to crack me up, which they managed to do, by dancing with each other! There was a limited audience in the control room with me and everyone was laughing loudly over the Smith-Chaney bits while I attempted to do a radio show. Good thing was, Hal Chesnut was in Houston and couldn't be with me during my opening night. Trouble was, I knew he was listening to the program in Houston!

I'll never forget the wire I received after that first show. It read: "Congratulations! Great show! So very, very good to have you with us! You made me proud!" It was signed: "Hal".

From that telegram on, I knew everything was going to be fine. My prayers had been answered.

The radio show was an overnight success. It was Judy who selected what she thought would make a good theme song, *"Orange Blossom Special"* by Felix Slatkin's Orchestra featuring my old friend, Gordon Terry, on the country fiddle. It was the first sound heard on that March 2, 1969 morning and as I write this, almost 35 years later, the old masterpiece continues to open my shows on XM Satellite Radio. I have never done a single radio show without the *"Orange Blossom Special"* opening the gig.

I remember the first telephone call I received was from a trucker in Minnesota. WBAP was a 50,000 watts <u>Clear</u> <u>Channel</u> facility where the coverage area was stronger during the late night and early morning hours than at any other time. The clear-channel offered the protection from having any other stations crowding into the 820 spot on the dial. Unfortunately, the *Federal Communications Commission,* in Washington, eliminated "Clear-Channel" several years ago and those once-powerful stations lost a tremendous amount of coverage power.

I couldn't believe my show was being heard in Minnesota ... and I'll always remember the words that trucker spoke to me on the telephone. Roughly, they went something like this:

"Well! I see we have a Texas midnight cowboy out there with us this morning! Play a good country song for all of us old lonesome truck drivers up here in Minnesota, Midnight Cowboy!"

I've wished so many times that I had recorded that telephone conversation and had the name of that truck driver. It was because of that phone call that I proclaimed myself as being radio's *"Midnight Cowboy"*. To this day, many people know me better as *The Midnight Cowboy* than as Bill Mack.

The truckers have been that <u>special</u> audience since 1969 and I know, without a single doubt, that I would have never been as successful with my stuff on radio had it not been for this special group. Now, of course, we have thousands of little lady drivers as well as the husky old boys. God bless 'em all! I owe them so much. When I smell diesel, it's pure <u>perfume</u> to me!

My first sponsor on the midnight show was Al Miller who owned a place in east Texas called *The Winfield Truck Stop*. I remember Al walking in during the second week of my show and, tossing a couple of hundred dollars on the table, saying, "I don't know how many spots this will buy, but I want to get on your show." *The Winfield Truck Stop* remained one of my leading sponsors for years and I will always be grateful.

My wife, Judy, was answering the telephone for me. I gave her the name, Big Tilda, although she was actually a beautiful, tiny lady, and it wasn't long before truckers all over the country were calling, asking to speak to "Big Tilda". One truck stop in north Texas even had a steak on their menu named the "Big Tilda Special".

Another very important person who added so much to my show was Harold Taft. Harold had been presenting the weather forecasts on WBAP-TV since 1948, and was recognized as the *Godfather* of the *Elements*. Although he was primarily recognized as a TV weatherman, he took the time to drop by my program and discuss the weather and other topics. He became a very important and respected personality, via his off-the-cuff contributions to the late-night brigade.

I named Harold, *The World's Greatest Weatherman* ... and the title stuck! Especially in the Fort Worth/Dallas area, Harold is still referred to as "the world's greatest weatherman".

When this good friend died of cancer, I was honorary pallbearer at the memorial services. As I recall, the skies were clear and the temperatures were perfect.

Seems to me, the weather hasn't been the same since Harold went to Heaven.

Then, there was the *Hogman!*

Bruce Carter came on my show one night from out of nowhere and, without warning, began squealing like a hog! It was a perfect squeal and you could almost smell the bacon! Soon, the truckers, and other late-nighters, had accepted the *Hogman* as a part of the *Midnight Cowboy's* assemblage of radio rowdies. Trouble was, *Hog* had a heart condition and was worsening it with a drinking problem.

Sad to say: My friend, Bruce Carter, better known as the *Hogman*, died before his time.

You may not remember my "announcer", Adrian Proctor, unless you were with me during the first year of my WBAP doings. Adrian was from England. He had come to the United States to attend a school-of-broadcasting in Dallas, and had asked to visit my show in order to "pick up a few tips". Since he had a heavy British accent, he was a unique addition to the program. The women seemed to love him, but some of the truckers thought he "sounded a little strange."

One Sunday night when I was off the air, a trucker-pal named Joe West and I decided we would take Adrian "*Snipe Hunting*". This is where the saying, "left holding the bag", originated. There is really no such thing as a *snipe*. The victim is ordered to hold a bag while those accompanying him on the "hunt" escape into the darkness of the night, leaving the impression they will be chasing the *'snipes'* toward the poor soul holding the bag. The chump is also ordered to beat on a big iron skillet with a hammer and scream, "Caw! Caw! Caw!", a sound resembling a big crow, supposedly.

We gave Adrian his bag, a big skillet, a hammer and a small flashlight. Then, Joe, Judy, a friend named Tonya and I escaped into the darkness. We ran to my car, opened the cooler, popped open some drinks and laughed as we heard the beating of the skillet and Adrian's "Caw! Caw! Caw!" from a far distance. This hum-drum went on for over an hour. Then, we decided to sneak up on him in the darkness where we would growl like fierce animals. This was the goal of the stupid trick … to scare the hell out him. Joe and I growled some serious sounds but Adrian didn't seem to. be afraid. He stopped beating the skillet, ceased the "Caw! Caw! Caw!" for a moment and shouted, "Here, little wolf! Here little coyote!"

Then, we decided to get closer to him and let the ladies release screams, following our growls, to leave the impression they had been attacked by the vicious animals, hoping this would really instill more fear. As we approached Adrian, Joe West fell into a huge dumping pit filled with broken beer bottles, rotted old tires, some barbed wire and assorted other damaging items. He let out a serious yell, receiving numerous scratches and bruises. Then, Tonya let out a scream from the darkness, "The car has backed into a ditch!" Seems we had failed to place the car in gear and lock the brakes when we exited the vehicle a few minutes earli-er and it had rolled backwards into a deep ditch on the side of the road.

Finally, we yelled at Adrian, informing him the *Snipe Hunt* was finished. His reply: "Great fun!"

We had to awaken an old farmer who lived about a mile from where the car had hit the ditch. He pulled his tractor up to the Chevy, tied a chain to it and managed to pull it out, charging me $50.00 for his time and labor. He also brought a small box of Band-Aids and some sort of salve for Joe West's scratches and bruises. In the meantime, Adrian was standing at a distance from us, beating on the skillet in the darkness, and practicing his "Caw! Caw! Caws!"

As we finally headed back to Fort Worth, all of us out of our minds from fatigue, Adrian sat in the back seat and continued beating the skillet while shouting, "Caw! Caw! Caw!" without let-ting up. Then, he paused long enough to say, "I say, old chaps! That snipe hunting is fun! Let's please do it again, soon. Maybe I'll have better luck." A pause and then, beating the drum came another "Caw! Caw! Caw!"

Joe West, rubbing his sore arm and leg growled, "Shut th' hell up, Adrian!"

Incidentally, we had taken a cassette recorder with us that night and caught most of the crazy action on tape. I played the bit on my radio show and the reaction was absolutely unbelievable, although it made fools of everyone involved ... except Adrian.

Beecher Wyatt, also a trucker, and I decided to pull another trick on my British announcer. I was scheduled to go to the *Radio-TV Commission* in Fort Worth and record some promos at 7:00 AM. When I finished my radio show at 5:00 AM, Beecher, Adrian and I got in my car and headed for the studio. I had lied to Adrian, say-ing a fellow British lady had telephoned, wanting him to stop by her house for breakfast. I also added that the lady's home was located near the studio where I was set to do my recording at 7:00 AM. It was pitch dark as we drove around the neighborhood on the west side of Fort Worth looking for any house that might have their lights on at 5:30 that morning. Finally, we found one, stopped the car and told Adrian to go knock on the door, that this was where the lady from London lived.

Excited, Adrian walked toward the strange house, rang the doorbell and, after a minute or so, the door opened and Adrian walked inside! "My God!" I shouted to Beecher. "They may kill him!"

Over an hour rolled by as Beecher and I sat in my car in a state of fear for Adrian's life. However, we were both too chicken to go to the door and check on him.

Finally, around 7:00 AM, the door to the house opened and Adrian came walking out with a big smile on his face. As he got into the car, I said, "I'm running late! What have you been doing in there?"

Adrian: "What a nice lady she was, although she is not from Britain. She is actually from San Antonio, just moved here a month or so ago. Quite lonely, she was, and she was so glad to make a new friend in me, dear soul. She fixed me a popping hot breakfast of scrambled eggs, bacon and buns. Sweet lady that she is … she's invited me to be with her Sunday for lunch!"

Beecher and I were both speechless as we made our late arrival at the *Radio-TV Commission*. Adrian broke the silence with, "Don't know why she would claim to be from England. The dear soul couldn't even remember making the call to you. She's a bit up in years, though. Possibly a memory disorder."

Adrian lived with Judy and me for over a year. He was a treasured friend and when the time arrived for him to return to jolly old London, we drove him to his plane at Dallas Love Field. There, he tapped on the top of the car after exiting and said, "So long, dear loves. Do hope to return some day."

While my little British pal walked briskly toward the airport entrance, Judy and I both broke down in tears.

Don Edwards, the Fort Worth singer, and Bobby Boatright, the great fiddle player, came to visit me at the radio station shortly after returning from a tour of England. They said they had visited an auction house in London named Sotheby's, where they were waited on by a strange little man. After informing him they were from Fort Worth, the little man smiled and asked, "Do you, by chance, know my friend, Bill Mack? He's a disk jockey of sorts there."

Don and Bobby informed him that they knew me and were also good friends of mine.

Adrian smiled and said, "Really? Well, tell the good chap that his announcer, Adrian, sends his best!" Then, he autographed a catalogue for Edwards and Boatright to deliver to me, which they did.

The autograph reads: "I'm now in this place. Lots of <u>love</u> and <u>luck</u> — Adrian"

I haven't seen or heard from Adrian Proctor in over 30 years, yet I think of him regularly. He was a nice chap.

The radio show was peaking in popularity in the 70s. Every night, there would be special guests and a limited audience on the show and I am certain this was one reason for its' success. I had complete freedom with my show. I could do as I damned well pleased.

One of the most popular questions submitted to me in interviews: "What is the secret to your success after over thirty years with your show, Bill?"

My honest reply: "It's no secret. I simply listen to the people! After all, the people let it be known what they want to hear on radio and it's the people who purchase our country music CDs and cassettes. Therefore, it doesn't take a genius to come to the simple conclusion that it all rests in the hands of the real experts in our business, the <u>people</u>."

During the past few years, some of our so-called country music experts and consultants in programming and record production have attempted to ignore the people, costing our industry millions of listeners and billions of dollars. What is most serious here is the fact that even though the results of their bad decisions have been sadly proven in radio ratings and the declining sales of our recorded products, most of those responsible for the decline are still in charge.

An entertainment writer for one of our newspapers said to me recently, "Sad to say, Bill, but I'm afraid you're in the minority with your feelings which are, obviously, correct."

I said, "I take that as a compliment. However, most of those manning the microphones have similar feelings. They just don't feel it's the right time to allow their feelings to be known to management.

"In other words, their butts would most likely be fired by sundown!"

Courage comes with age.

It was also right after the show began in 1969 that the great extraordinary opportunities began to come on strong. Although I had been a disk jockey since I was in my teens, I had no idea of the benefits until WBAP began charging the nation nightly with its

50,000 clear-channel watts. Ralph Emery was still doing his thing on WSM in Nashville, also a 50,000 watts clear-channel power-house; old friend, Mike Hoyer, was stationed at WHO in Des Moines, along with Billy Cole, and there were others, but it seemed I had the winning horse at the time, perhaps because of the heavy promotion and the fact WBAP had the best coverage at the time. Doug China, a rock disk jockey, would come on the scene a few years later out of WWL, New Orleans, switching from "rock" to "country" and changing his name to Charlie Douglas.

The extra ordinary opportunities also brought a split with Judy. I allowed the radio show to take complete control of my life while Judy attempted in every way she could to keep things together for me. The show was going strong; my second marriage was growing weak.

Marty Robbins during one of his many visits to my
all night radio program at WBAP.

CHAPTER EIGHTEEN

My radio show had caught on so strong in 1971 that WBAP decided to change the radio format to "all-country". Of course, some of the older veterans at the station thought this was an insult to the ancient ship.

The switch to "Total Country" was set for August, 1971. It was decided we would present a free outdoors country music show in order to celebrate the occasion.

I flew to Nashville in order to line up some acts that might want to come to Fort Worth and join us for the "Country Gold" blowout. I met with Wesley Rose, the chief honcho at Acuff-Rose Music, one of the most influential people in country music, inviting him to be one of our guests of honor. Wes was happy to accept the invitation and, as a surprise, said he would bring Mr. Roy Acuff with him to Fort Worth. Since Roy was known as The King of Country Music, I knew this would be the supreme compliment, something like having Arnold Palmer as a guest at a local golf tournament!

I had invited several acts to be with us at the celebration party, several saying they would do their best to make it. The acts were not to be paid. They would appear voluntarily.

WBAP had been heavily publicizing the upcoming event, hoping we would have a crowd. Hal Chesnut, the radio station manager, strongly believed in what we were about to do. He realized

I would have been terribly embarrassed if the show turned out to be a flop. He had a lot to lose too, if our plans fizzled. Hal had stuck his neck out, battling some very important people within the organization, in order to switch the format to "all country".

I approached Rupert Bogan, the chief engineer with WBAP, informing him we would need a big public address system set up to handle the crowd.

Rupert, always the grouch, said, "We'll set up a couple of speakers. I doubt we'll need more than that."

The show was scheduled to start at 7:00 p.m. The big bed of a truck was to be the stage for those who would be kind enough to donate their services.

As the afternoon grew later, the guest artists began to arrive. Among those making the scene were Charley Pride, Johnny Duncan, Connie Smith, Tony Douglas and his band, Leona Williams and a cute little newcomer named Tanya Tucker who had just recorded a song titled, "Delta Dawn", her first 45 rpm for Columbia Records.

It was a typical August day in Fort Worth, the temperature several degrees above the 100 mark.

While Bogan and one of his engineers were stringing wire to the two small speakers he had agreed to provide, the cars began rolling into the huge parking lot. The radio station was located on a hill about a mile off Interstate 30, which connected Fort Worth and Dallas, and the traffic was back-to-back, edging toward WBAP.

Suddenly, police cars arrived to handle the crowd.

I walked up to Rupert Bogan and said, "We're going to need a huge sound system and a bunch of speakers, Bogan! Look at the crowd coming in ... and it's not even five o'clock!"

Bogan growled: "You don't honestly think all of those cars are headin' here, do you?"

He shook his head in disgust, gave me a fiendish smile and spouted, "There must be a ball game around here somewhere."

An accurate head count wasn't made on that hot summer night, but it's estimated that over 20,000 people were in attendance as we presented our "Country Gold" shindig.

It was to be one of the most successful country music shows I have ever seen and, of course, I was a bit proud. After all, it had been my idea to put the powerhouse play together, realizing there were still those in command at WBAP who literally hated me for being responsible for the switch to country.

Of course, most of those who were attempting to block the country music move changed their opinions rapidly when the loot began piling in. My radio show was "sold out" with commercials and, immediately after going "Total Country", money was filling the hoppers at the radio station at an unbelievable pace, something the company had not enjoyed in years.

Although the acts were performing at no cost, it was a profitable gesture for those who donated their services. WBAP was the most powerful full-time country music station in the world and had the top ratings in the huge Fort Worth-Dallas area. Every country music star that played on the bed of the truck in the steaming humidity that night was reciprocated with heavy airplay of their recordings long after the party was over. We would never forget how they had gone out of their way to be with us, helping us celebrate the auspicious occasion.

After the shindig was finished that night, I did my radio show before an audience of hundreds. The acts that had appeared on stage agreed to hang around with me for interviews.

The first 'star' I interviewed was the little girl named Tanya Tucker. She had come with her daddy, Beau. And even though she wasn't the super star yet, she didn't seem to feel intimidated by those who had been on stage singing their big hits. As a matter of fact, her *"Delta Dawn"* wouldn't rise high in the Billboard charts for several months (*"Delta Dawn"* peaked at #6 in Billboard May 13, 1972).

Tanya has always been special to me. I've always considered the entire Tucker family to be a branch of my own.

From the first time I met her that August night in 1971, to the present, Tanya has been a personal favorite. I love her works, of course, but there has always been that special "something" in the lady, herself, that has placed her in a very important part of my heart.

I realize the "Texas Tornado" has had her share of publicity, some of it not too complimentary, and this has caused me a lot of personal concern. In reality, Tanya is one of the most gentle, caring and giving people I've ever known. Of course, a lot of this warmth was instilled by her parents, Beau and Juanita.

I've been around Tanya dozens of times, ushering her to different events in Nashville, and have never heard her make a negative remark toward anyone; a quality a bit difficult to find in today's show business community.

Even when Glen Campbell laid some heavy statements in print about her in his book, Tanya refused to get revenge when her *"Nickel Dreams"* went into book stores. I'm sure this may have cost her some sales of her biography, since many people were waiting to read what 'Terrific Tanya' might have to say about her ex, Campbell, and their sizzling sessions together.

When I attempted to get Tanya to chit-chat about old Glen in secrecy with me, she merely laughed and said, very simply, "Oh … those were yesterdays."

During a special bio of Glen Campbell on television, he pointed his finger at Tanya, hinting that she had caused him to get heavy into drugs and booze. As I write this (December, '03), Campbell was arrested in Arizona a few days ago for being drunk while driving and punching a police officer.

Sad situation.

It's easy to see why Tanya has her fans. It's also not difficult to realize why she has a lot of men hot on her trail. She is a very glamorous lady. In many ways she reflects the image of *Hollywood's Hallway-of-Beauty* that, back in the 30s and 40s, produced the likes of Lana Turner, Liz Taylor and a few others. Honestly, it's beyond beauty. There is also the "mystique". TT is one of the few ladies I have met who projects an indescribable "happening" when she comes on the scene. However, she is so real. Sometimes, her honesty constructs inquisitiveness. You wonder what makes her tick?

Miss Tucker (no, she's never been married) is not the kind to shy away from parties and fun! And, in the process, has caused her share of the heartbreak of a few old boys who attempted to get her to the altar.

One night, on my radio show, she was given a ten-karat diamond ring by a wealthy businessman from Dallas who was obviously madly in love with her. Her daddy, Beau, was also with her that night and seemed to be a bit shocked by the presentation.

Next night, I emceed a show featuring Tanya and asked her if she was in love with the Dallas suitor. She replied, "No. I barely know him! Can't understand why he'd give me a ring as beautiful as this!"

Then, she stuck her finger under a light in her dressing room, giggled, and said: "It sure is good to have those fans out there, Bill!"

Several years ago, when she was my guest at the *Mid-America*

Trucking Show in Louisville, Kentucky, I asked her if she still had the gorgeous diamond ring the millionaire had given her when she was visiting me on my radio show in the 70s.

"I lost that sucker!" She replied.

In an obviously sincere afterthought, she added, "I wonder what ever happened to that old boy that gave me that ring. It was so nice of him."

Then came that silly little-girl giggle.

Of all the people to compliment my radio show, no one was more popular than Marty Robbins.

Marty was to appear with me many times on the all-night radio gig. He would stroll into the control room with his guitar and, for four or five hours, he would simply pick and sing. The studio was always filled with guests, giving the show the sound of a 'come-as-you-are' party, which was what it was.

I referred to each show as *"A Marty Party!"*

Years later, Marty Stuart would utilize the title, "Marty Party", for his TV appearances.

The audience would shout requests ... and Marty would fumble around for the right key on his guitar and begin singing. It might be a song he had never performed, but he would make an effort to bring it to life, which he always did.

After I had asked him how he managed to remember the lyrics and melody of every single song that was requested, he laughed and said, "Oh, I don't know near all of them. I just strum th' ol' guitar and make up some lyrics, if I don't know them. Then, I just hum around, faking them." He added, "Th' good folks don't seem to mind. I guess most of them, like me, remember th' melody but don't take special interest in every single word in the lyrics.

"A song is like a movie," he stressed. "The lyrics are like a movie script. As long as you stick to th' general story ... and know the melody ... you can make it work!"

During my tenure with the midnight radio show on WBAP, the mornings spent with Marty behind the microphone were, by far, the most memorable; the most popular of them all.

At his own expense, Marty would fly into Dallas, grab a cab and come to the radio station in Fort Worth. During the span of 5 hours, I might play a half dozen recordings. The rest of the time was taken up by Marty and his guitar. I was always in awe of this giant talent as he "did his thing". He made it look so very easy. Here was a man picking his guitar and singing the songs the people wanted to hear. And he enjoyed those parties more than anyone.

"I love to sing for th' people," he said. "I'm not th' best singer in th' world, but those fine folks make me feel like I am! And as long as they like what I'm doin' ... I'm gonna continue doin' it!"

Marty's fans considered him to be <u>the best</u>. And they still do!

I recorded every visit with Martin David, collecting over thirty-five hours of his singing and his clowning around. He was a very funny person. He loved pulling pranks on me.

One morning in the early 70s, Marty telephoned me and said he was set to do a movie for *Universal Pictures*. "I want you in 'th movie!" He laughed. "I'm gonna make you a movin' picture star!"

He told me I would need to take a week off in order to do the film and WBAP was very cooperative, realizing it would be good publicity for my radio show.

I flew into Nashville and Marty met me at the airport. He told me they were taking a break for a couple of hours and that we would shoot my part in the film later in the afternoon.

As we stopped for a hamburger, he said, "This movin' picture business is tough! You've got to be on your toes and be able to remember your lines!"

"Do you have a copy of my script?" I asked.

"No. We'll get that when we get back on th' 'set'."

Naturally, I was concerned. After all, *Universal Pictures* was a giant motion picture studio and I certainly didn't want to foul up in front of millions! I was just hoping I could remember my "lines". I was also of the opinion that Marty should have brought a copy of my script with him. I could be looking it over as we sat in the booth munching on our hamburgers.

We finally made it to the set where everyone seemed so busy amidst the lights, cords, cameras and assorted bits of unfamiliarity. Marty introduced me to the director, who wasted no time in saying, "Good to meet you. We're about ready to shoot your part."

I was led to a makeshift dressing room where a nervous looking dude shaved me. Then, a pretty girl applied makeup. There was very little conversation in the room and I'm sure my nervousness was obvious.

The makeup girl said, "Take off your pants!" Then, handing me a pair of jeans and shirt, she shouted, "Put these own ... and make it fast! Also put your boots back on!"

What made me feel even more uncomfortable was the fact she remained in the room with me, twiddling her thumbs, while I changed into my outfit, leaving the impression it was routine procedure with her.

She led me back to the set where the director gave me a fast study and shouted, "Get on the set, Mr. Mack!"

An assistant led me to the set, which resembled a control room in a radio station. I was seated behind a microphone. Then, the director said, "I want you to ad-lib something like you normally do on your radio show. Then, Mr. Robbins and Mr. Jackson (This was Sammy Jackson, the former disk jockey and actor, Marty's co-star in the picture.) are going to enter your 'studio'. You will turn around and ask Mr. Robbins what he is doing in town. Mr. Robbins will say, 'Sammy and I are on our way from Las Vegas to Nashville and decided to stop by and see you, Bill.'

"Then, you will say, 'Marty, will you sing me a song?' Mr. Robbins will respond by saying 'Yes, I will, Bill', then you will say, 'Will you sing my favorite song? 'The Hands You're Holding Now'?'

"Then Mr. Robbins will say, 'Of course I will, Bill', and then, he will take the guitar and sing the song.

"Do you have that?" Asked the director.

For some reason, I felt like I was set to do the 'run-through'.

"Action!"

The lights were bright and there was complete quiet as I pretended to be on the air, ad-libbing about how good it was to be with my listeners, etc. Then, Marty and Sammy came running into the set where I continued with the ad-libs, telling Marty I was so glad he had surprised me with his guitar and, as directed, asked him to sing my favorite Marty Robbins song, *The Hands You're Holding Now*.

Marty said, "I should have known you would ask me to sing that song, Bill ... and I'll be happy to do it for you."

Then, Marty sang the song, told me he and Sammy "had to hurry to Nashville", and, after shaking my hand, rushed out the door on the set.

Thinking I must have done all right in the "run-through", I was anxious to do a serious "take".

Then came the words: "That's a wrap!"

I couldn't believe what I was hearing! I looked at Marty, who was laughing like mad, and asked, "Is this some kind of joke?"

He continued to laugh, replying, "No! It's no joke! Now, you're a movie star!"

Marty took me to the hotel where *Universal* had reserved a suite for me and handed me an envelope, telling me he had to rush back to the movie set. Inside the envelope was a check for what I considered to be an extreme over payment for what little I had done. He also enclosed a note of thanks, adding, "Now, take the rest of the time off from the radio station and enjoy yourself."

I spent a few days in Nashville and then hopped a plane back to Fort Worth where I rested in the sun.

When *"Country Music"* opened in Fort Worth in 1972, I literally slid down in my seat when my part in the picture hit the big screen. The simple movie, with several big-name country music "guests" in it, besides Marty, didn't make any big splashes when it was released, but it was such a memorable experience.

I can still hear the Marty Robbins laugh as I recall the day he "made me a movin' picture star".

When it came to personal appearances, Marty told me Texas was his favorite state. He loved Texas. Rumor has it his grandfather was, at one time, a Texas Ranger. It didn't matter where Marty was booked in Texas. He always filled the halls.

One night, Marty was booked in the Fort Worth Convention Center. Also on the program were Dottie West and Kenny Rogers.

I had been playing Kenny Rogers' recordings for years, but had never met him. Since I was to be the M.C. for the big show, I thought it would be a good idea to get acquainted with the big star. He was in the basement of the convention center, where the busses were parked, talking with a young girl. I approached him, stuck out my hand and said, "Excuse me, Kenny, I just wanted to shake your hand and introduce myself. I'll make it fast."

Rogers gave me a perfectly constructed 'Go-to-hell' glare, looked down at my extended hand, ignoring it, and turned his back on me! As I stood there, feeling like an idiot, he turned his attention back to the young lady. I thought I should attempt to apologize for what was obviously an intrusion. I said, "I'm sorry I ..."

Before I could finish the sentence, Kenny growled, "Why don't you get your ass lost?" Then, shaking his head in disgust, he and the girl walked toward his band bus.

Dottie West was a dear friend. Just as Rogers made his stroll to the bus, Dottie walked up to me as I was attempting to hold back my fuming anger. She gave me a big hug, telling me how happy she was by being in Texas. She and Rogers had recorded some duet hits together. She asked, "Did you meet Kenny?"

Still fuming over Rogers' actions, I kept my reaction short by saying, "No. He was busy."

Dottie said, "He'll want to meet you! Stay here just a minute!" Then, she walked rapidly to Kenny's bus.

Within a minute, Kenny exited his bus and, with Dottie by his side, rushed towards me with his familiar CBS smile planted on his bearded face. As he approached me, he extended his hand and said, "Why didn't you tell me you were Bill Mack, the disk jockey? I wouldn't have been so rude!"

I looked down at his extended hand, ignored it, looked square into his smiling eyes and said, "Why don't you get your ass lost?"

Dottie looked a bit shocked.

When I told Marty what had happened, he went into convulsive laughter. He said, "I'll get one of my band members to introduce old Kenny tonight, since he's th' star and I go on just before he trots on stage. I don't think your heart would be in it!"

From that moment on, Marty would telephone me from time to time during my radio show and, changing to a high-pitched voice, he would shout: "This is Kenny Rogers! I haven't heard you play one of my *hits* tonight!"

Then, without further conversation, he would hang up the phone.

As I mentioned, Dottie West was a very dear friend. She was also the perfect singer, a beautiful lady. However, for some reason I will never understand, Dottie never received the recognition she deserved. The only awards she received from the *Country Music Association* were those handed to her in 1978 and 1979 as *Vocal Duo of the Year* ... with Kenny Rogers!

Dottie died of injuries from an accident in Nashville on September 4, 1991. Her car had stalled as she was attempting to get to the Grand Ole Opry, where she was a member. She was running late and had hitched a ride with an old neighbor. The old man, driving at high speed, missed a curve and crashed into a ditch. Dottie, not realizing she was so seriously injured, told one of the passers-by to rush the old gentleman to the hospital. She said she would wait for the ambulance.

The old man survived, but Dottie died.

One morning, on the air, I asked Marty Robbins how he felt about the fact he had not been inducted into the *Country Music Hall-of-Fame* in Nashville.

I still treasure his reply, which I have on tape: "I don't want to be inducted into the *Country Music Hall-of-Fame*. And do you know why?"

"Why?" I asked.

"Because they don't put you in there unless you're dead ... or about to die!

"I'm not dead, yet ... and I don't feel like I'm dyin'! I want to keep it that way!"

Marty Robbins was inducted into our Country Music Hall-of-Fame in October, 1982. Two months later, on December 8, 1982, he died of a heart attack.

Marty Robbins: Irreplaceable as a singer and entertainer.

More important to me, Marty was a friend.

CHAPTER NINETEEN

1973 was a very special year for me. My radio show was voted the top country d. j. show on the scene and, more important, I married the most beautiful little lady I have ever known: Sweet Cindy.

Jo Bryson was the manager of the apartment complex where I was living. Almost on a daily basis, I would meet Jo, either at the pool or in her office, for a chat. Jo and her husband, Bill, had two very good-looking daughters, Linda and Cindy, who were also on the scene most every day.

I enjoyed my visits with the Bryson family, and when I told a funny story about the 'happenings' of the day, Cindy always caught my attention with her cute, unrestrained laugh. Little by little, I was finding this bit of prettiness a lot of fun to be with, although I certainly had no thoughts pertaining to anything more than our daily gabfests. The last thing on my mind was making a serious attachment to a female, especially one quite a few years my junior.

One Labor Day weekend, I had just returned from a trip to San Antonio in my little *M-G* convertible, and was flopping around the pool. There was hardly anyone in the area at the time, and I was resting up for the Jerry Lewis Telethon I was scheduled to co-host from Dallas that night. Jo walked up to me and we did our regular bit of chatting. She casually mentioned that she felt a bit sorry for Cindy, because she didn't have anything to do over the holiday weekend, and I yawned the fact that she could go with me to the telethon.

That's how it started. Little did I know that within a few weeks I would find myself in love with the little lady. Even less expected was the fact that we would be married within a few months!

I wanted to write this while she is out of the house. It gives me time to think. I have no idea what I'm going to write, although I know it will be easy in some spots ... maybe a bit tough in other areas.

If I ever had a pal, it's Cindy. She's also my wife. Sometimes, I believe *pal* is just as important as *wife,* when the entire scope is taken into consideration. I could never be completely happy without Cindy's friendship. She's a stump (she'll hate that word). By that, I mean she's a dependable creation I can lean on ... and be comfortable in doing so. And God! I've leaned on her so many times. What's so important to me is the fact she has *never* let me down.

When Cindy and I married, over 30 years ago, many considered it a terrible mistake. Neither of us has ever doubted the vows, thank God. When Cynthia came into my life, I had a reputation of being inconsistent in the love department. For sure, I wasn't bonded to any individual lady ... although they <u>all</u> thought I was. I wasn't a Casanova, I just considered *several* to be beautiful and friendly, and I was jumping here and yon.

Cindy's parents were very "put-out" by the marriage. Now, looking back, I really can't blame them. I was hard-crusted at the time. I'm sure I would have become a lighted fuse, had one of my daughters stepped into a similar situation (I erased the word, "trap").

Now, all of the attitudes and anger have healed. Bill and Jo, my in-laws, are top grade. I love them both very much. This also applies to Linda, Cindy's beautiful sister, and her husband, Dennis.

Everything's fine on the home front, I'm happy to say.

Besides being the most beautiful lady I have had the pleasure of knowing, Cindy comes accompanied with a good working mind. It's not flawless, of course, but her thinking power has been put to the test many times, and she seems to answer-the-call as good as any so-called expert I've ever known. I've never known a more dependable individual than Cynthia Ann. She runs the company, *Bill Mack Country,* Inc. She keeps the books, and hands out the paychecks.

My main gripe: I never see a paycheck, and I haven't been given a raise-in-pay in years! She did manage to give herself a raise here recently ... but she deserved it.

Cindy loves to shop at Wal-Mart and Target. She has a

Neiman-Marcus credit card, but has only used it a couple of times. I think those times were when she was purchasing something for me. That's her style.

Adding to the blessings that have entered my life, since attaching to Cindy, are the three beautiful children. Misty and Sunnie are the gorgeous daughters. I'm not exaggerating here. Then, there's my good-looking son, Billy. Even his sisters claim he is the best looking dude in town.

Now, there are the grandchildren. Cody, going on eight as I write this, is my best pal. He's also super sharp, of course. Then there's Brittany (Brit), the gorgeous princess who doesn't look her age (5). I've recently begun referring to her as *Scout*. She reminds me of the little girl with that nickname, played by Mary Badham, in one of my favorite films, *"TO KILL A MOCKINGBIRD"*. Miss Badham was a bit older than Brit in that movie, but there was a resemblance. I believe it was the hair.

I'm in awe of Cindy's complete control when approaching situations that would normally blow my mind. She simply sets herself into a pattern of steadiness. Sometimes, though, I fear for her. I know she is holding back in order to settle the atmosphere, good ol' girl that she is. I've seen her "explode" maybe a half-dozen times during the over 30 years we've been together, and these explosions were simple *whiffs*, compared to my *blast-offs*, which she has witnessed dozens of times.

Adding to her preciousness is the fact she forgives me without my making countless apologies. Most times, I don't have to apologize at all. Even when the fault is all mine, she will hug me and whisper: *"Let's don't fight."*

This lady is one beautiful and loving individual.

Cindy is still my greatest 'audience' ... and my best friend.

Best Man at our wedding was a rustic old cowboy known as Big John Brigham. He would have made a perfect star in those old Saturday matinee westerns. John was about 6 foot-3, sported a heavy beard and mustache, was always dressed in floppy western gear and wore a dusty black cowboy hat.

Big John's business was stagecoaches. He was hired by WBAP to hitch his beautiful horses to his coaches and proudly strut down the streets of various cities in Texas and Oklahoma with the radio station disk jockeys sitting on top of the stagecoach, waving to the crowds.

Big John was my best pal. His favorite food platters consisted of "calf-fries" (fried bull testicles), pork ribs and bacon. "I eat a pound of bacon ever' mornin' for breakfast!" He would boast.

We lost Big John Brigham several years ago. He was still in his 40s, and I've always wondered if it wasn't his love for bacon that brought on the massive heart attack.

His body was carted to the cemetery on a horse drawn wagon. I rode 'shotgun', next to the driver.

It was a very sad day.

The reaction to WBAP and the *Country Gold* format was unbelievable in the '70s. Every night, a top entertainer would be with me on my radio show. Since the station was playing country music around the clock, artists were in the studio on a daily basis, visiting with the other jocks as well.

I have never seen a radio station receive the public reaction WBAP received during those so-called *"golden days"* in the '70s. Every d. j. made extra loot by making personal appearances as emcees at various events, and the pay was very good.

Among those on the payroll, in the beginning, were Don Harris, Jim Baker, Don Day, Jimmy Stewart, Hal King and Joe Martin. It was a very good lineup.

I was receiving great opportunities to make extra money, and those opportunities weren't restricted to the Fort Worth-Dallas area.

I received a telephone call one day from an advertising agency in New York, telling me I had been selected to be the "intro announcer for *Coca-Cola*" and their country music personality radio ads. It was a great chance to make some good loot and, of course, I accepted the offer. The ad man said I would have to fly to Nashville, where he would meet me at the air terminal, fill me in on what I would be required to do, and would drive me to the recording studios where the commercials were to be produced. "You'll be able to recognize me at the airport. I'll be wearing a brown beaver hat," he said.

When I arrived at the Nashville terminal, the fellow from New York, in the brown beaver hat, shook my hand, introduced himself (sorry to say I've long since forgotten his name), and said, "Good to see you! Let's get this show on the road!"

When we arrived at the recording studio on Nashville's 16th

Avenue, I was handed a printed script and told to step to the microphone for a voice-check.

"Read the first line of your script and let's see how it 'feels'!" Shouted the producer, through the studio speaker from the control room.

Holding the script, I announced: "Here is Tammy Wynette … singing for *Coke!*"

There were a few seconds of discussion with the man wearing the brown hat before the producer yelled, "That's good! Now, let's make a take of your first line!"

Again, I announced: "Here is Tammy Wynette … singing for *Coke!*"

I noticed the producer and the man in the brown hat nodding their heads in the control room. "Good!" Exclaimed the producer. "Now, read the next line!"

I announced: "That was Tammy Wynette … singing for *Coke!*"

There was no immediate reaction from my second 'take' and, looking into the glassed-in control room, I could see the producer talking with the man wearing the brown beaver hat. After about thirty seconds of what I presumed was a deep discussion between the two of them, the producer smiled at me through the window, opened the speaker mike and shouted: "That's it! Perfect take! That wraps it up!"

I couldn't believe I had flown all the way from Dallas to Nashville to do such a simple chore. What really caught my attention was when the man in the brown beaver hat walked into the studio, shook my hand and said, "You were great! Next week, we'll cut one of these introducing David Houston!"

He handed me a very nice check, took me back to the Nashville air terminal and, within an hour, I was in the sky headed back to Dallas.

"Way to live," I thought to myself … as I gazed out the window of the plane at the friendly skies!

Cindy told me the good news! She was pregnant … and I couldn't have been happier. I had missed some good times with my daughter, Debbie, and felt that now was the perfect time for us to become parents.

On the morning of April 9, 1974, Cindy was sitting with me as I did my radio show when, suddenly, she shouted: "Oh! My water broke!"

At first, I thought she was referring to the plumbing at the radio station. It didn't take long, though, for me to realize it was time to head to the hospital! I telephoned my old friend Joe Martin and asked him to rush to the radio station and relieve me.

Within a few hours, our daughter, Misty Dawn, was born. Like her mother, Misty was gorgeous. Still is!

Cindy, Misty and I were living in an apartment near the radio station with thoughts of purchasing a house. It was time to locate something bigger than an apartment. After all, the money was rolling in nicely.

To quote a well-known movie line, shouted by James Cagney in "White Heat": "Look, Ma! I'm on top of the world!"

Just as everything was moving at a perfect pace, the news was released that the Amon Carter Company was selling WBAP to a huge outfit out of New York, *Capitol Cities, Inc.* There was also the attached announcement: *"Nothing to worry about!"*

After hearing a similar announcement years before in San Antonio when KENS was sold, a chill of disappointment shattered my body.

Capitol Cities was a huge broadcast group. Eventually, it would purchase *ABC* radio and television and, years later, hitch up with Disney to become one of the most important conglomerates in the entertainment world.

The new general manager of WBAP was a figure named Warren Potash. Warren was both, my boss and my neighbor. And to be honest, I didn't find either title anything I could brag about. Even though he was ultra friendly, I just didn't feel any tranquility when I was in his presence.

Although Potash was very good to me, he was a terror to some of those working under his banner. This was especially evident in the sales department. There was all hell to pay if radio sales dropped. Guy Woodward, a salesman who had been with WBAP for years, and had been placed in the unenviable position as Sales Manager, became a basket case from receiving his daily butt chewings from Warren.

He told me, in confidence, "I'm scared to death of the man, Sweetie!"

No, he wasn't gay. He just called everybody, male and female,

"Sweetie", which might have been one reason Warren kept the whip on his tail.

Potash, New York bred and New York raised, loved the image of the cowboy. He kept a saddle on a wooden sawhorse in his office. One day, I made a bet with Guy, the nervous salesman. I said, "I'll bet you fifty dollars that I can talk Warren into putting on a cowboy outfit, and getting on that saddle in his office, and shout, 'Hi, ho, Pal!'"

The salesman whispered a jittery, "It's a bet, Sweetie!"

Potash had told me several times that he had always wanted to be an actor. Remembering this, I told him I was going to produce a home-made movie with my little 8-MM sound camera, and I wanted him to be in the film. He thought it was a great idea, and next day, as I had instructed him to do, he wore his western shirt, jeans and boots to his office. He also brought a pair of chaps and a big, obnoxious, western hat.

After he had closed all the doors to his office, he put on the chaps and placed the big hat on his head. Then, I directed him to place his skinny body in the saddle, setting on the sawhorse. Excited, he did as ordered. After checking the lighting, I started my camera and yelled, "Action!"

I still have a clean copy of the film, with perfect sound, of Warren Potash, the head of WBAP, straddled to the saddled sawhorse. With his legs stretched out, holding his hat in his hand, he yells, *"Hi, ho, Pal! Giddyup!"*

It was an easy fifty bucks … and I must admit … Potash was rarin' to go, on this bit of action.

One hot summer day, I was set to emcee a *Willie Nelson Picnic* just outside of Dallas and Warren invited himself to go with me in my little *M-G* convertible. As the two of us sped east, I decided to stop at a *7-11* store, about six miles from my house, and purchase some crushed ice for the drink cooler I had setting in the back of the car.

"What are we stoppin' for, Pal?" Asked Warren.

"I forgot to get ice. I'm going to buy a bag for our drinks in the cooler." I replied.

Potash growled: "Take me home."

"What?" I asked, in a state of confusion.

Potash: "You heard me, Pal. Take me to my house."

Thankful that he had changed his mind and wanted to go back home, I whizzed back toward our townhouse complex. I realized

I might be running a bit late for Willie Nelson's gig, but it would be worth it, having Warren exit the car. In my mind, I presumed he found the weather too hot to travel in a little car without the comfort of air-conditioning.

I drove Warren to his door and he jumped out of the *M-G*. I was about to drive away when I heard, "Wait here a minute, Pal! I'll be right back!"

Dumbfounded, I killed the engine and waited for the dude. "Probably had to use the restroom," I thought.

Within a couple of minutes, I saw Potash rushing out of his townhouse with an armload of ice trays! "What are you doing?" I shouted.

"I got some ice here for the chest," he said, unloading the trays in the cooler. Then, he tossed the empty trays toward his door and said, "Now, we can go!"

I was highly ticked and speechless as I headed back east with my alien passenger.

The silence of the angry moment was broken when Potash released one of his *classic* statements: "Never buy ice, Pal! It's just frozen water!"

I was late in arriving at the Willie Nelson Picnic, in order to save seventy-five cents in ice.

Incidentally, it was at this event that Willie pulled a wild joke on me. Just as I introduced him, he handed me his cigarette while he pretended to adjust his guitar as the crowd was going wild. Photographers were shooting pictures of Willie smiling and waving at the crowd ... with me standing beside him, holding his smoking cigarette.

Next day, on the front page of the entertainment section of the Dallas Times Herald, there was a photo of Willie in his honesty ... and me holding a 'joint'!

WBAP's FM affiliate, *KSCS*, was just beginning to show some strength. This was when almost all of the FM stations were giving away big bucks on a daily basis in order to grab the listeners.

KSCS decided to promote a real audience grabber on the air: "Listen carefully to *KSCS*, where you'll hear *ten recordings in a row* ... with no commercials! Now, if you happen to hear a commercial inserted *before* ten recordings have been played ... and you are the first to telephone *KSCS* ... you'll win *ten-thousand* dollars!"

The poor disk jockey on duty one night had to rush to the restroom. After zipping up and returning to the control room, he thought he was hearing the end of his tenth recording, believing it was time to insert a commercial.

Just as he punched the button, he looked at his music log ... and took note of the tragic fact he had played only <u>nine</u> recordings before hitting the spot!

As the commercial was loudly penetrating the airwaves, he was in the midst of a silent prayer that no one had caught his 'mistake' when, almost immediately, he noticed the contest phone line lighting up like mad. After picking up the receiver very slowly and mumbling a nervous, "Hello", he heard a loud, responsive, "Gotcha!"

A good old boy from Burleson, Texas had just won the $10,000 ... and the unfortunate d. j. had just lost his job!

Normally, a radio station would utilize this occasion to pick up tremendous press coverage over the fact one of their listeners had, indeed, won ten-thousand bucks by listening. And *KSCS* <u>did</u> pick up a ton of press. However, it was over the fact Warren Potash, the manager of the outlet, had become enraged because the company was going to have to fork over the loot and had decided to <u>fire</u> the "non-thinking disk jockey!"

There were those who attempted to persuade the "boss" that *KSCS* was in a position to pick up press from all over the country worth much more than ten-thousand dollars, but Potash just couldn't stand to let-go of the loot!

Eventually, after attorneys from both sides had discussed the issue, the disk jockey was put back on the KSCS payroll.

Bill and Cindy with President George Bush

CHAPTER TWENTY

In 1980, I was offered a job at *KRLD* in Dallas. This was, as it is today, the leading competitor of WBAP, since it is also a mighty outlet with 50,000 watts of power and has a very good reputation. The job would consist of more money, although the hours would be similar, all night long.

I was ready for the move since I was feeling less devotion to WBAP. Warren Potash wasn't giving me any problems to speak of, but there was that 'gut-feeling' I seem to have built in, which is seldom wrong. I still utilize it today.

I accepted the *KRLD* job and was anxious to make the move. I walked into Potash's office and told him I was leaving, that I wasn't happy. Old Warren went goofy! He began yelling, "No! No! You can't leave this station, Pal!" Of course, he was thinking of the big bucks my show was pulling in. There was no love or friendship attached to his actions.

I told him I had my mind made up, that it was time for a change.

Warren promised me everything within his reach to hang in with WBAP and, for some reason I will never understand, I allowed him to talk me out of making the move to *KRLD*, something I have always regretted.

That night, the doorbell rang at our house and there stood Warren and his wife, Marie, in their pajamas, holding a bottle of champagne. "Celebration time, Pal!" He shouted. "You'll never regret staying with good ol' WBAP!"

I'll never forget one of the sales people telling me: "Warren Potash will never forgive you for even <u>thinking</u> of moving to *KRLD*. Just wait and see."

Within a matter of weeks, I could see the writing on the wall. The boss had plans!

A bulky dude out of Buffalo, New York was hired as Program Director of WBAP. It was to become a case of *Instant Hatred ...* on both sides.

Immediately, the new whiz lit the neon on his charmed ego by calling the WBAP disk jockeys together for what he categorized as a 'friendly meeting'. He caught the attention of those blessed by his holy presence when he blurbed: "I'm Italian! I don't get mad, I get revenge!"

Holy Buffalo!

After this ho-hum approach, *PD* began his duties as Potash's muscle man. I was told he had been hired to make things a bit *uneasy* for me and to eventually have me axed. Immediately after *PD* hit the scene, the agreements Potash had made to me in order to keep me from moving to *KRLD* began to fizz out. *PD* plastered up memos stating *"No More Visitors or Guests Allowed Unless Going Through Me!"* This, of course, placed a slab on my program, since the guests were so very important to the structure of the show.

WBAP had moved to a new, smaller building down the road from where it had been housed for years. The control room was smaller and there was no room for a studio audience. When Marty Robbins made his last appearance on my show in January, 1982, he had to be "cleared" by *PD* before being allowed to bring his guitar into the control room and do what he had been doing for over ten years with me. With no live audience ... and realizing I was miserable under the 'leadership' of the new program manager ... Marty was extremely sad. He sang for a couple of hours, but his heart wasn't in it. The excitement that normally accompanied Marty into the studio had fizzled. The air was filled with discomfort. Finally, my pal made some sort of excuse to cut his time short.

As he left the radio station that morning, heading back to

Nashville, he said, "Get out of here, Billy Boy! This gig ain't gonna work!"

A big fence with a locked gate was placed around the new studio building and there was no place to park the big rigs, should truckers want to drop by for a visit, as they had been doing regularly for over a decade. Besides, *PD* had let it be known that truckers would have to go through him in order to pay me a visit. It was easy to spot the fact that he was attempting to sever my connection with those very special people, the truckers!

To test his attitude, I made it a point to telephone *PD* around one o'clock in the morning a couple of times to get permission for truckers to be admitted through the locked gate. His response: "Don't <u>ever</u> wake me again, Mack, unless it's an emergency!"

Next, *PD* had the toll-free number to my show disconnected. The 800 Number was one of the first things I had demanded from Potash before I backed out on KRLD.

"No problems, Pal! You'll have your 800 Number for the truckers!"

Now, the toll-free phone number, like my patience, had been whacked!

While *PD* was in action with his hatchet, Warren Potash was nowhere to be found. I telephoned his house a few times, but he was always *"out of town"*, according to his wife, Marie.

Again, I was reminded that "Potty" had never forgiven me for accepting the job with KRLD, even though I had remained with WBAP. Every agreement Potash had made, in order to make me drop the *KRLD* offer, had been broken. I was stupid for not having the agreement drawn up by an attorney. Texas handshake agreements aren't worth a damned when it comes to a New York 'high-roller'.

What really added to my anger over the situation was the fact those who were a party to the agreements also turned their backs on me.

One supposedly good friend, Gary Hill, encouraged me to "stick with the team" and was selected as one of four people who were to help direct my show and make certain everything that had been promised me, in order to change my plans with *KRLD*, was delivered.

It just dawned on me: I haven't seen or heard from Hill in over twenty years, although he lives within thirty miles from my house.

Not long ago, I was asked to videotape some kind words about Gary, since he was being given a *tribute* in Dallas. I agreed to do so, and I did. I am told the videotape was played at the tribute, although there has never been a 'thank you' note from Hill.

A mutual friend informed me: Good old Gary still can't look you in the eye. He still feels awful about the way he failed to back you up when you were kicked out of WBAP."

Oh, well, what th' hell.

There were a couple of others who were to turn their backs on me when the chips were down, but they're not important. Besides, they were afraid it might cost them their jobs if they didn't bend with the boss.

Melinda Butler, a very sweet little lady who was the producer for my show … and a very good friend … told me, "Watch out for *PD!* He and Annie Gee are now 'very, very close' … and he has promised her your job!"

Annie Gee was working the all-night bit on weekends at the time, calling herself the "*Weekend Wonder Woman*". Melinda, who chummed around with Annie from time to time, was given "first hand reports" by Annie of the *whoopee* goings-on between her and *PD*.

Melinda said Potash was also becoming friendly with the 'Wonder Woman', according to Annie.

I was receiving daily reports from Melinda … who was receiving daily reports from Annie.

Funnsville!

One day, Melinda said: "You won't believe this! *PD* told Annie that you are going to be fired! Annie told me he said, 'Just think what this will do for your career, Annie? You're going to be given Mack's job!'"

He added: "Don't tell Melinda about us!"

Annie did!

It was a cold night in February, 1982, and snow was falling when Teddy and Doyle, the Wilburn Brothers, came to the locked gates of WBAP, wanting to visit with me. For some reason, there was no guard on duty that night as the Wilburns stood outside the fence in the cold. Since I couldn't leave the control room to attempt opening the gate and I realized Teddy and Doyle had the radio on in their car, I opened the mike and said, "Sorry, Wilburn Brothers, I can't let you in the gate. I don't have a key!"

A few days later, I received a call from *PD*, ordering me to meet with him in his office. As I walked in, he turned his bulky frame toward me and said, "Mack, you are fired. Our attorney is Phil Bishop. I've boxed up your things."

The reason for my getting axed, according to the grande leader: "Bill Mack divulged confidential radio station information *on the air!*"

That confidential info was my informing the Wilburn Brothers that the gates were locked!

Potash's reaction to the heavy press over my firing: "Talk with th' *PD!* That's <u>his</u> department! He's Mack's boss!"

Although thirteen years of all night broadcasting had been slugged by Potash and his axe-man, there was a feeling of relief in realizing I wouldn't have to be a part of the shoddy atmosphere any longer.

CHAPTER TWENTY ONE

Leaving WBAP after thirteen years was a shock. It had been the hub of my professional life and, prior to arrival of Warren Potash, had been pure enjoyment.

Melinda Butler and a couple of other people working at WBAP told me that *PD* was strutting around the hallways of the radio station wearing a big lapel button reading, "*I FIRED BILL MACK!*".

Firing me seemed to be an obsession with this guy, from what I was told. I received a tape from a couple of WBAP pals consisting of *PD* utilizing his interpretation of the voice of Superman, going into a weird spiel about firing me! I was told that he also had a bumper sticker placed on his car, reading "*I FIRED BILL MACK!*" However, my sources of voluntary information also told he removed the bumper sticker after some truckers blared down on him as he was driving to work one morning.

Striking a very happy note was a petition delivered to me that had been signed by hundreds of truckers, asking me to "get back on the air".

God bless 'em! The truckers have always been there.

PD left WBAP within months after my exit. Some said he was fired, others said he couldn't take the 'heat'. Either way, it was obvious that Warren Potash had hired him to do the dirty work and then shoved him out of the picture.

I wasn't suffering over my split with WBAP. I was remaining busier than ever. In May, 1982, I was asked to be the emcee for Bob Hope's 80th birthday blowout in Port Arthur, Texas, home of a hospital named after the super star. What an honor that this great man had chosen me. A private jet was sent to Dallas where Cindy and I, along with my friend Charley Pride and his sweet wife, Rozene, were whisked to Bob's shindig.

The birthday bash for Bob was a tremendous success, of course, with lots of important people on the scene, paying tribute to who, possibly, was the greatest comedian-entertainer of all time. After the party was over, Bob and his beautiful wife, Delores, excused themselves. Bob had been through a full day, playing golf and doing interviews, and was extremely tired. The rest of the bunch went to an after-the-party blowout.

As Cindy and I were mixing with the rest, Jim Batson, part of the Hope group, walked up to us, asking us to follow him. He eased us out a side door and took us to a small reception room where Bob and Delores were standing. They gave Cindy a hug and, as Bob shook my hand, he said, "Thank you, Bill, for being with me."

Shaking Bob Hope's hand will always be referred to as a most memorable experience. I'll always be that kid from Shamrock, Texas who feels a bit awestruck when I'm in the company of giants. I hope I never lose that feeling. There will never be a bigger giant than Mr. Bob Hope. God, I loved that man after meeting him! When he passed away recently, that special night in Port Arthur, Texas became even more important to me.

A dude named Terry Bean came up with the idea of "*A Tribute To Bill Mack*", held at *Billy Bob's Texas* on May 26, 1982. It was quite a compliment. Showing up for the 'tribute' were Ernest Tubb and his Texas Troubadours, Reba McEntire, Boxcar Willie, Rose Maddox, Tony Douglas and his Shrimpers, Mae Axton and several others. Also on hand were my special family members, including my mom and dad. Proceeds from the event were to go to charity. However, Terry Bean escaped with the proceeds before the show was over and I haven't seen the character since that night. Bean never returned my phone calls. I was told by his wife, who finally picked up on my telephone efforts, that " poor Terry needed the money."

BINGO has been called!

I was also keeping busy with *"Country Crossroads"*, the syndicated radio show I have hosted for several decades.

It was in 1969 that Jim Rupe with the *Radio-Television Commission* in Fort Worth approached me with an offer for me to co-host a radio program that would be syndicated through several radio stations throughout the United States. My co-host would be Leroy Van Dyke, the talented country singer. I liked the idea of hooking up with the program, which would be titled, *"Country Crossroads"*. It was to be a commercial free half-hour presentation consisting of country music, interviews with the top country stars, and religious overtones, something very different from the programming structure today.

In October, 1969, our first broadcast of *"Country Crossroads"* was set to air on 32 radio stations throughout the nation. Leroy and I were in Nashville for the grand kick-off.

We had no idea that *"Crossroads"* would soon be heard on over 800 stations, making it one of the most powerful syndicated radio shows in the world!

"Country Crossroads" has picked up many awards including the *"Angel"* Award; a gold medal from the *International Radio Festival* in New York; the *SESAC* Award; and was nominated for *Billboard Magazine's Radio Award for the Best Syndicated Country Music Program.*

In 1972, comedian Jerry Clower joined Leroy and me, adding strength to the show.

I was sad to see Leroy Van Dyke leave *"Country Crossroads"* after being with the show for several years.

My old friend Jerry Clower was funny, loud and loving. Jerry, who could come on strong with his comedy, and in real life as well, was misunderstood by some. As a fertilizer salesman out of Yazoo City, Mississippi, he had literally backed into show business when someone recorded one of his funny speeches at a gathering in Lubbock, Texas in 1971. The recording *"The Coon Hunt"*, would soon make it to *MCA Records* where Jerry was to become one of their biggest selling artists. He joined the *Grand Ole Opry* in 1972.

Clower wasn't known to be calm. He could be a bit overwhelming in his approach to just about any subject, leaving the impression he was high-strung to the point of being a loud intrusion to some of his peers

Several years ago, I received a telephone call from the *North*

American Mission Board informing me that Clower had been placed in a hospital in Georgia. They said he was suffering from fatigue and wasn't accepting any calls at the hospital. I thought I would call and check on his health, not expecting to talk with the man, himself.

Shortly after reaching the Georgia hospital and telling them I was Jerry's friend and wanted to check on him, I heard the familiar, "Whooee! Knock him out, John! Hello, Bill Mack! I love you!"

Jerry told me he had a strange thing happen to him. It seems he was doing a show in Georgia and after waking up in his hotel room, he suddenly couldn't remember if he had already performed the show or was to do it that night. "My mind just flipped out on me, Bill. The doctor thinks it's 'over-stress' or something like that. They are doing some tests and then I'll go home to Mississippi and rest up."

A few days passed and I was driving to WBAP to do my overnight show, listening to *ABC Radio News*. The announcement caught my attention: "Another *Grand Ole Opry* star has died."

Immediately, I thought it might have been Johnny Cash, since he had just been admitted to a Nashville hospital. Then came the more detailed information from *ABC*: "Country comedian Jerry Clower has died at a hospital in Mississippi ... of heart failure."

I was so shocked, I had to stop my car. Here was a man who was so full of life, gone. I loved Jerry Clower.

Today, *"Country Crossroads"* is still going strong on radio. Kirk Teegarten and his crew make it more enjoyable than ever as I sit down behind the mike. I am the single host on that very special radio program that has been such a treasured part of my personal and professional life for almost 35 years.

One of the greatest compliments of my life took place on October 15, 1982 when I was placed in the *Country Music Disc Jockey Hall-of-Fame* in Nashville. This is the honor-of-honors, presented by my peers. Here, again, I was so very thankful to God ... and to those who had made it all possible.

I was receiving radio offers from affiliates outside of Fort Worth and Dallas, but was determined to stay in Fort Worth. Cindy, of course, was there with the encouragement. She knew that although I was handling the split from WBAP very well, I needed to get back into broadcasting. I believe she was picking up on my boredom. In 1983, I accepted a job with KLIF, located in

Arlington, just outside Fort Worth. Dan Halliburton and his crew gave me complete freedom to do my own thing, and it was an enjoyable hook-up.

It was while doing the KLIF bit that I met Connie Francis, one of the most popular female singers of our time. We became very close friends and she took me into her confidence. Connie had made the move to Dallas and was going through a very tough era. Although she had plenty of money, her career had taken a slip because of her emotional anguish. She was raped at a Howard Johnson Hotel and her only brother had been murdered … sending her into a downward spin of depression, as would be expected.

I should mention here: Because of Connie's lawsuit against Howard Johnson, new lock assurances are now on the doors of hotels and motels all over the world.

I love Connie Francis, as does my wife, Cindy. She is a class act; a good person. I couldn't detect the mental problem because she was always smiling and laughing when we were with her. I did detect some hangers on who were taking advantage of her loving, giving nature. One disk jockey, in particular, had wormed his way into Connie's personal life, borrowing money with no intention of repaying. He was also utilizing her name value to open some doors that would have normally been closed to him.

I was aware of the fact Connie's dad, a very demanding force in her life, was putting pressure on her to drop those people who were surrounding her in Big D. I, too, told her she should drop the clowns, which she eventually did. She moved from Dallas to Florida where some more people were waiting for handouts.

When Cindy became ill, Connie telephoned from Florida. Seems she knew a doctor who specialized in the problem and wanted to "fly Cindy to Florida for a visit."

Thankfully, doctors in Fort Worth handled Cindy's health issue very well and there was no need to make the trip to Florida. However, Connie's call was a very important reflection of the caring nature of the lady.

Connie Francis is back home in New Jersey, now, and makes limited personal appearances. There are still those very sad memories, of course, but she has been freed of the fierce emotional thunder.

I decided to leave KLIF when what sounded like a golden opportunity came my way.

I was approached to do a radio show over *XERF*, that power-ful radio station in Ciudad Acuna, Mexico … just across the bor-der from Del Rio, Texas. This was a dream come true! Mr. Arturo Gonzales, a very important attorney in Old Mexico, was owner of what used to be a powerhouse radio outlet, which first grabbed my attention when I was a kid in Shamrock, Texas.

Although the transmitter was in bad shape, Mr. Gonzales had hired technicians to get the sleeping monster back on the air with plans calling for at least 250,000 watts. This would be five times the power of any radio station in the United States! The addition-al good news was that I would be pre-taping my shows in my home studio and shipping them by bus to Del Rio.

Wayne Martin, a very good radio sales person, decided he would like to get on board *XERF* with me. He, too, turned in his notice at KLIF. We had made an agreement with Mr. Gonzales to do the four-hour nightly show on a percentage basis. There would be no salary involved; we would receive the bigger part of profits accumulated during my show.

There was a lot of energy circulating, pertaining to the big news I would soon be doing my radio programs from "across the bor-der". A press conference was set up at *Billy Bob's Texas* and sever-al good pals were on hand to strengthen me as I talked about our plans with the mighty *XERF*. Tanya Tucker and her mother flew in from Las Vegas, at their own expense, to be with me. Boxcar Willie was on hand, along with several entertainers from the Fort Worth-Dallas area. Mr. Gonzales and his son, a pilot, flew into Fort Worth in their private plane for the big meeting with the press.

I laid it on the line: We were going to be doing a show out of Fort Worth that would be fed to the big mother in Old Mexico, blowing out a signal consisting of a quarter-of-a-million watts. The press seemed to be impressed, although there were a few questions.

Question Number One: "When will the transmitter be ready for you to begin these powerful radio shows?"

Answer: "Very soon. As a matter of fact, we will be broadcast-ing in the beginning with a limited signal of 50,000 watts until the transmitter is set to full power."

Question Number Two: "Will you be selling junk such as baby chicks, table cloths that have been spiritually blessed … and har-monicas … like in the 'old days' at *XERF?*"

Answer: "No. We will sell only quality merchandise. My partner, Wayne Martin, already has some important sponsors set up. (Big hand here for Wayne, who was smiling with excitement of things to come.)"

Several weeks went by without any progress with the transmitter in Mexico. I was sending tapes by *Greyhound Bus Lines* every day, but we could barely pick up the signal in Fort Worth. I attached all kinds of wires as antennas at my house in order to hear my big, big sound on *XERF*. Strangely, the strongest signal was when Cindy wrapped one of the antenna wires around her toe and held on to a doorknob.

The engineers on duty at *XERF* were having all kinds of problems. Undoubtedly, they couldn't comprehend the English instructions on the reels of tape they were receiving, normally shipped in four separate boxes. One morning we heard the <u>end</u> of the show played at the <u>beginning</u> of the program. They had placed Tape #4 on the playback unit instead of Tape #1! I came on the air with: "Well, we're just about to say goodbye to all of you fine folks ..."

That great radio entertainer, Wolfman Jack, who received his big break on *XERF*, kept assuring me, "Stay in there, Baby! The 'Big X' is gonna rise again!"

Meeting Wolfman Jack was a real thrill. This dude was a howling personality, even when he wasn't on the air.

When I picked him up at the DFW airport one night, he shoved his big body into my car and began smoking a cigarette. From time to time I would glance over to him and see his wild, weird eyes glaring at me whenever I passed under a streetlight. He was on his way to *XERF* for a Radio Reunion Special. All the way to the hotel in Dallas, he raved, "We gonna go out to th' *Big X* and lay some new noise on them cats, baby! Yeah! Ol' Wolfman Jack and '<u>Coyote Mack</u>' are gonna lay some midnight shine on them babies that like to wallow after midnight!"

Unfortunately, the grand old station never got back on line in power because of a combination of economical problems and politics, and we had to drop the program. I will always be grateful to Mr. Arturo Gonzales and his son, Sergio, for their belief in me. I am also grateful to Wayne Martin for his confidence.

Wolfman Jack passed away a few years ago. I've always thought we could have made a good team ... howling under the midnight moon at *XERF*, together!

I wasn't hurting, emotionally, because there was still lots of excitement in the air during this period in my life. There were many radio offers and I was also attempting to catch up on my lousy golf game. I had given some serious thought to getting into a new avenue of entertainment, record production. I had been approached by some very strong people to jump aboard the production train. After all, I had done a bit of producing and was sure I could make it work on a consistent basis. Besides, some of my old pals who had started out in broadcasting had moved into the record production business and seemed to be both, happy and wealthy.

Trouble was … I didn't want to move to Nashville, although I loved the old town and have a lot of very close friends in Music City U.S.A. There is too much Texas in my blood, I suppose.

One day I received a telephone call from *KXOL* in Fort Worth, making me an offer I couldn't refuse. This was one of the legendary affiliates in Cowtown that had exploited the likes of George Carlin, Norm Alden and several others. Now, they were playing country music and, although the ratings didn't reflect the fact, they had a tremendous, loyal listening audience.

Doing an early morning show, I received a good weekly paycheck from *KXOL*. Also, the station made "trade-outs" on anything I wanted … ranging from riding lawn-mowers to refrigerators! I had as much real fun at *KXOL* as I had ever enjoyed in radio. As mentioned, the radio station had a following as big as any I had worked at. Anytime there was a remote broadcast, you could expect a crowd. The *'XOL' fans were super-loyal!*

Ever since working at *KXOL*, I have had serious doubts about the rating systems that are the judges and juries of the radio survival game. Many sponsors informed me that *KXOL* pulled a bigger crowd for them than the other outlets.

One day, *KXOL* was sold to a gospel group that immediately dropped the country music format and switched to "religion".

For me, it was back to the golf course.

I was approached about doing a daily or weekly television show. One of the biggest firms in Dallas was willing to "take a chance" with me on TV. I turned them down when they casually uttered, "taking a chance". I simply didn't want to take any more chances, especially in the dog-eat-dog business of television. A daily show out of Dallas would be a bit perplexing, requiring too much time for too little money. Also, since there wasn't a mainstream of high-marquee talent available for entertaining on a daily basis, I was afraid it wouldn't work.

Looking back, I believe I could have done a television "Talk Show" and I might have enjoyed it. Trouble is, I have always considered radio to be a more "personal" avenue than television.

TV has always been more of a job, while radio has been a plaything with me. Therefore, radio should never sound like it's a job.

I can always tell by listening when an air-personality is 'under-the-gun' by his boss. He (or she) sounds like he is at work; on-the-job. I've always thought the real winners in broadcasting were those who never released a hint they were 'at work'. Arthur Godfrey always sounded like he was sitting beside me in my car when I listened to his shows while driving. Regis Philbin, one of my real favorites on television, never leaves the impression he's on-the-job. Therefore, you can relax with him; enjoy his company!

Might add: I also like Kelly, his beautiful and talented little sidekick. *Regis and Kelly* make a good team.

Recently, when a newspaper columnist was interviewing me, he mentioned that he always considered my show to be as much "talk" as any of the so-called talk shows, and I agreed with him. If I had someone hot on the telephone, whether it was a recording artist or just someone who happened to call in with something of interest, I held up the music.

When I was doing my WBAP radio show in the beginning, without the wadded commercial load, I considered it to be "*Talk-Music Radio*". The enjoyment was placing people on the air and checking their attitudes. Now, of course, I'm doing that very thing on XM Satellite Radio and it's truly more fun than ever.

During the time span when I was shiftless, with no demanding schedules to meet, I was back to writing songs, writing my news-paper/magazine columns and whacking at golf balls. However, I'm not the kind who can stay off-the-air for an extra long period of time. After all, I have been in radio since I was a kid.

One day, as I was sitting around the house, I received a telephone call from Ted Stecker, the program director with WBAP.

Ted, whom I will always consider to be one of the true professionals in broadcasting, got right to the point: "Bill, now that we have new management, would you be at-all interested in coming back to WBAP?"

I replied, "We could talk about it."

"Drop by tomorrow," said Ted.

I dropped by … and stayed awhile.

Bill and Lefty Frizzell

CHAPTER TWENTY TWO

Ted Stecker and I reached an agreement in 1988 that stated I would go back to the old midnight till 5:00 am shift on WBAP. There was a lot of publicity about my coming back on the scene. Stecker was a very honest program director and, to this day, I consider him among the best. He expected things to be done in a professional manner … and stood his ground against management if he believed he was correct in his direction of the programming on WBAP.

He wasn't the typical *'yes man'*.

One reason I was called back on the scene at the old station was because sales on the overnight show had dropped in a big way since my departure a few years earlier. The brigade of jocks handling the wee-hours bit just didn't connect with the audience and the commercial log was lagging.

I've always known that it takes a certain type of chemistry for an "air personality" to attach to those who are up during those so-called "ungodly" hours, listening to radio. A special 'styling' is required. Some say it's the voice, others say it's the 'honesty' or 'sincerity' of the individual who is behind the microphone. I honestly believe the radio host must communicate perfectly with those listening. The late night listener is completely different from those who utilize the radio while driving to and from work, checking traffic and news reports during the morning and afternoon hours.

Many of those who were destined to become big names in broadcasting rode the late-night shift before hitting the big marquees. Arthur Godfrey, who became the super personality on CBS Radio and CBS-TV over fifty years ago, was one of the original "all-night radio jocks". Larry King, who I personally believe is the best interviewer on television today, was a late-night radio host in Miami ... and very good at it. When he moved to the Mutual Radio Network, I was one of his biggest fans. I even placed a call to him one night back in the early 80s when he was interviewing my friend, Johnny Cash. And would you believe it? I was too intimidated to reveal my name!

Larry has the talent to "listen" to his guests. Most of today's radio and television talk-show hosts do too much blabbing, not enough listening. They seem to be of the opinion that they "own" the program and those seated in the hot seat or placing the phone calls to the show are at the owner's mercy.

Let me insert the fact that I also enjoy and admire Mark Davis' talk-program and Randy Galloway's radio sports show. Coincidentally, both of these exceptional talents are heard on WBAP!

There is no teaching method when it comes to doing "overnight radio". It's built-in. And if it's not built-in, it can make for a long, lonely night for both, the radio personality and the listener!

I've heard disk jockeys who are a whiz during the daylight hours, but put them on after the moon comes up and they flop. As I'm writing this, I am twisting across the dial and, at a little after 2:00 a.m., am bored to death with what I'm hearing! The jocks are either "pushing it", voicing at high speed like robots, or playing back-to-back music with little conversation.

I found out a long time ago that people want to hear the human voice during the wee hours, but they want it to be real.

My return to WBAP caught on very well and, before long, there were plenty of sponsors back on the ship. One reason was my very good sales rep, Sandra Johnson. Sandra ran an honest and professional game. She had both, sales knowledge and *class*: A most needed combination. She is also a beautiful lady.

To celebrate my return to WBAP, Sandra and Ted Stecker came up with the idea of me broadcasting from the *Opryland Hotel* in Nashville. Naturally, I was very excited about going back to Music City.

Accompanying me on the trip were Sandra Johnson and Robert

Shiflet, the WBAP public relations guy who had made all of the arrangements ... presumably. On our arrival at the *Opryland Hotel*, Shiflet told me there was a problem. "Things have fouled up, Bill! You don't have a room!" Then, in an act of mercy, he added, "But I was lucky enough to find you a room at another hotel *across town!*"

This tossed me into a state of shock! I was set to host a radio special at the *Opryland Hotel* and, according to the dynamic PR man, didn't have a room? Give me a two-dollar break! There was, undoubtedly, something completely haywire. Things like this just don't happen, accidentally! Normally, the public relations genius would gladly forfeit his room at the *Opryland Hotel* in order to preserve an atmosphere of tolerance for the guy set to host the radio show. Instead, Shiflet hauled me to a cheap rate hotel located miles from the *Opryland!* Adding to my fury was the fact I was left without the benefit of a car! Shiflet was very generous, though. He said, "We'll pick you up in a few hours for dinner!"

I didn't tell Sandra or Shiflet of my plans after being placed in the idiotic situation at the flimsy hotel. Instead, I telephoned my wife, Cindy, informing her I was catching a plane back to Fort Worth. She fully agreed, shouting, "Get back here!"

From that day on, Cindy would refer to Shiflet as, *"Shifty!"*

I made arrangements to fly out of Nashville. I had no intention of following through with the much heralded radio show.

While making plans to catch a return flight, I telephoned several people in Nashville, since I had set some plans to meet with them while in town, and informed them of what had happened. It was my call to bluegrass idol, Bill Monroe, that caused me to change my mind about flying back to Texas. Bill said, "Bill Mack, you're gonna stay here in Nashville! I want to see you! Now, promise me you will stay! I'll get you a room at the *Opryland Hotel!*"

I decided to cancel the return flight, although I was still highly ticked over the idiotic, "fishy" situation that the PR man had placed me in.

I did the radio show from the Opryland Hotel on Friday night. Several veteran country music acts made the scene that night, including Bill Carlisle.

"Jumpin'" Bill Carlisle was definitely from the old school of country music entertainment. His biggest hit was released in 1953.

It was titled, *"NO HELP WANTED"*. To make the happening a little more fun and exciting, Bill would jump high in the air while performing this song on the *Grand Ole Opry*. When he reached his eighties, I asked him if jumping while singing *"NO HELP WANTED"* wasn't a bit difficult to do at his age. He looked at me, laughed, and said: "I can still jump as high in the air, I just don't stay up there in the air as long as I used to!"

One night back in the 50s, Tillman Franks brought Bill Carlisle and The Carlisles to Wichita Falls where I booked them at the Wichita Falls Memorial Auditorium. This was back when Bill and his group were still members of the *LOUISIANA HAYRIDE* out of Shreveport, Louisiana and *"NO HELP WANTED"* was riding high in the charts. They played to a full house in Wichita Falls. Next night, I had them booked for an appearance in Frederick, Oklahoma, about one hundred miles from Wichita Falls, where they played to another big crowd, even though the weather was miserable. It was snowing and the temperature was about ten degrees above zero.

After the show was over, Tillman Franks and I headed back to Wichita Falls, wanting to get there before blizzard conditions set in, as had been forecast. Bill Carlisle and his three musicians were set to follow us as soon as the instruments and sound equipment had been loaded up in the trailer that was attached to Bill's Cadillac. This was before most bands utilized busses.

As Bill and his group were traveling the lonesome Oklahoma road, headed for Wichita Falls, there was a blowout on the *Cadillac*. Bill jumped out of the car and opened the trunk, only to notice he didn't have a jack! He waved a flashlight at every vehicle that passed him, but no one seemed interested in helping the stranded guitar picker. Remember, this was about midnight, it was snowing fiercely, and Bill was still dressed in his white stage cloths, complete with rhinestones! Oakies were not accustomed to seeing such a sight on a cold winter night!

Finally, a pickup truck stopped directly behind Bill's *Cadillac*. By now, it was two o'clock in the morning and the snow was blowing wilder than ever. A good old Oklahoma boy, wearing a cowboy hat and releasing regular wads of chewing tobacco into the snow, volunteered to help Bill out of his misery. He pulled a jack out of the bed of his pickup, shoved it under the car and, with Carlisle holding the flashlight, began pumping the flat wheel off the snow.

Bill informed me that the good old boy had nothing to say.

"The only time he opened his mouth was when he had a notion to spit his tobacco," he said.

Just as the Oklahoma citizen was loosening the bolts on the wheel, Bill decided to strike up a friendly conversation. "You like country music, do you?" He asked.

The Oakie spit a wad and grunted: "Yep."

Carlisle: "Ever listen to th' *Louisiana Hayride*, out of Shreveport?"

The Oakie spit again and mumbled, "Sometimes."

Getting a bit deeper into the matter of importance, Bill asked, "Ever hear '*NO HELP WANTED*', by Bill Carlisle an' th' Carlisles?"

Bill said the Oakie was a bit hesitant in answering, but finally spit a big splatter of tobacco in the snow and growled, "Yeah."

Carlisle proudly announced, "I'm Bill Carlisle! I'm th' guy who wrote and recorded '*NO HELP WANTED*'!"

The Oakie looked up at Bill, unloaded the final wad of tobacco on to Bill's boot and then twisted the lever that lowered the jack! After the flat flopped back onto the ground, the old boy from Oklahoma got up off his knees, tossed his jack back into the bed of the pickup, entered the cab and slid off into the icy Oklahoma night, leaving Bill standing in the snow, holding his flashlight!

"Guess he didn't like my song," laughed Carlisle. "We didn't git another car to stop 'til the sun came up. And then, I had to wave a twenty-dollar bill at 'em!"

Bill Carlisle, the loveable old pro, passed away in 2003 at the ripe old age of 95.

My little friend, Connie Smith, was also with me as a guest on the *Opryland Hotel* radio show.

I've known Connie since her first recording, *"ONCE A DAY"*, became a hit in the mid-sixties. I love Constance June, although our relationship has been a potpourri of diversified moods.

Connie, a beautiful lady, is a top-of-the-line singer. I consider her the best female singer of them all. She can belt a country song, a "pop" tune, a "rock" ditty or rip your heart out with a good old gospel favorite. Gospel is her choice of music and she handles these special songs with respect and dignity. When she sings *"HOW GREAT THOU ART"*, you expect the heavens to open! And when Constance takes a notion to sing my *"CLINGING TO A SAVING HAND"*, you can expect tears of rejoicing from the soul!

Connie is a very religious lady. She lived on the brink of fear, terror and thoughts of suicide before becoming a born again

Christian. Her dedication to God is real. There are no loopholes in her belief.

One night, Connie took me to Reverend Jimmie Rodgers Snow's church in Madison, Tennessee, on the outskirts of Nashville. Jimmie is the preaching son of the country music giant, Hank Snow. It was a Wednesday prayer-meeting service and I was the only man in the small group that had gathered for prayer. One of those in attendance was Alice Frizzell, Lefty's sweet little wife.

During the service, Reverend Snow asked everyone to bow their heads in prayer, inviting any backsliding sinners to make a walk to the alter for a special "gathering", where the laying-on of hands is a part of the ritual. There was no reaction. I presumed that all of the ladies in the small crowd had already set things right with the Lord. It was then that Reverend Snow got a little more personal as heads were bowed. He shouted, "If anyone here tonight isn't set right with God, raise your hand!"

No response.

Then, he shouted: "What about any <u>man</u> who is among us tonight? Is there any <u>man</u> who has strayed from the fold? Raise your hand!"

Since I was the only man in attendance, and feeling he was pin-pointing me, I raised my head and said, "I'm o.k.!"

Connie gave me a firm stare. Then, she couldn't hold back a giggle, making the scene even more traumatic!

Johnny Cash also attended Jimmie Snow's church for awhile.

One Sunday morning, Johnny made a walk to the alter and was kneeling in prayer when he felt a loving arm on his shoulder. He presumed someone was laying-on-the-hands, a common practice in the church. It was then that he heard a whisper: "Johnny, I wrote a song that you'll love! It fits your style just right!"

Johnny looked up at the old boy in total disbelief as the stranger added, "After this service is over, we'll go to my car an' I'll take my guitar and sing you th' prettiest damned country song you ever heard!"

I mentioned that Alice Frizzell, Lefty's wife, was also a member of Reverend Snow's church. Lefty had never attended.

One night, Alice returned home in tears. She had been to church while her hubby had chosen to stay at the house, drink beer and watch TV.

Noticing Alice's sadness, Lefty set his *Pabst Blue-Ribbon* on the table and asked, "Why are you cryin', Honey?"

Alice sobbed: "Reverend Snow says I need to divorce you, Lefty."

"Divorce me? Why in th' world would Reverend Snow say such a thang?"

Alice replied: "He says that since you don't attend church, you're sending us both to Hell!"

By this time, Lefty was holding Alice tightly in his arms. He said, "I guess I ought to call Brother Snow and talk with him."

"Oh, would you do that, Lefty? Would you please call Reverend Snow? Do it for me!"

Lefty asked Alice for the preacher's phone number and within minutes had Jimmie Snow on the line.

"Brother Snow, this is Lefty Frizzell!"

"Yes, Brother Frizzell! What a pleasure to talk with you! Can I be of service?"

Lefty said, "Well, Brother Snow, my little wife, Alice, came home in tears after attendin' your meetin' tonight. She tells me that you said she ought to divorce me."

Reverend Snow: "No, Brother Frizzell! I didn't tell Alice she needs to divorce you. I told her the Lord told me to tell her she should divorce you, since you never attend church services with her.

"The Lord told me to tell her that, Brother Frizzell!"

Lefty cleared his throat, swallowed a bit of his *Pabst Blue-Ribbon* and asked: "Well … did th' Lord also tell you that I'm gonna be over at your house in about ten minutes to kick yore ass?"

Alice remained Lefty's wife until his untimely death in 1975. He was 47.

Keith Whitley, a big fan of Lefty Frizzell, was also with me during my radio special at the *Opryland Hotel*. With him was his wife, Lorri Morgan. Little did I realize that Keith would die a few weeks later, at age 33. He was an alcoholic. I was told he mixed booze with tranquilizers. I'll always believe if Keith Whitley had not died, he would be sitting on top of the heap in popularity today. He was a tremendous talent and a very good friend.

Other guests on my *Opryland* radio broadcast included Johnny Russell and Johnny Paycheck. Johnny Russell and Johnny Paycheck have also passed away since that memorable night, I'm sad to say. Russell was one of the most gifted enter-tainers I've ever known. Paycheck was second-to-none, when it came to singing a song. Unfortunately, he couldn't handle the accompanying personal problems.

What a waste.

The next night in Nashville, Sandra, Shiflet and I went to the *Grand Ole Opry* where we had special guest passes to backstage. All in all, it was a good night. As is always the case when I visit Nashville, I had the blessed opportunity to visit with those special people who had been with the grand old show for years. Sad to say, many of those acts have passed on. The vets at the Opry have seemed like family to me for a long time. I treasure the memories and the friendship.

After running into Bill Monroe backstage, he shook my hand and asked me to "hang around a minute". Then, he went on stage and summoned me to "come out and take a bow" on the stage of the *Grand Ole Opry*, after laying some very complimentary words in my direction.

Can you imagine my feeling as I walked out on that special stage at the invitation of that great man? To this day, I still feel the "shakiness"! I've been told by several *Grand Ole Opry* veterans that "it's a natural reaction."

Following his *Opry* performance, Mr. Monroe took me aside and said, "The Bluegrass Boys and I have to leave in a couple of hours for an appearance up in the Midwest. Would you and your guests come over to my restaurant for a little while? I want to visit with you before we head out of town."

One could never refuse an invitation from the "*King of Bluegrass*" and, after bidding the *Opry* gang goodnight with a few hugs and kisses, Sandra, Shiflet and I headed for "*Bill Monroe's Restaurant and Show Place*". However, when we arrived at the door, we noticed there was a big sign in the window marked, *CLOSED*. I thought that perhaps I had misinterpreted what Mr. Monroe had said to me earlier at the Opry. As we were walking away, the door of the restaurant opened and James Monroe, Bill's very talented son, invited us in. "Dad will see you in a few min-utes. How do you like your steaks?"

"Aren't you closed?" I asked.

James said, "We're not closed to you, Bill Mack. You folks sit here at this table."

We told James how we wanted our steaks cooked, still trying to rationalize what was going on. Besides James, a waiter and the cook in the kitchen, we were the only people in *"Bill Monroe's Restaurant and Showplace"*. Suddenly, the lights dimmed a bit and we noticed the Bluegrass Boys setting up on the stage. Then, out walked Bill Monroe … and the music began! For about 40 minutes, Bill and his great band gave us a private show!

Sandra and Shiflet are still around as witnesses to what I consider being one of the supreme compliments in my life. Who else has had the honor of having Bill Monroe and his Bluegrass Boys entertain them with a <u>private</u> performance while they devoured the tasty steaks he had arranged to feed them?

We visited with Bill at the table for a few minutes following the show. Then, he had to rush out and board his bus for another appearance with his Bluegrass Boys somewhere far from Nashville.

The kind and thoughtful man *thanked us* for coming by!Bill Monroe was to give me many compliments and happy moments throughout the years. He even recorded my gospel song, *"Clinging To A Saving Hand"*, giving it that special "Monroe" touch.

When Bill passed away September 9, 1996 at the age of 84, it was almost impossible to accept. He was a very special man.

Ted Stecker, the program director who had done such a good job for the company, left WBAP and moved to Chicago. He was replaced by a guy named Tyler Cox. Honestly, I never considered Cox to be a *replacement* for Ted. Cox was more *in-frame* with most of the other directors of programming of that era. Obviously, he didn't care for *traditional* country music, the type I was featuring on my program. One day, Tyler met me in the hall and said, "I'm hearing a lot of *Hank Williams* music on your show. Do you think you might be playing too much of old Hank?"

Almost certain that Tyler seldom listened to my program and that someone else, possibly management, had told him to approach me, I replied: "Name me the title of <u>one</u> of the Hank Willliam's tunes you've heard me play, Tyler."

Subject dropped.

Several years later, when "BLUE" became a big hit, Tyler caught me in the hallway at our new location, smiled and said, "I'm hearing you play a lot of the lady singing your song, 'BLUE', Bill."

I returned the smile and said, "You ain't heard nothin', yet! I'm gonna lay a lot heavier on that one, Tyler!"

Subject closed.

After working with me for a couple of years, Sandra Johnson was replaced by a young lady from the San Antonio area named Mindy Baker. Everything seemed to be in order ... except for the fact Mindy simply did not strike me as having any knowledge of country music. She seemed to tolerate what I was doing on radio because it was making money for her and the radio station, but it was obvious that her thoughts toward traditional country music didn't consist of high rankings.

One year, we were attempting to book a guest star for the big *Mid-America Trucking Show* in Louisville, Kentucky. We always brought in big names to sit at the WBAP booth and sign autographs. Most of those stars were "traditional country" artists, those the truckers wanted to meet.

I really knew we were in trouble when Mindy asked, "Why don't we get Patsy Cline?"

Patsy had been dead for over thirty years!

Another time when Mindy's lack of country music knowledge caught my attention was when I was doing a remote broadcast from a truck stop in Hillsboro, Texas and Willie Nelson decided to drop by and visit with me.

Willie was dressed in his normal summertime garb consisting of shorts, a well-used T-shirt and tennis shoes. As he sat down at my desk, Mindy attempted to "chase the scummy looking dude away!"

Even she laughed about this bit, later.

Certain that WBAP would be broadcasting the all-important *Texas Rangers* baseball games, as it had for years, the radio station paid a ton of money in order to move to Arlington, Texas, home of the Rangers ... and closer to Dallas. I was told John Hare, the WBAP bigwig, had made it a point to have his office set to overlook the new *Ballpark-In-Arlington*, across Interstate 30.

As Cindy and I were driving around the new ballpark one day, we noticed *KRLD* chiseled in stone on the wall of the huge structure. *KRLD* was the strongest radio competition for WBAP and I had a strange feeling they may have snuck in and ripped the *Rangers* from the paws of WBAP. I told Cindy, "That's not a hamburger joint they're putting in there."

Mindy Baker kept assuring us, "There's no way *KRLD* can lift the Rangers from WBAP! We have the deal locked up!"

Just before WBAP made the move to Arlington, an important staff meeting was called at the old offices on *Broadcast Hill* in Fort Worth. Presuming it was a sort of "farewell to the hill" get-together, Cindy went with me to the meeting. Immediately after entering the hallways, you could almost smell funeral flowers as John Hare bawled out the news: "The Rangers are going with *KRLD!*"

Tyler Cox, the program director, took me aside and whispered: "Just think! The *Rangers* games won't be running overtime into your show anymore!"

Somehow, I didn't feel Cox's *happy* statement was from the heart.

Today, the grand office that was constructed for the workings of Mr. Hare, overlooks the beautiful *Ballpark-In-Arlington* and the proud radio call-letters, *KRLD*.

Shortly after moving to the new studios in Arlington, I informed Tyler Cox that I needed help with the telephones. Since my beginning year with the station in 1969, WBAP had provided someone to answer the many phone calls that came in nightly. For some reason, the radio station hadn't found that that bit of help to me necessary since my return. I told Cox that my son, Billy, was available and could do a good job. Billy was about 16 years old, at the time, and was on summer break.

Tyler said, "Let me think it over and see if it fits our payroll."

Several days later, Cox handed me the good news: "The station is willing to hire Billy, but not for the entire five hours of your show.

"We are willing to let him work three hours per night. His pay will be five dollars per hour!"

Big '*B-A-P* deal!

Billy did work for a few weeks, in order to learn the game of broadcasting, but decided the "pay didn't quite fit the hours"!

I totally agreed.

I received a telephone call immediately after doing an appearance for WBAP at the Walcott, Iowa trucking show in 1996. My informant said, "Did you know WBAP flew the '*Trucking Bozo*' into town while you were doing the job for them in Walcott? They discussed the possibility of his taking over your show!"

The Bozo was supposedly my competition at the time, doing a radio show geared to the truckers and running at the same hours my program was aired on WBAP.

I was in the swimming pool when the call came in. After hanging up from my informant, I immediately telephoned John Hare, asking him what had happened, why they had called Bozo to my back.

At first, Hare denied having any knowledge of the news. Then, after I challenged his honesty, he admitted Bozo had been in town ... but not to discuss replacing me on the air!

After stating I knew he was "hiding the truth", Hare uttered a nervous laugh and said, "Tyler Cox really mishandled this!" He had been caught in an embarrassing lie, handling it like a kid who had been snapped stealing cookies.

After slamming up the phone from Hare, I received telephone calls from Cox and Mindy Baker, both saying something on the order of "Bozo just came to the radio station for a visit! We didn't ... and never would ... offer him the opportunity to replace you, Bill! Bozo could never replace you!"

My reaction: "Why did you fly him in? Did you want to take him to *Six Flags Over Texas*?"

After hearing the dishonest bit about Bozo, I would never trust Hare again and it added more distrust in my already tarnished feelings toward Mindy Baker.

Tyler Cox wasn't important.

Quite some time after the so-called "Bozo Incident", I was informed he had been flown into Arlington to discuss the possibility of him taking my place since it was almost a certainty I would be retiring after winning the Grammy and making the extra loot with my song, "BLUE".

My very simple question was: "Why didn't they ask me if I was about to retire?"

Let me mention: I don't place any blame on *The Trucking Bozo*. Flying to Texas in order to possibly take over my show wasn't his idea! He is a very talented man on the microphone and he has more than his share of listeners. Most important, Bozo is a very special friend.

"Th' Boze" should have been placed in the *Country Music Disk Jockey Hall-Of-Fame* years ago, a firm project now being pursued

by those who respect his tremendous talent and appreciate the many contributions he has made to the industry via his outstanding radio programs.

In 1996, The *Midnight Cowboy Trucking Network* was formed, allowing my show to be fed to several different radio stations throughout the nation and it was a very good 'hook-up'. The station had also hired Eric Harley as *producer* for my show. Eric did a good job and handled the phone calls.

Larry Scott, a disk jockey veteran for many years, was also hired to co-host the show. Unfortunately, the station didn't keep Larry on the program for long.

With the extra heavy commercial content and "features", the show was losing its personal touch. No longer was there a chance to chat in-depth with the audience or guests on-the-air, as I had done for so many years.

Over commercialism had taken over and I simply didn't want to continue with the radio show in the direction it was going. Also, the station was restricting some very important recordings by not allowing the play of any *ASCAP* licensed songs. It was a move to cut expenses ... but it also wiped out some strong recorded material. This was the only time in over thirty years that "restrictions" were creeping in and, with the dropping of *ASCAP*, it was most obvious that plans for the future of my show did not include music!

I was receiving so much mail pertaining to the fact the old show "just wasn't the same", because of "too many commercials", that I decided I would exit WBAP when my contract expired December 31, 2000.

I informed Keri Littlefield, the manager of the radio station, that I did not plan to extend my contract after January 1, 2001. I did, however, agree to lay over for three additional months, until the end of March, immediately after appearing at the *Mid-America Trucking Show* in Louisville, Kentucky. This was, presumably, a transitional period, allowing Eric Harley to take over the show after my exit. Problem was, I wasn't allowed to mention the fact I was leaving until mid-March, only two or three weeks before I was set to walk out!

There was no big going-away party held for me as I exited after my final broadcast, representing over 32 years with the company. The farewell feast was made up of bagels, muffins and one bottle of champagne for those who were kind enough to drop by for a friendly goodbye.

Oh, by the way. John Hare, the boss, was nowhere to be found … and I'm yet to receive a note of farewell or best wishes for the future from the big wheel-hoss. And that, I suppose, represents … in a nutshell … the "feel" of some of those who have been placed in avenues of guidance for much of today's radio.

True story:

The last time I saw John Hare was months before I decided to break with WBAP. It was a Sunday when Cindy and I had made a short drive to the radio station to pick up a big package that had been dropped off for me by a trucker. It was a huge basket filled with fresh peanuts!

Walking through the lobby was John Hare. He nodded a greeting and then noticed I was carrying the gob of peanuts. "What 'n hell is that?" He asked.

I didn't even slow down as I responded: "It's payday, John!"

I had known for years that with super technology bringing forth almost unbelievable creations in audio and video, it was inevitable that radio would eventually rise from the droll grave where it had been placed. Radio had allowed itself to become unbelievably staid at most outlets. If the listeners wanted music, AM could no longer compete with FM in quality. Thus, the gates were opened for the *"Talk Radio"* format on most AM stations, instead of music. Rush Limbaugh and the likes had replaced most music jocks on the AM affiliates. And, of course, news and sports still had a home on AM.

The listening audience is more finicky, nowadays. And they can afford to be choosy!

Enter *"Satellite Radio"*, a digital sound that can now be heard in vehicles, in the home … everywhere! *Satellite* radio allows the listener to channel in his favorite brand of music, his favorite news people, his sports and his preachers without having to "touch the dial" between the tip of Florida to Canada, from Maine to Old Mexico. And best of all, satellite radio is not crammed with commercials and fizz that isn't fit to be heard. There are 100 channels to choose from, everything delivered in perfect digital sound. Best of all, it is programmed by caring people!

I must admit that Keri Littlefield, the manager of WBAP, made some fairly good offers in order to get me to stay with the station I had been with for over 30 years ... but I was determined to walk into the excitement of the future in broadcasting. However, it wasn't an easy walk. After telling Keri that I was hooking up with *XM Satellite Radio*, she hit the roof. She growled, "You can't sign with *XM!*"

Without giving forethought, I told her I had already made a deal with *XM*. This was a costly statement. Within a few days, WBAP's New York attorneys had filed a *Breach of Contract* suit against me! Even though my contract was completed, the radio station was attempting to force me to sign an extension!

I had to hire an attorney to defend me from a broadcast facility that had allowed my radio show to become an over-commercialized piece of crap. There was no room for in-depth interviews and by dropping *ASCAP*, the music licensing establishment, there was the indication music would also be dropped, although programming and management had assured me that "dropping the music will never happen!"

Shortly after I had pulled out of the WBAP parking lot for the last time, all music was dropped on the "all-night program".

Soon, the newspapers headlined the news, *"ACCORDING TO WBAP ATTORNEYS, BILL MACK CAN NO LONGER USE THE HANDLE, 'MIDNIGHT COWBOY'!"*

The WBAP outfit thought they were really punishing me with the final punch by claiming they owned all rights to the words, *Midnight Cowboy*, a name I had utilized for over 30 years; a handle suggested by a trucker the first night I hit the midnight airwaves in 1969. I was the "Midnight Cowboy" years before *Capitol Cities* out of New York had taken control.

Really, I had no use for *"Midnight Cowboy"* any more. My agreement with the good people with *XM Satellite Radio* had placed me in a much more comfortable and enjoyable position. I would now be heard during the daylight hours ... as well as early evening, during "repeats" ... via satellites placed "high-in-the-sky".

Happy to say, I was about to become *The Satellite Cowboy!*

Bill's induction into the *Country Music Disk Jockey Hall of Fame* in Nashville in 1982. Presented by Chuck Chelman.

CHAPTER TWENTY THREE

I've been asked so many times: "What would you change if you had the chance to live your life over?"

That's an easy one to answer: I would spend more time with my kids. All of my children are adults now, but I constantly remind myself of how much precious time was wasted because I had become so involved in my professional life that I neglected my son, and my three beautiful daughters. Oh, they had plenty to eat, they dressed in clothing reflecting the fact they weren't beggars, and they all had their private little rooms, complete with television and video recorders. Eventually, they would have their own cars ... demonic bits of systematized marvels on four wheels that I would come to fear.

Yes, I've been blessed with three beautiful daughters and one very good looking son ... and I love them very, very much. Important thing here is the fact they all know both parents *love them.*

Debbie is the first born. Her mother is Jackie, my first wife. Jackie was very caring and loving to Debbie, making proper upraising a strong priority, which is most obvious in Debbie's attitude toward life. I am well aware of the fact that my splitting with Jackie caused tremendous pain to Debbie. However, she is a survivor; a beautiful person with a loving heart.

Misty, Billy and Sunnie are the children of Cindy and me. As I have mentioned several times, Cindy is the perfect mother. She is always <u>there</u>, when needed … and which is often! Her tolerance level is unmatched, thank God!

I've heard it mentioned, so many times, that children of people in entertainment, *show business*, are robbed of normal family happiness. I prefer to totally disagree with that statement, since I know many offspring of entertainers who have somehow managed to be happy <u>and</u> normal. Again, though, I believe my special four could have been much happier had I simply taken more time to show a deeper interest in their youthful activities. Problem was, I didn't realize at the time that I <u>wasn't</u> being the average dad.

He has never mentioned it to me nor to anyone else I am aware of, but I believe Billy may have been innocently neglected most by me. He is my only son, and I realize that I should have done more of those things *good dads* are noted for. We have fished together (once). I was most embarrassed because he had to teach me how to utilize the rod-and-reel. I believe he was about 10 at the time. We were in Branson, Missouri where I was set to appear at the *Boxcar Willie Theater*. Boxcar had brought the fishing gear to the lodge where we were staying, insisting that we take advantage of the beautiful lake nearby.

Neither Bill nor I caught any fish that day, but it was extremely nice.

I wish I had taken him to the lake several times. I'm certain we would have developed a more positive father/son relationship. I'm not so certain I would have ever become a good fisherman, though. I've never been drawn to fishing holes. Someone, I've forgotten who, told me one time that I didn't have the patience needed for the catching of the slimy little creatures, and I believe that might be a fact.

I've also failed to take my son hunting. One of my neighbors said, "You haven't really been a caring dad, until you take your boy hunting!" Here, again, is something I've never been attracted to. I'm not in that crowd you see regularly on television, condemning folks for wearing leather and eating meat. It's just that the killing of an animal, or bird, is not my cup of tea.

Here, again, is a matter I should have approached with my son. Could be, we would have had some great fun together at a hunting lease.

Of course, it's not too late to take Billy fishing and hunting, if he decides he would like to make the excursions. I'm not so sure I would be a good hunting or fishing companion, though.

I am certain of one thing: I wouldn't catch any fish.

Another thing of importance: I've heard several men say they find it difficult to say, "I love you", to their sons. That's never been a tough thing for me to do. I take the time, regularly, to tell Billy how much I truly love him. It's a natural statement.

Some of the genuine moments in my life have been with my son. Like all boys, including myself, when I was his age, he has had his share of stressful and downright ridiculously bad days and nights (mostly, nights) of uncalled-for activities, but he's always managed to re-group, and make me proud. A lot of the re-grouping, however, must be credited to his beautiful, loving mother. Cindy is the epitome of goodness and understanding as a wife, and mom, and I must admit there are many, many times when I'm a much bigger problem to her than any of the kids. As a matter of fact, my daughters and son have grown up much more maturely than their dad.

I also know they must have checked out many of my shortcomings. Perhaps they have learned a bit from my obvious weaknesses.

I certainly hope so.

Another important area where I know I have failed tremendously is in church. I've been weak in encouraging Sunday school attendance to my kids; something I know is so needed. This, I suppose, is where I place an overwhelming amount of blame on myself. I am certain that the church is a most important area ... where there is hope. Without God's help, I honestly don't see any easing of the terrible happenings that are occurring today. I am aware of the fact that *strength* for our youth should begin at home. However, my belief is that without God in the home, very little *strength* can be found.

Allow me to mention here that all of my children are Christians, and we do attend church. I just wish I had been a better leader toward God and the church for my babies to rely on. Of course, it is also my belief that there is an opportunity to change courses and attitudes with the help of our Good Lord, if we make a firm decision to do so.

I want to insert here: One of the most moving and loving moments I have ever witnessed took place on a special Easter Sunday when my daughter, Sunnie, took our precious Cody, my baby grandson, to the alter of our church and dedicated him to

God. When you experience something so wonderful as this, you rapidly realize it is a blessing of *hope*.

There is absolutely no fear in my mind, pertaining to the future of my grandson.

Now, there is Brittany Ann, my granddaughter, who is five-years-old, as I write this, and is, without a doubt, one of the most gorgeous little creatures I have had the pleasure to *snuggle* in my arms. And we *snuggle* regularly!

Then, there is Nick, my *first, wonderful* grandson. His parents have instilled the perfect ingredients of love in him, and he is one of the finest young men I have ever known. He is also a very sharp hombre! I am so proud of him, and he knows I love him very, very much.

Might add: My daughters also consider Nick to be a very handsome dude!

I presume you have noticed by now that I strongly believe *beauty* and *good-looks*, run in my family!

Allow me to rapidly insert that I now have a gorgeous daughter-in-law, April. When Billy married this very precious creature, he presented his mother and me with a true blessing. God, she is special!

April and I are very close.

Adding to that special blessing is Julio, my latest grandson, whom Cindy and I love dearly. Julio is not only *good-lookin',* he is also super-sharp!

Then comes the inevitable: "Do you want your kids to be in country music?"

This question, of course, brings many thoughts into focus in my mind. First, there is nothing wrong with being in country music as entertainers. Fact is, though, it is difficult to point to true happiness in entertainment, in general. Divorces are as common as guitars, and the reasons are, basically, temptations and time-away-from-home. Most of the time, it's the absence from home that brings on the temptations. Now, we all know that temptations are going to occur to all of us. Whether you're a teacher, a preacher, a plumber, a trucker, it doesn't matter. There will always be the temptations. It's the yielding to the temptations that brings on the hurt and the splits in most cases, and there are more temptations in entertainment than just about any other frame in life. The reason for this being the simple fact that most stars, male and female, are absolutely idolized by the masses.

Of course, everyone knows the money in country music entertainment is also very good, if your name has any value via radio, television and hit records. Naturally, many people are of the opinion that country stars have it *"made-in-the-shade"*. Believe me, it ain't as easy as it looks, most of the time. Like trucking, teaching and plumbing, entertaining the masses can also become an uncomfortable chore. After all, it's a job!

Then, there are the drugs and the booze.

The reason so many tabloids dwell on the subject of booze and drugs in entertainment is simply because there is a strong combination of booze and drugs in entertainment!

Not long ago, a very well known country singer told me that it was almost <u>impossible</u> for him to walk out on that big stage and face those screaming, yelling look-a-likes, without something to ease him. Preferably, something that comes on strong, but will get you tossed in the city jail should the local fuzz or the feds find it in your possession.

The star said," I hate to admit it, but I've been on the stuff for years. I'm not hooked, I just need it to calm me down before a show."

The fact he does approximately 300 shows per year, and needs a "lift" before every gig, is an indication he is, indeed, <u>hooked</u>. Trouble is, he doesn't slow down long enough to take inventory of the fact the tours have taken their toll on him. He looks drawn and ragged, but the pretty girls on the front row could care less. To them, he's a handsome hunk!

Let me again insert the honest truth that the majority of the big names in country music are strictly *against* the use of drugs and alcohol abuse. Several have had experiences with narcotics and/or booze, but realized that it was a dead-end street, and had the good sense to halt.

The country music entertainment neighborhood is fairly close-knit. Practically everybody knows *everybody else* and what *everybody else* is doing. They're well aware of their co-stars' sins and their habits, and some have witnessed tough drug and alcohol abuse in action; a few seeing their closest peers die while under the influence.

Back to the initial question ... would I want my children to become a part of the country music industry:

I would certainly encourage it, if they could find the happiness with real friends such as I have been blessed with down through the years, a treasured bunch of them living in Nashville.

Nashville has been my 'second home' for over 50 years. I have experienced the love, encouragement and excitement generated there by some loving, caring people ... many of them referred to as *'giants'* in entertainment.

I am genuinely proud of our country music industry because I am certain it will always reflect *heart* and *soul* in the lyrics and music it releases for millions to absorb and enjoy.

Responding to what makes up a perfect country song, someone, somewhere, once put it perfectly: *"Ain't nothing that hurts better than a good old hurtin' song!"*

TRUCKERS

As long as I can remember, truckers have been a very important part of my life. I have had the opportunity to become acquainted with this special breed of people on both, a personal and professional level.

It used to be that truckers were regarded as traveling rednecks. The image of the driver was a big, not-too-bright hombre with dirty fingernails and multi-day growth of beard, sitting at the counter of a greasy spoon café while wolfing down a bowl of chili. Now, times have changed drastically, as has the attitude toward the trucker. True, you may still find a few who run close to this rumpled description, but in most cases, the 'knight-of-the road' is among the most intelligent crowd in today's sophisticated society. He (or she) probably knows more about governmental issues blasting out of the nation's capitol than you do. You can also rest assured that he knows more about what should be done to ease the problems associated with the economic situation than the average man on the street.

Don't get him on the subject of fuel prices unless you're prepared to spend a few minutes listening to a well-informed oratory. And he's not going to back down from his stand on the issue!

I keep referring to "he", when discussing the trucker. This is simply a matter of habit. We're finding more ladies behind the wheel, maneuvering the big rigs, than ever before. She may be cute and dainty, but she can handle that truck as well, if not better, than some of her male brethren.

I've also found the trucker to be among the most caring people I have ever known.

Following the Oklahoma City bombing, the haulers were among the first to volunteer their services. When a tornado or earthquake occurs, you can rest assured the truckers will be their with their rigs, more than willing to get the goods to those caught up in the catastrophe … most of them expecting no reciprocation for their efforts.

I have personally witnessed the giving, caring nature of these special people.

Back in the early 70s, I announced on the air the sad fact that one of my young listeners, who telephoned nightly, was battling leukemia. I referred to her as 'Darlin' Debbie', mentioning that she was a very sick little girl, although barely past ten years old. Of course, I made no mention that she probably had less than six months to live.

Debbie would telephone me and I would chat with her on the air. She always talked about her dreams for the future, closing every conversation with, "I'm going to get well very soon, Mr. Bill!"

I found out that the doctor and hospital costs for Debbie's parents were astronomical, and thought it would be a good idea to have a *"Darlin' Debbie Blowout"* to help ease those expenses.

I called several country music performers and bands in the Fort Worth-Dallas area, arranging to get them to donate their time and talent for the *'Debbie'* event. I can't remember one single act refusing the invitation. I also called an automobile dealership located just off one of Dallas' most highly traveled interstates and arranged to use their huge parking lot to accommodate what I hoped would be a crowd. Then, I started announcing on my show that we were set to have the "big show for little Debbie" and that I hoped some of the truckers would stop by for awhile that night.

When the warm summer night arrived and I drove up to the automobile dealership, I was absolutely astonished. Had they not been holding a parking spot for me near the makeshift stage, I would have had to park blocks from the area where the show was to be presented.

Immediately, I noticed there were literally <u>hundreds</u> of rigs in all sizes and shapes parked in the area near the automobile dealership, and on both sides of the interstate!

Little Debbie had been released from the hospital for a few hours, long enough to enjoy the tribute being paid to her by such caring, loving people. As she sat in her special chair on the stage while the entertainers performed in her honor, I saw hundreds of truckers, male and female, pushing money into the hands of those taking up the donations.

Thousands of dollars were raised that night and when I handed the microphone to Debbie, giving her a chance to thank all of the good people who had made "her night" so special, I watched those truckers as they sobbed unashamedly under the bright lights in the parking lot.

It was only a few weeks later when Darlin' Debbie died. That night, as I announced her death on my radio show, I received dozens of telephone calls from those special haulers, many taking her passing very personal.

I also heard more weeping.

More recently, when another youngster, named James Lee Henry, was detected as having cancer, the truckers were again on standby. While the six-year-old dandy was receiving chemo treatments and blood transfusions at *Cook Children's Hospital* in Fort Worth, dozens of toys began arriving at our post office for James and other kiddos who were in that very good medical center. Money was also sent by drivers, after realizing there would be an extra financial strain placed on James Lee's family.

Incidentally: James Lee Henry has become *super-special* to Cindy and me. This little fellow has a courageous heart and an over-abundance of strength. He is surrounded by total love from his family and everyone who has the opportunity to know him.

James Lee has allowed us to be a part of his life, and it's been a rewarding venture.

Cindy and I feel very blessed in knowing ... and loving ... this fine little gentleman.

Most certainly, the gifts from truckers presented happiness to James Lee Henry and the other children who were isolated to the hospital during the Christmas season, but the thoughtfulness of those good people also instilled a completely new attitude in Cindy and me. We were witnessing unrestricted care and love as we had never seen before. And this "giving" was from people within an industry where money was sometimes "tight" because of high fuel prices and reciprocation was limited.

There is something within the mainstream of most trucking people that creates concern for others! It's *built-in*! And this was again obvious when my darling little pal, Linda Plowman Fikes, was caught by cancer.

Linda Plowman, who is one of the most talented singers God ever created, openly discussed the importance of *lady drivers* getting those important breast cancer tests after her doctor presented her with the dreaded news that she was facing surgery and chemo treatments.

Immediately, the calls came piling in from truckers, informing Linda that she was now on their gigantic "prayer-list". Linda also received gobs of personal messages from some wonderful people, folks she had never met, instilling confidence, love and hope.

See why I place truckers in a special spot?

During my thirty years doing the 'all night' bit on radio, I received countless gifts from the truckers. They would stop at the radio station just long enough to hand various items to the guard and then rush back into their rigs in order to get back on the road. Some would visit with me on my program for awhile, but most times they wouldn't even leave their names while dropping off their 'goodies'. They were giving, with no strings attached; not even expecting a mention of their names, or what they had done, on the radio.

I'll always remember the giving nature of a huge hunk who went by the name of Big Red.

Big Red made it point to telephone me every morning while on the road, or from his home in Fort Worth. One morning as I was leaving the radio station after doing my show, I noticed a big rig parked near the entrance to the station, it's engine idling. It was then that I noticed Big Red running toward me with something in his hand. Since it was still dark outside, I couldn't focus in on whatever it was he was holding, but did notice it was squirming.

Big Red was sobbing as he handed me a tiny, fidgety monkey!

"I want you to have this, Bill," he sniffled. "He's the cutest, sweetest little creature in the world! He's just like a baby to me, but I can't take him with me on the road … and there is no one to watch over him at my house!"

258

He added: "Be good to th' little feller!"

As I stood there, speechless, holding the monkey, Big Red ran back to his truck and spread gravel as he whizzed away.

I was single at the time, but took my 'gift' to my apartment. Since I didn't know what to feed a monkey, I offered it several bits from my pantry and the fridge. It jumped around on the furniture and climbed up my drapes, completely ignoring the food I laid out for it on my kitchen floor. Undoubtedly, Big Red had given the little fellow his final meal, as far as he was concerned, before shoving it into my hands.

I didn't sleep well that day because the monkey was chattering and jumping all over the apartment. He managed to pull the drapes loose, and left bits of his natural droppings all over the furniture and the floor!

Two days went by and my apartment was a shambles. I noticed Big Red hadn't telephoned during this trying time and I was certain he was hiding out in his rig somewhere. He knew I would demand he come back and retrieve his *gift* to me, should he make his regular call.

I decided I would put an ad in the classified section of the Fort Worth *Star-Telegram*, our newspaper, announcing I would be happy to give the monkey to <u>anyone</u> who was willing to take it. Of course, I also wanted the assurance that it would be given a good home.

The very day my ad ran in the paper, I received a telephone call from a lady who was anxious to see the little creature. After giving her instructions on how to reach my apartment, she said she would be over in less than an hour.

When the lady arrived and I introduced her to what I thought would be something she was seeing for the first time, she turned white and screamed: "It's him! It's him!"

At first, I didn't know whether she was referring to the monkey or to me.

Holding the little monster tightly in her arms, she said, "Oh! I can't thank you enough! My husband is going to be so very happy!"

I wasn't interested in her reason for making such an exclamatory statement, but she wanted to share the good news with me.

"I gave this little darling to my husband as a birthday gift a few weeks ago and he was absolutely crazy about it. And then, a few days ago, it got out of our house in the middle of the night and ran away! One of us accidentally left the back door open!"

Kissing on the mini-ape, she purred, "I don't know how in the world it ever got this far from our house, but I want to thank you for finding him! And my husband, who is a truck driver, will be so thrilled when he gets back home tonight!"

Thanking me again, the lady walked to her car as the nervous little creature squirmed, screeched and pulled at her hair.

Next morning during my radio show, I received a call from Big Red. It was short and to the point: "Thanks a hell of a lot!"

Then came the click.

One of my very first sponsors on the midnight 'til dawn show was a product called, *Superderm*. It was an ointment utilized for the treatment of hemorrhoids, manufactured by Cas Walker out of Knoxville, Tennessee. Cas bought time on my program because he had heard I had a lot of truckers dialed in nightly … and that truckers, seated in their rigs most of the time, had a long history of serious bouts with hemorrhoids.

Cas would fly into Fort Worth to record his commercials, praising the fact that *Superderm* would bring comfort from itching, burning "piles", immediately after applying.

Don Harris, possessing one of WBAP's better voices, was given the job of producing the commercials. It was his added assignment to correct Cas when it came to the word 'piles', asking him to please utilize 'hemorrhoids', instead.

"I had to take the scissors and literally cut out the word, 'piles' from the reel of tape … and then splice in 'hemorrhoids' after taking Mr. Walker to the airport in order for him to catch a flight back to Knoxville. It took me a full day to whack 'piles' out of those sixty-second spots!" Said Don.

He didn't want to correct Cas too often, since he was the first sponsor to lay down some big loot on my show.

Since *Superderm* was one of the very few products aired on my show during those beginning months, it was obvious when one of the sixty-second commercials hit the airwaves, proclaiming its soothing effects to the burning, itching disorder. And, since it was selling so well, Cas Walker bought extra spots on the show.

One night, I received a telephone call from a trucker who was in a hospital in Wisconsin. I had him on the air as he informed me he had just had surgery performed on his rear because of *hemorrhoids.*

I'll never forget the obvious agony he was going through when he said, "You know, Bill, I've been listening to your ... your show for the past few months ... hearing you praise that stuff called ... called *Superderm.*"

Then, pausing for a moment, he moaned: "I'll tell you what you can do with that ... that *Superderm ... "*

Before he could continue, I said: "That's what you were <u>supposed</u> to have done with it!"

Next day, Cas Walker telephoned from Knoxville. Seems he happened to be listening in when I was talking with the hospitalized trucker about his 'amazing' product.

Cas cancelled his sponsorship on my show.

Snuffy and Granny Smith are a husband and wife team that I treasure as friends. Besides driving their rig, they are entertainers and are seen at most of the major truck shows. Granny wears an old-fashioned bonnet and granny-style dresses. Snuffy wears overalls, a hat with the front brim pinned up like Gabby Hayes and sports an untrimmed mustache and beard. He has no teeth, which is obvious when he picks his banjo and sings. Most times, he picks and sings duets with Granny.

The *'Swingin' Smiths'* have been at practically every trucking show during the past years, walking among the folks and singing their songs.

Even though Mindy Baker, who was the sales rep on my WBAP radio shows, found them to be embarrassing and made it a point to say, "Ignore Snuffy and Granny", I always ignored her demand, determined to mention the good news they were with us.

And they <u>were</u> always there.

I was parade marshal on *St. Patrick's Day* in my hometown of Shamrock, Texas several years ago. While standing on a special float and proudly waving at the big crowd, I heard a honk, looked behind me and there were Snuffy and Granny in their big rig ... <u>in</u> <u>the</u> <u>parade!</u>

Later, when there was a big ceremony naming a street after me in Shamrock, I was on a big outdoor stage, seated to the left of the podium, with members of my family, while the mayor was speaking. The mayor asked me to come to the podium where he presented me with a special green and white sign reading, *BILL*

MACK STREET, making me so very proud. I then stepped to the microphone to thank his honor and, glancing to my right, I noticed several dignitaries seated. There was the mayor's wife, a couple of well-known politicians from West Texas and a few more important people.

However, what really caught my eye were Snuffy and Granny. They were seated next to the mayor's wife, dressed in their regular garb, smiling at me!

I shouldn't have been surprised.

Not long ago, during *Fan Fair* in Nashville, I was on the big outdoor stage with several country music stars. Looking out at the huge audience, I spotted Snuffy and Granny on the <u>front</u> row, waving wildly and smiling! And this was when tickets for the show were always sold out well in advance and were considered "impossible to find".

I hope they will always be there. My life has been made much happier by Snuffy and Granny Smith.

For over twenty-five years, I have attended various trucking get-togethers and they are always big events for me because I have the opportunity to visit with truckers I've known for years —- and there are chances to meet new friends who make their living on the road.

Especially outstanding is the *Mid-America Trucking Show* in Louisville, Kentucky.

I've been making the yearly journey to Louisville since the '70s. This blowout gathers approximately 70,000 people associated with the trucking industry, mostly truckers, every March ... and there is never a dull moment.

Truckers come in all shapes, sizes and ages.

In 1993, I was made a *Kentucky Colonel,* by Governor Brereton C. Jones of that great state. What an honor! Another time, they proclaimed it *'Bill Mack Day'* in Louisville. I was given the *'Keys To The City'* of Louisville — and I have been given numerous other awards, including one I treasure from the veterans.

Every year, I had a special guest (or guests) at the *Midnight Cowboy* booth, just inside the lobby at the huge coliseum. Among those to be with me were Ray Price, Marty Stuart, Tanya Tucker, The Oak Ridge Boys, The Bellamy Brothers, LeAnn Rimes, Waylon Jennings, Jessie Colter and Loretta Lynn. As a matter of fact, Loretta was with me two times.

Also appearing as a special guest was Willie Nelson.

Willie doesn't like to fly. Instead, he likes to take his big old bus with him everywhere he goes. In order to be with me in Kentucky, he and his driver drove for hours from Austin, Texas. After arriving in Louisville, Willie signed autographs for four hours that afternoon and then appeared with me on my broadcast from Kentucky from 1:00 a.m. until 3:00 a.m. the next morning. Then, he and his driver drove all the way back to Austin in order to play a dance that night!

Talk about a special friend.

While talking with Willie recently, I asked, "Why did you go to all that trouble? You could have easily turned me down ... and I would have understood."

His reply: "You would have done it for me."

Subject closed.

In Walcott, Iowa ... a spot in the road ... there is another annual trucking affair that rates among the greatest, drawing thousands of truckers. It usually takes place in July at the I-80 Truck Stop — - and it's always super hot.

I haven't been to the Walcott show in a couple of years but am looking forward to going back.

The last time I was set to appear there, I told WBAP sales rep, Mindy Baker, that it would be impossible because I wanted to be with my mother, in Houston, on her birthday. Mindy informed me she fully understood.

Well, after the Walcott show had closed, I began receiving calls and letters from truckers, telling me how sorry they were to hear about my mother, many saying she was in their prayers. I also received a caring telephone call from my pal, the *Trucking Bozo*!

The girl working the booth in Walcott, said Mindy had instructed her to announce to those who inquired about my whereabouts that my mother was "extremely ill" ... and that I had been forced to cancel out at the last minute.

Mindy had known for several weeks that I wasn't going to appear in Walcott!

I telephoned the I-80 Truck Stop to get a verification on this bit of mis-information and was assured this had, indeed, occurred. The good people working at the truck stop were still concerned about my mother's "critical" condition and seemed a bit shocked when I informed them she just had a fantastic, healthy, happy birthday!

It would have saved a lot of mistrust had the real reason for my backing out on the gig been announced at the booth.

The truckers would have fully understood. They have mothers.

One 'happening' that will always ring a sad tone in my memory occurred several years ago.

A trucker, on his way back home in Louisiana, had what was apparently a heart-attack while driving near the Texas-Louisiana line. Utilizing his CB radio, he put out a message for help and managed to pull his rig to the side of the road. However, he was dead by the time the police and an ambulance had arrived on the scene.

An officer with the Texas Department of Public Safety telephoned and told me that my program was running at high volume in the cab of the trucker as they placed him in the ambulance.

"Your voice was the last thing that poor trucker heard, Bill," said the officer.

I've often wondered what I said during those early morning hours.

One thing is a certainty:

I would never have made it in the business of "all-night radio" without those special people, the truckers. I owe them so very much.

Shortly after hitting the air that March morning in 1969, I was made an *Honorary Member of the Teamsters* and was told that I was the only disk jockey, at that time, to receive such an honor.

I am so very proud to have a strong association with my friends behind the wheel.

This would be a good time to say thanks to a beautiful little friend, Megan Cullingford, with *TRUCKER'S CONNECTION* magazine. Megan approached me several years ago about writing a monthly column for this fine magazine. As I write this, I've been doing that column every month for 8 years, and it's given me an even closer connection with the drivers.

Thanks, Megan!

I've also been doing the weekly *OVERDRIVE TOP-TEN COUNT-DOWN*, syndicated on a bunch of radio stations, for years. This is a pleasant assignment that is presented by the good folks at Randall Publications *(OVERDRIVE MAGAZINE)*.

Special thanks to another sweet little friend, Diana Davis, the Overdrive Radio Network Director, for many years of friendship … and super confidence, when it was needed!

A HAPPENING

I spoke with Lee Abrams about the possibility of joining *XM Satellite Radio* after I had decided to leave WBAP, as soon as my contract with the old radio station had expired. Basically, it was a short conversation. Lee, an old pro who has fought in many trenches in broadcasting, simply laid it on the line, telling me *XM* would deliver what the people wanted to hear!

I will always be grateful to Lee for welcoming me to the beautiful community of *satellite radio*!

I'll never forget my reaction, many years ago, when I was allowed to work on an AM radio station that boasted 50,000 watts, clear-channel! This was assurance that my radio show could be heard hundreds of miles away from our transmitter site. Of course, there would be static and, eventually, a complete fade-out, but it was what was referred to as a *"powerhouse radio station"*! Picking up the telephone in Fort Worth, and chatting with a truck driver in Chicago, was an almost unbelievable happening!

Let me repeat: I will always be grateful to Hal Chesnut, and Mr. Jim Byron, for giving me that wonderful opportunity back in 1969.

Times change.

When I made the announcement I was leaving AM radio, and hooking up with a satellite radio outfit out of Washington D.C., there were those within the broadcasting and country music communities who whispered, "Mack has lost his damned mind!"

XM Satellite Radio built the most elaborate broadcast facility on the Planet Earth in Washington DC. More important to me, they allowed me to put my studio in my home in Fort Worth, Texas! It's known as the *XM Satellite Ranch*!

Ken Johnson, my producer and friend, is stationed in Washington. Here again, I was blessed with a producer who is a country music expert. Ken can tell you Webb Pierce's shoe-size!

Think I'm kidding? Ask him sometime.

Seriously, Ken is a tremendous help to me. He relieves a lot of pressure. When listening to my *XM* show, you get the impression he is in the studio with me when, actually, we are hundreds of miles apart. I may see Ken twice a year. He and his pretty little wife, Jackie, are very special to Cindy and me.

As all of my *XM* family knows, Cindy is a very important part of my program. She had worked with me on WBAP back in the early 70s, before we started our family, and is now with me on *XM*, daily.

Cindy doesn't care for stardom, and her becoming a fixture on my show took a lot of persuasion from me. Now, she receives more mail than I do (dammit!) and sincerely enjoys what she is doing.

When you're hearing Cindy on *XM*, you're actually hearing her *as-she-is*. The infectious laugh is uncontrollable. Sometimes, when we're listening to a re-play of one of the shows, she'll question her laughter. Next thing I know, she's laughing <u>at</u> her laughter!

Strange, but beautifully true.

I'm very proud of this lady. She not only helps me when I'm on-the-air, she runs our company! I realize her job is a tough gig, but she never complains. She's a beautiful pro.

Even though I was certain *XM* would be a great success, I had no idea *how great* it would become!

You've got to remember that we're not talking about a *single* radio station, here. We're talking about *one hundred* radio stations … all in one marvelously constructed magic box that allows music, news, sports, *Nascar*, talk, comedy, weather, traffic — you name it — to be spread, clear-as-a-bell, to *any* spot in the United States, with no static; no fade-out!

I realize it's almost impossible to believe you can hear me just as clearly in Boston, Mass as you could hear me if you were seated next to me in my studio in Fort Worth, but it's a fact!

It's *unlimited* digital sound!

All of the *XM Satellite Radio* music channels are commercial free, making it super nice. Those selected channels consisting of commercials, such as my show, have a limitation on verbal peddling. You'll never hear "too many commercials" on *XM*.

God, I'm so proud to have the opportunity of being on the ground floor of the greatest thing to happen to radio, since the beginning of the gadget!

I was becoming extremely bored with AM and FM and, to be honest, was ready to exit broadcasting and setting my focus on writing songs and books. Then, Lee Abrams and I chatted on the phone, and I discovered "new life"!

I did my first *XM* broadcast from the ranch on September 10, 2001. I don't have to tell you what happened the next day!

Were there moments of doubt after 9-11? Yes. And they were normal doubts. After all, *XM* was the new kid on the block ... and the block had been hit by explosives!

I might have hit a panic button or two had Lee Abrams released any negative statements about the future of *XM* after September 11. Instead, his notes to the hundreds of employees and air personalities consisted of *absolute encouragement.*

Certainly, Lee was concerned about our nation, but he also realized it was a time for the spreading of *hope* and *determination.*

I've worked at several radio stations where management went goofy over a small drop in ratings! Not Lee Abrams. He retained his "cool" after the towers were hit in New York and the plane had crashed into the Pentagon, just a few miles from the *XM* studios in Washington!

Lee's comments were on the order of, *"Let's make radio fun again!"* ... *"Our satellites are in the air!"* ... *"Let's make the people happy!"*

Fun! Fun! Fun!

Hugh Panero, another one of the good *XM* leaders, maintains that same attitude of genuine *"belief in the product"!*

All-in-all, *XM Satellite Radio* consists of the perfect combination in leadership. Certainly, those leaders are determined to deliver the greatest sound ever heard in the history of radio, but there's something else that catches the attention: They sincerely care about those who are working on the big boat ... the employees.

It requires faith, strength, dedication and unlimited confidence to fulfill what Lee Abrams, Hugh Panero and the ultra-talented crew at *XM* have managed to accomplish in a little over two years, and it rubs off on the other folks working on the flashy new ship!

As I write this, we are approaching 2-million XM subscribers, and it's getting stronger every day. *XM* is no longer the "strange, new kid on the block". Now, it's a leader, setting new paths never before traveled in radio.

Of great importance: It's a genuine pleasure to be on the same channel with my old radio competitors, Dave Nemo and *Truckin' Bozo*, thanks to *XM Satellite Radio*. Even though we were competitors on AM radio, it was a friendly competitiveness. The radio stations, and those representing us in the sales departments, considered our programs battlefields, as is normal. Nemo, Bozo and me have always had a friendly relationship.

The Trucker's Channel, 171 (Open Road), has become a genuine family. And because of the people who have joined that "family" ... God bless 'em ... I am now happier in broadcasting than at any time in my professional career.

I've got to be honest with myself: There was that special morning, about a half-century ago, when I saw the red "ON-THE-AIR!" sign flash, and heard Bob Beller announce, "This is K-E-V-A, the <u>Five-Town-Station</u> in Shamrock, Texas. It's time for the morning livestock report ... and <u>with</u> that report ... here is Bill Mack Smith!"

That may have been the most exciting moment in my life. After all, it was a short, introductory sentence, spoken by an underpaid announcer in a tiny studio, that indicated I had entered radio ... a game I dearly love!

Certainly, there have been the trenches ... but the occasional battles have been most interesting.

FAITH

One of the most precious individuals I have met is Linda Plowman Fikes. Her professional name is Linda Plowman. Her story would make a good screenplay.

Conway Twitty introduced me to Linda, back in the early 70s. He said, "Bill, I want you to meet one of the greatest singers in the world!"

She was 14 at the time.

Shortly after meeting the beautiful little creature and hearing her turn the old Hank Williams composition, *"I'M SO LONESOME I COULD CRY"*, into a hit, I was in total agreement with Conway.

Linda informed me: "My big break came when my mom landed me a "gig" where I opened the show for Conway Twitty in Mississippi. Conway took me under his wing and flew me to his home in Oklahoma where he produced a "demo" record session on me. I was 14 when my version of *'I'm So Lonesome I Could Cry'* charted nationally. This secured a guest spot for me on the hallowed *Grand Ole Opry,* some moments I'll forever cherish."

Although one of the best singers in the business, Linda never considered entertainment as being priority. She retired after a few years to answer her first "calling", becoming a full time wife and mother.

This is where the real story begins.

Linda: "God blessed me with the husband of my dreams, Bobby, and 3 beautiful children. Our son, Clint, is an engineer with Mercedes Benz, like his daddy. Brandon is 10 and is president of his student body. Our daughter, Barbara, moved to Heaven four years ago. She was 16."

Barbara was absolutely gorgeous. And, along with that beauty was goodness. She had been "raised right", as they say in Tuscaloosa, Alabama.

About 6 p.m. on October 28, 2000, Barbara was pulling from the family drive onto the busy street. Since it was a "football" Saturday, excitement may have caused higher acceleration in the vehicles. One of them smashed into Barbara's car.

Linda: "Barbara moved to Heaven around 6 p.m. next day, Sunday. In many ways, we feel her spirit left on Saturday, because she never breathed on her own after the crash. Her funeral, "Going Home Service", was on November 1, 2000, which was *All Saint's Day.*"

The story doesn't stop with death.

Linda: "My grandmother passed away just weeks prior to Barbara. This had prompted a family discussion on organ donation. It is so important that we each consider this important decision and discuss our wishes with our loved ones. As Barbara's parents, we were so thankful that it was an automatic response to sign the paper granting permission to donate her organs. We had heard her wishes from her very own lips. Therefore, we knew the answer, without having to discuss it among ourselves during this traumatic time.

"Our family has been blessed to meet two of Barbara's recipients, in person, and we've spoken with two more by telephone. Steve Wallace received one of Barbara's kidneys, and Penny Thompson, a hairdresser in Florida, received her heart ... and both lungs. During a visit with her to Barbara's grave, Penny allowed us to place our ears to her back. We could hear our daughter's heart beating within Penny!

"Both Penny and Steve have "adopted" Barbara as their own and proudly carry her photos and writings to share with others.

"We have been blessed to see how God has continued to use Barbara to make a difference in other lives here on earth, as Barbara lives in Heaven."

There's more:

Linda: "I must remind women (and men) of the importance of

monthly self-breast-exams … and to get those yearly mammograms! I have to credit "Sweet" Cindy for her mammogram reminder on your *XM Satellite* radio show, Bill, for giving me that extra 'push'. My husband, Bobby, had recently prodded me because I was overdue for my mammogram. It was *Breast Care Awareness Month* when Cindy laid heavy on the subject. Upon hearing her advice, I went straight to the phone and made my appointments.

"Thanks to Cindy's timely urging, the doctors were able to find my cancer early. However, early detection is the 'key' to survival!

"The breast cancer battle is 'doable'. Attitude and faith are everything! I am so thankful to have survived seven months of surgeries, chemotherapy and radiation … all by the grace of God. God's grace came to me through reading His word, personal prayer time spent with Him … and the prayers and loving support of my precious family and friends. I'm also grateful for the caring doctors, nurses and medical staff."

During Linda's months of cancer treatment, we stayed close-in-touch, mostly by e-mail. We referred to those months as "the jungle". She survived that jungle and, after sharing her thoughts and attitude toward the loss of her daughter and the uncomfortable cancer months with my listeners, Linda picked up a new family. It's difficult to realize how her words have brought so much hope and consolation to those who have lost children through accidents and illness. Several ladies have sent word to me … and to Linda … that she may have saved their lives by urging them to "get those tests!"

Because of the heavy demand for Linda's time, she and her husband, Bobby, have constructed a website as a helping hand to others: www.lindaplowmanfikes.com. Her email address is: LindaF41@aol.com.

No, you won't be imposing.

Several weeks ago, Linda's mother went through the torment of a Mastectomy. Faith sustained. As I write this, there is a note from Linda on my desk reading, "I took Mama to the Cancer Center today. Good news! For sure … NO chemo needed, and NO radiation! All is well, thanks to early detection."

To add to this good news, Linda Plowman (Fikes) will have a new CD released later this year. Like the rest of this beautiful soul, the voice is stronger … and prettier … than ever!

Linda: Bill, just think about it: NOTHING can separate us from

God! He is with us for the long haul ... the whole trip. Every mile ... all the way.

"All we have to do is trust Him ... and <u>keep on *truckin'!*</u>"

BOOK ENDS

After spending hours, days and years behind the computer while typing out memories of yesterdays, and pecking in thoughts of today, struggling to structure some sort of a manuscript, I realize I've come up short.

I could never pay ample tribute to all of those who have made it possible for me to be a part of an atmosphere that has produced an over abundance of happy moments.

Certainly, there have been agonies, but, thank God, those dark moments were secondary to the good times; the blessings.

FRIENDSHIP:

Someone said, "If you make it through this life with *one* true friend, you've been lucky."

I've been super lucky, here.

I met Bill Setzler when I was 5-years-old. He was almost 7. I had spent the night with my grandmother in Shamrock, Texas and was walking up the sidewalk from her house. Setzler was approaching me in the opposite direction, with a long stick in his hand. As he passed me, he popped me on my butt with the stick. I picked up a rock and hit him in the back of his head.

Instead of becoming angry, Bill asked, "Want some hot chocolate?"

I replied, "Yes."

Bill took me to his house, where his mother made us some hot chocolate and bologna sandwiches.

It was the beginning of a strong, untarnished friendship that lasted over 60 years.

When Bill Setzler died a few years ago, I realized my childhood had ended.

I mentioned Big John Brigham earlier in this book. He was a friend who saw me through many personal battles. He was built like a scrubby giant, but had a heart that was the most allegiant I have ever known. God, what a pal!

One night, after appearing at a dance hall in Dennison, Texas, an ex-cop approached me and began an argument. Seems his wife had enjoyed my show and he was a bit jealous. After informing me that he was once an important policeman and "didn't take no crap off of nobody", he shoved me against my car. I punched him, knocking him to the sidewalk.

When I looked behind me, there stood Big John, holding a huge rock in his hand. He yelled, "Better keep your hands off of Mister Mack! Cop or no cop … I'll bust your head in if you so much as get up on your feet!"

Big John never called me *Bill*. It was always, *Mister Mack.*

When he died, while still in his 40s, there were many tears.

Big John was very special. Our friendship was *brotherly.*

I will never have a closer friend than Asa Johnson.

Asa isn't an entertainer. He doesn't sing, and he doesn't write songs. He simply projects *real* allegiance as a friend, asking for nothing in return.

Asa is one of the most unselfish people I've ever known. He is also one of the finest human beings I've ever met.

I realize those are fairly strong words, but I'm not exaggerating a single bit.

Asa is from the old school of friendship, where "your word is bond." He has been an auto dealer since I first met him, many years ago. Sometimes, car dealers can lay it on a bit heavy while attempting to sell you a car. Not Asa. Honesty is also a very important part of his makeup.

Asa Johnson's only fault is spotlighted every time he calls me on the phone. Without exception, he'll say, "I hope I didn't disturb you!"

Every time Asa takes the time to "disturb" me, it's a genuine pleasure. What a pal!

We may go weeks without communicating, but I know Asa is *always there*, if needed. And he realizes I will *always be there* for him, if needed.

Asa and his wife, Charlotte, are very close to Cindy and me. It's a treasured friendship.

Asa will be embarrassed when he reads the deserving acclaims I have *set to print* about him, but there's not a damned thing he can do about it!

Thank God, Asa Johnson, my best pal, is still going strong.

Then, there is Cindy: *Friend, Woman, Wife.* Her unparalleled understanding has been so very significant in my life for over 30 years.

MEMORIES:

I didn't have time to reflect on several memorable events in my life and the people who made them so special.

Some thoughts that come to mind:

During my first trip to Nashville in the Fifties, I had set plans to visit *Acuff-Rose Music*. My dear friend Mel Foree worked as a representative for *Acuff-Rose*, and had made me promise I would drop by and visit the publishing company, when I made that first trip to Music City.

Arriving late at night, I stayed at the *York Motel*, located directly across the street from *Acuff-Rose*. Next morning, I walked across the street, entered the building and was met by an older gentlemen, wearing thick glasses. He informed me that the place was closed, although the doors weren't locked.

He said, "This is Saturday. We're closed." Then, he asked me my name. This was before *Acuff-Rose* became the giant music publishing house it was destined to become, but it was the biggest publisher in the city … and was growing rapidly.

I told the friendly man my name and informed him that I was a disk jockey from Wichita Falls, Texas.

I was a bit shocked when he said, "I'm very familiar with you and your programs out there in Texas! Welcome to Nashville!"

He said, "I'm Fred Rose. Glad to meet you."

This was the man who was solely responsible for the initial success of my idol, Hank Williams! Hearing that he recognized my name was a moment of professional inspiration I will never forget.Mr. Rose said, "Since you're here in the building, you can help me fill some mailers for radio stations!"

For over an hour, working beside Fred Rose, I placed 45-rpm records in dozens of mailers. The title of one side of the record was *"MOODY'S GOOSE"*, by Bill Carlisle and the Carlisles ... on Mercury Records ... published by *Acuff-Rose*.

After finishing with the mailers, Mr. Rose asked, "Is there anything I can do for you while you're in town?"

I said, "Well, I want to go the *Grand Ole Opry*, but I didn't arrange for advance tickets and was told it's sold out for tonight."

Fred went to the telephone, placed a call and then walked back to me. He said, "Tickets for you and your little wife will be at the box-office at *The Ryman*, in my name."

That hot summer night in 1954, I was to see Nashville in action for the first time. Not only did Mr. Fred Rose arrange for admission to the *Ryman Auditorium* for Jackie and me, the seats were *front row!*

Pure excitement was in the air, as such stars as Roy Acuff, Ernest Tubb, Bill Monroe, Jimmy Dickens, Minnie Pearl, Carl Smith, Hank Snow, Sam and Kirk McGee, *The Gully-Jumpers*, and others, presented their works on the microphone ... marked *WSM!*

After the program had run for about an hour, I felt a gentle nudge to my shoulder. Looking around, it was Fred Rose! The gentle man whispered, "I just wanted to come here and make sure everything was taken care of for you."

Since that one special night, everything has been taken care of *"just fine"* for me ... in the wonderful world of country music.

I'm very thankful to all of those who have presented that beautiful sound for over fifty years of my professional life.

God bless 'em!

AWARDS PRESENTED TO BILL MACK

2003

FORT WORTH COWTOWN HERITAGE AWARD (WESTERN HERITAGE DAY) – Honored by Fort Worth and Texas Christian University, November 15, 2003.

2002

INDUCTION INTO THE TEXAS RADIO HALL OF FAME – As proclaimed by Rick Perry, Governor of the State of Texas, October 26, 2002.

2000

MEDIA AWARD – In recognition of *Excellence in Broadcasting*, voted on by peers within the industry, Nashville, Tennessee.

1999

MARCONI AWARD NOMINEE – *Major Market Personality* by *National Association of Broadcasters*, September 2, 1999, Orlando, Florida.

INDUCTION INTO THE TEXAS COUNTRY MUSIC HALL OF FAME – August 21, 1999 in Carthage, Texas.

INDUCTION INTO THE TEXAS COUNTRY MUSIC D.J. HALL OF FAME – August 21, 1999 in Carthage, Texas.

1998

"BLUE" is selected by *Red Lobster* restaurants for radio & television ads.

LUNAR BIBLE – A very special gift presented to Bill on February 5, 1998: The first bible on the moon aboard the *Apollo XIV Mission*. This microform of the Holy Bible, consisting of 1,245 pages of the King James Version, was carried in the spacesuit of astronaut Edgar D. Mitchell.

MILLION-AIR AWARD – BMI SPECIAL ACHIEVEMENT AWARD – In recognition of *DRINKING CHAMPAGNE* being aired over one-million times in broadcasting.

MULTI-PLATINUM ALBUM – *"BLUE"* – For sales of over 5,000,000 CDs & cassettes.

PLATINUM ALBUM – *"YOU LIGHT UP MY LIFE"* album by LeAnn Rimes that included *"CLINGING TO A SAVING HAND"* – Composed by Bill.

GOLD SINGLE FOR *"BLUE"* – For sales of over 500,000 copies.

Award celebrating 32 years with the Nationally Syndicated radio program, *"COUNTRY CROSSROADS"*. Six years with *"COUNTRY CROSSROADS"* on cable television.

TEXAS #1 DISC JOCKEY **for** 23 years.

OWNER-OPERATOR INDEPENDENT DRIVERS ASSOCIATION AWARD – In acknowledgement of continuing support of Owner-Operators.

1997

GRAMMY AWARD – For the composition of the song, **"BLUE"**, voted *Country Song of the Year 1996*. **"BLUE"** was also nominated for *Song of the Year 1996* by The *National Association of Recording Arts and Sciences*. February, 1997.

ACADEMY OF COUNTRY MUSIC AWARD (ACM) – *"BLUE"* voted *Song of the Year 1996"*.

FLAG OF THE UNITED STATES OF AMERICA – This flag was flown over the United States Capitol on February 27, 1997 at the request of the Honorable Kay Granger, Member of Congress. This was in recognition of being selected as the songwriter for the *Grammy* winning song, **"BLUE"**.

GOLDEN PICK AWARD **BY COUNTRY WEEKLY MAGAZINE –** As voted by the fans.

PLATINUM BOXSET *"STRAIT OUT OF THE BOX" by George Strait* **–** Which included Bill's composition, *"DRINKING CHAMPAGNE".* This commemorates the sales of more than 1,000,000 copies.

COUNTRY MUSIC ASSOCIATION (CMA) AWARD – Finalist for *"BLUE"* in the category of *"Song of the Year"".*

BMI POP AWARD – *"BLUE"* by LeAnn Rimes.

BMI COUNTRY SONG AWARD – *"BLUE"* By LeAnn Rimes.

NATIONAL SONGWRITERS ASSOCIATION AWARD – *"BLUE".*

GOLDEN MILE AWARD – Presented by *RPM EXTRA* – For distinguished Service, Friendship, Entertainer and Leadership to the trucking industry and the truckers for 28 years.

Dedication of BILL MACK STREET in hometown, Shamrock, Texas.

EAST FORT WORTH BUSINESS ASSOCIATION – For bringing the *Grammy* and *Academy of Country Music* awards "home" … to Fort Worth.

1996

HONORARY CITIZEN OF LOUISVILLE, KENTUCKY, CITY OF LOUISVILLE, OFFICE OF MAYOR – "In appreciation of your outstanding involvement in *The Mid-America Trucking Show.*

1995

Inducted into the TEXAS MUSIC HALL OF FAME in Carthage, Texas – March 5, 1995.

Worked with Clint Eastwood and *Warner Brothers Pictures* to supply and coordinate music for the motion picture *"A PERFECT WORLD"*, co-starring Kevin Costner.

GOLD ALBUM – *"TEN STRAIT HITS"* – *"DRINKING CHAMPAGNE"*, recorded by George Strait.

Inducted into *THE OKLAHOMA COUNTRY MUSIC ASSOCIATION.*

1994

CERTIFICATE OF APPRECIATION – *Vietnam Veterans of America.*

1993

COMMISSIONED A *KENTUCKY COLONEL* **By Governor Brerston Jones** – February 16, 1993.

1991

GOLD ALBUM – "LIVIN' IT UP" – For the composition, *"DRINKING CHAMPAGNE"*, recorded by George Strait and released as a *single record.*

1990

HONORARY SOUTHERN PACIFIC LOCOMOTIVE ENGINEER – March 9, 1990.

1984

HONORARY FIRE FIGHTER – City of Duncanville, Texas – July 6, 1984.

1982

Inducted into the NASHVILLE *COUNTRY MUSIC DISC JOCKEY HALL OF FAME* **FOUNDATION** – For accomplishments in Country Music Radio and Television. FICAP Banquet and Awards in Nashville, Tennessee – October 15, 1982.

BILL MACK DISC JOCKEY HALL OF FAME DAY **IN TARRANT COUNTY, TEXAS** –PRESENTED BY THE COMMISSIONERS COURT – October 25, 1982.

TEXAS MUSIC ASSOCIATION – FOR LIFETIME CONTRIBUTION TO EXCELLENCE IN BROADCASTING – October, 1982.

BILL MACK DAY **IN FORT WORTH, TEXAS** – AS PROCLAIMED BY MAYOR BOB BOLEN – MAY 23, 1982.

BILL MACK DAY **IN TARRANT COUNTY, TEXAS** – PRO-CLAIMED BY COMMISSIONER B.D. GRIFFIN – April 22, 1982.

Proclaimed as: *HONORARY CHIEF OF THE CHOCTAW NATION.*

THE AB ADAMS COMMUNITY SERVICES AWARD – Tarrant County, Texas *UNITED WAY.*

1981

AWARD OF APPRECIATION – Tarrant County, Texas *UNITED WAY.*

1977

HONORARY CITIZEN of BIG SANDY, TEXAS – July 23, 1977.

COMMUNITY Leaders AND NOTEWORTHY AMERICANS AWARD.

1975

JERRY LEWIS MUSCULAR DYSTROPHY AWARD **for** outstanding dedication in the fight against Muscular Dystrophy.

COWBOYS FOR CHRIST AWARD – September, 1975.

C.B. POLICE REACT TEAM Award.

BILL MACK DAY – Ruidoso Downs, New Mexico – May 24, 1975.

BILL MACK DAY – Ruidoso, New Mexico – May 24, 1975 (Separate from Ruidoso Downs).

HONORARY DEPUTY SHERIFF **OF TARRANT COUNTY TEXAS** – Proclaimed by Sheriff Lon Evans.

1974

GOLDEN D.J. Award – August, 1974.

HONORARY MEMBER of the ***INTERNATIONAL FRATERNITY OF DELTA SIGMA PI CHAPTER*** – April 27, 1974.

1973

HONORARY DEPUTY SHERIFF **in San Augustine County, Texas** – MAY 26, 1973.

HONORARY LIEUTENANT COLONEL AIDE – DE – CAMP In The ALABAMA STATE MILITIA – Presented by Governor George Wallace – March 27, 1973.

COUNTRY MUSIC ASSOCIATION (CMA) ***DISC JOCKEY OF THE YEAR*** – Nashville, Tennessee – October, 1973.

1972

HONORARY MEMBER OF LA TUNA, TEXAS JAYCEES – June, 1972.

HONORARY MAYOR OF LANCASTER, TEXAS – January 20, 1972.

1971

FAVORITE D.J. OF THE TRUCKERS WIVES **AWARD.**

AWARD OF DISTINGUISHED SERVICE – Southern Baptist Radio/Television Commission – "COUNTRY CROSSROADS" Syndicated Radio Program.

Proclaimed as MEMBER OF THE FLORIDA COUNTRY MUSIC HALL OF FAME.

HONORARY MEMBER OF *TEXAS CONFERENCE OF TEAM-STERS* – May, 1971.

1970

***BILL MACK DAY* IN FORT WORTH, TEXAS** – November 30, 1970.

***MUSIC AMBASSADOR AWARD* – Press Club of Fort Worth, Texas.**

Proclaimed HONORARY CITIZEN OF TUSCALOOSA, ALABAMA.

***MR D.J. U.S.A.* - 1962, 1970.**

SPECIAL NOTES

**BILL MACK served two terms on *THE COUNTRY MUSIC ASSOCIATION* BOARD OF DIRECTORS.

**BILL MACK was voted among the 13 MOST POWERFUL PEOPLE IN COUNTRY MUSIC by *"COUNTRY MUSIC MAGAZINE"*.